CRITICAL ACCLAIM FOR
JUDGE JAMES PICKLES

'He is the Geoffrey Boycott of the Bench'
Martin Kettle in *The Guardian*

'Pickles promenades where other judges fear, decline or disdain to tread'
Charles Newin in *The Daily Telegraph*

'The notion that Pickles has somehow diminished the dignity of the Bench by writing as he has is a nonsense: in my view he has enhanced it. He has made an important contribution to an important debate, and deserves our thanks for doing so'
Ludovic Kennedy

' . . . a judicial cheeky chappie, ever determined to Have a Go at what he saw as the conformist, conservative, complacent legal establishment'
Auberon Waugh

**Also by the same author,
and available from Coronet:**

STRAIGHT FROM THE BENCH

About the author:

James Pickles was born in Halifax, Yorkshire in
1925. He read law at Leeds University and received an MA from Christchurch, Oxford. He
married in 1948 and has two sons and a daughter.

He was called to the bar in 1948 and is known
principally for his work as Circuit Judge from
1976–1991, sitting in the Crown and County
Courts, mainly in Yorkshire, but also in London.

He is also the author of *Straight From The
Bench* which was published in 1987, and has
written many articles for national newspapers,
including *The Guardian* and *The Sun*.

Judge For Yourself

His Honour
James Pickles

CORONET BOOKS
Hodder and Stoughton

First published in Great Britain
in 1992 by Smith
Gryphon Limited

Coronet edition 1993

Printed and bound in Great Britain
for Hodder and Stoughton
Paperbacks, a division of Hodder
and Stoughton Limited, Mill
Road, Dunton Green, Sevenoaks,
Kent TN13 2YA (Editorial Office:
47 Bedford Square, London
WC1 3DP) by Clays Ltd, St Ives plc.
Photoset by E.P.L. BookSet,
Norwood, London.

British Library C.I.P.

A C.I.P. catalogue
record for this title
is available from the
British Library

ISBN 0-340-58347-9

CONTENTS

To my children
Roger, Carolyn and Simon

ACKNOWLEDGMENTS

I am deeply indebted to Sheron Boyle, a journalist, for her advice on editing, and for the time she spent shaping, reading and typing the manuscript.

David Chambers, a sub-editor on the *Daily Telegraph*, did an excellent research job. Professor Bryan Hogan and his colleagues at Leeds University Law Department kindly advised me before I began the book. The Home Office was very helpful in providing statistics. Mrs S. L. Chambers typed early drafts and, as always, interpreted my handwriting skilfully. My daughter-in-law Christine Pickles coped well with my word processor on the early chapters. Ms Maria Boyle also assisted in typing several chapters. Esther Jagger edited my manuscript brilliantly.

My wife, Sheila, put up with the inconvenience of living with a writer who got up sometimes at 3 a.m. and often at 5 a.m.

I owe a great deal to Mark Leech, who is referred to in Chapter 9; he provided me with much essential information. I am grateful to the *Guardian* for permission to reprint my articles in Appendixes 1, 2 and 4. Finally, I thank all the many people I have met in the law over the years and who have contributed to my thoughts: lawyers, judges, court staff, police, probation officers, shorthand writers and the media. Nor must I forget the most important people of all – litigants and defendants. Without them I would have had no work and no living.

None of the above is committed in any way to the views I express, which are mine alone.

FOREWORD

Friday, 30 June 1991. Bradford County Court. I ended where I had begun in the law forty-two years previously – twenty-seven of them on the Bench, including fifteen as a full-time circuit judge. This was the same court room in which I had conducted my first case on 27 January 1949.

In my part of the north-eastern circuit a farewell ceremony for a judge is usually held at Leeds Crown Court, where I was due to sit on 1 July, my official last day as a judge. But it was suggested that Bradford was more appropriate, and I agreed. In Leeds a senior judge would have been expected to say something, and he might have found it embarrassing. After all, I was not exactly top of the popularity parade with some of my judicial colleagues, though I always got on well with the administrative staff.

So words were spoken in court by a QC who had been with me in Bradford chambers. A Bradford solicitor also spoke. Both men were tactful, choosing their words carefully. I did not expect or deserve fulsome tributes from either legal profession: I had criticised both.

In my response I spoke of compensations. At the Bar, for every defeat there was a victory. On the Bench, for every Hailsham there was a Mackay. Going from one role to the other was like standing in a crowded train corridor, then suddenly being thrust on my own into a first-class compartment and the door being promptly locked. Life on the Bench was comfortable and prestigious, but solitary.

I was about to change trains, I went on. Where the next one would take me, at what speed and in what safety, I did not know. Life could begin again at sixty-six, and I hoped to live more productively, more intensively. Then I rose and left, never again to wear wig and gown.

It was as if I had fenced my way up a maze of staircases, against a succession of opponents, one conflict after another. Then I stepped into a room, closed the door and – silence.

I sat and looked back. How did it all start, this love/hate life in the law? How did I come to be a judge, and how well did I perform? Those clashes with Lords Hailsham, Lane and Mackay: what were they all about? What were the rights and wrongs? Regarding my sentencing on particular notorious cases and my general approach: why all the fuss and how far had I got it right? There was so much to set down before it was too late; so many things to tell the public – wrongs that should be righted, injustices that should be ended, flaws crying out for reform. I have tried to deal with all this as fully and fairly as I could. This book is my final summing-up on my life in the law. You, the readers, must act as judge and jury and decide on the verdict.

1

What made me as I am?

Perhaps I missed my way and should have been an investigative journalist. When I was a student I found it hard to choose between that road and the legal route. Did I start off on the wrong track and get stuck on it – not knowing how to get off – and did I therefore end inappropriately on the Bench? Some would say 'Yes'. I often felt, at the Bar and on the Bench, that I was among alien people who – with all due respect to those who have remained on friendly terms – tended to be narrow, stuffy and rigid. I seem to get on better with those media people who have uncluttered, questioning minds.

I probably went for the law because my father unknowingly nudged me in that direction. But I have always been combative, argumentative: useful qualities for one type of advocate, though not necessarily the best. What made me so? We are all products of early influences: our parents and the place where we grew up.

I yelled into life on 18 March 1925, the day after St Patrick's. The Irish doctor wanted my mother Gladys (how the name dated her: she was born in 1900, a Victorian) to name me after the saint. The alliteration – Patrick Pickles – may have put my mother off, though having left school at thirteen she would not have known that word. She knew no Shakespeare either, but typically condemned it as nonsense.

I was born in a small, stone terraced house in Warley, a village in Halifax, West Yorkshire – then the West Riding. That town has been the backcloth to my life. It has moulded

1

me. I have always lived here, as did my parents and grand-parents and my wife Sheila and her forebears. Ours is a town of millstone grit: solid stone-built mills, many silent now, and rows of stone-built terraced houses.

Like many northerners, Halifax people are blunt in speech and independent in attitude. My mother was (she died in 1989, aged eighty-eight). Untutored, outspoken, honest and frank, she was strong-minded and determined – and I get much of that side of me from her. I am not easily put off. I can stand up to those set over me. I follow things up. I speak my mind. It has got me into trouble and isolated me from the herd ever since I was a child. But I prefer to be so, rather than smooth, soft-soaping, creeping and crawling: more than a few in the law are like that.

The sort of person we are depends a lot on how we got on with our mothers, and I did not get on with mine. Gladys – I would never have dared call her that, and it would have horrified her – cared well in the material sense for my four younger sisters and me: we were amply fed and clothed. But in the emotional sphere she had few clues. There was kind-ness underneath, but so far down that I rarely glimpsed it. Gladys was a quick-tempered scold. She and I could not talk to each other without arguing. The fault was as much mine as hers, and in her last decade or so she did soften her tongue. I must have learnt my snappiness at her unyielding knee. I do not remember being cuddled, though she did kiss me once when I was eighteen and in hospital. She did not understand how to deal with children, from whom unques-tioning obedience was expected. But she was strong and told no lies.

My sister Christina Pickles – as she now calls herself (we knew her as Christine) – went to RADA and then emigrated to America to escape Gladys. She is still an actress, and had a part in the TV series *St Elsewhere*. My sister Angela went to live in New Zealand, though mainly for other reasons. Sisters Gwen and June (a magistrate) are still in Halifax.

2

Gladys did not get on with her mother, Margaret, who was illegitimate. Margaret's mother, my great-grandmother, was only fifteen years and ten months when Margaret was born in 1878. The father, whose identity is as unknown to me as it was, I think, to Margaret, was probably a fellow servant at the big house where my great-grandmother worked (I am speculating here) or one of the sons of the family who employed her. Whoever the father was, and however discreditable the seduction, as they called it then, I must not be too hard on the man. He was one of the millions of chance happenings that made me.

A photograph of me as a baby, with my mother, grand-mother and great-grandmother, shows the latter as a stout, bustling, self-confident lady. She had married a Mr Fudge – for better, for worse, but not for long – and then went without him to work as a cook in the Yukon Gold Rush. For many years after that she was housekeeper for a big shipping family called Brown who lived in Rhode Island.

Her daughter Margaret, my grandma, did not have as adventurous a life. She was in service until she married, and I recall her making remarks like, 'Such things' – owning a car, perhaps – 'are not for the likes of us.' She knew her place, and was humble in the presence of those whom she thought her social superiors. That photo reveals a tight-lipped, suspicious, resentful woman, though as handsome as her mother and mine were. Bastardy was a stigma when Margaret grew up. But grandma was good to me, and I got on well with her. I still have the small blue case she gave me for my twenty-first birthday; I keep family documents in it, including letters and homework by our three children and the oldest two of our six grandchildren.

I got on even better with grandpa William Crampton, Margaret's husband. Like his father, he had gone to work as a gardener at a big house. Surprisingly, William had first worked for a short time for a solicitor, and his handwriting was copperplate. When I knew him he had a small jobbing gardening business and employed two men. He was quiet and solid, stoically suffering the railings of his censorious wife. My mother cried at her father's funeral but not at her mother's; I was at both.

Grandma Crampton's attitude to life was reflected in my mother, and my mother's in me. There were reasons for the bad feelings between my mother and grandmother beyond the latter being a bastard. Gladys resented having to bring up her three brothers as a sort of assistant mum. She also resented her mother's harsh and restrictive control over her spare time.

Did I have a father, then? Oh yes, and a remarkable one. Arthur Pickles was small in stature – my height comes from the Cramptons – and the child of a poor family, probably a notch or two lower in the social scale than my mother's if one has to assess these things – and the English love doing that. I cannot trace the Pickles line far back – or rather, I have not yet tried to. When I told my father that I was thinking of paying money to trace the family tree, his comment was: 'And you'll soon be paying hush money, too!' Father thought he was the first-born, until he went to the local church and found he had been number two.

My great-grandfather George Pickles was a stonemason who went to London to work on the Law Courts, that stone Victorian Gothic 'cathedral' where the Strand becomes Fleet Street. There he met Louisa Cornaby, a Cockney from Bow. They went back to Halifax and got married, and their children included my grandfather Fred, whom I knew. The product of Yorkshire grit and Cockney wit, he was a most amusing man: his spontaneous humour kept many a pub in an uproar. He was less successful in business, and my father had little respect for him on that account. Fred would rather build a wall for nothing for a friend than buckle to as a stonemason or a small builder. Fred and his second son, Wilfred (later a well-known radio personality) went bankrupt as builders. The youngest son, Richard, a retired architect, survives. The brothers were all talented.

My father won a scholarship to Rishworth School, a boarding establishment near Halifax, but had to leave at the age of thirteen in 1914, as his father Fred had gone to the war – more to escape his personal troubles than to serve his King, as my father quipped to me. Arthur now became, in effect, the head of the family, helping his ex-weaver mother Margaret, a nice warm woman with whom he got on well. Hence my father was kinder, blander, more tolerant and balanced than me. He went to work for an architect, and at the age of nineteen was in a practice on his own; he also built a pair of semi-detached houses speculatively. He and a re-markable Halifax businessman, Charles Holdsworth, built acres of houses in Halifax, Sheffield, Chesterfield and London before the Second World War. During the war my father was chairman of the Civil Defence Committee, which earned him the OBE. After the war he sold his architectural practice to his brother Richard and headed several companies, finishing his business career running unit trust companies in the City: Ebor, Janus and Jascot in turn. He became prosperous and ran a new Rolls-Royce for a time, but never had a million. Until his final few years he lived a very active life.

Father became Mayor of Halifax, stood for the town as a Liberal in the 1950 General Election, and was chairman of the town's magistrates. He was a Rotarian, and at one time a Freemason – though he let that lapse, I am pleased to record; I do not like secret societies with silly rituals which for most members mask pushy self-interest. He was on a Cheshire Homes committee with Lord Denning. Father was also a noted amateur actor, and one of my first visits to the theatre, at the age of six, was to see him play the lead in *Adam the Creator*.

In his life, Arthur created a great deal. Viewed as a whole, he was a remarkable man who achieved much through nothing but ability and effort. I owe him a lot in several ways, and I was glad to be with him when he died, aged eighty-two, in 1983. 1 try to be as generous and understanding with my children and grandchildren as he was with his. That is the only way to repay your parents.

My father would have been a much better judge than I was: he knew how to get on with people. Without intending to, he inspired me to do what he once said he would have liked to do but could not afford: go to the Bar. Father would have excelled. He was subtle, sensitive and intelligent; he knew how others' minds worked and he could deal with anybody, fearlessly though without aggression. In vain moments – and I have a fair number of them – I flatter myself that I inherited my mother's frankness, honesty and strength of will, and my father's intelligence and subtlety. But that presents a picture that few will recognise as they look at me and my record as a barrister and judge.

I recall an early example of my rebellious nature and anti-authority attitude. At ten I went to a boarding prep school. It was rather a barbaric place, though I was as much of a barbarian as any of my contemporaries. I did not enjoy it at the time, but never said so to my parents, who thought I liked the school. The experience must have made me thick-skinned: I had to stand up to the others, who were soon affronted by my outspokenness, even rudeness, to my seniors – among the boys almost a capital offence in that school. When in trouble there was no one to turn to – a bit like prison in several ways. In both institutions you can go to those in authority, but they cannot guard you all the time; the others will get you eventually. All that toughened me and prepared me for later, when I had to stand up to educated barbarians including Lord Hailsham.

One day a master chastised me with a whip, instead of the usual cane which used to leave ridges on my backside. The whip was less painful than the rod, but we boys decided that someone ought to complain. The prep was attached to the senior school then, so I volunteered to go to the headmaster,

6

a reverend gentleman, who said he would speak to the master concerned. Not long afterwards the latter was called up for the war, then captured in Norway after which he spent five years in a prison camp: the Almighty was surely too hard on him. The point is that I believe I enjoyed going to the headmaster, nervous though I was when I went. I was a rebel then, and have remained so – a characteristic which has not sat easily with my Establishment position on the Bench.

After prep school I went to a minor public school, Worksop College in Nottinghamshire, and from there to Leeds University where I studied law. Then I left the north of England and came south, to Oxford, where I took an MA at Christ Church, an élite establishment favoured by the products of Eton and Harrow and their like. Here I came into contact for the first time with these expensively educated future pillars of the Establishment – Quintin Hogg, for instance, had been at Christ Church, though a little before my time. It was all a long way from Halifax.

But I cannot leave the subject of my Yorkshire background without saying something more about my Uncle Wilfred, whom I have only mentioned in passing – he deserves more. At about thirteen he became a 'half-timer', spending half the day at school and the other half at work in a shop. After that he became a bricklayer and then there was the bankruptcy. When Wilfred became famous as an entertainer the creditors took an interest, and Wilfred bought himself and his father out of bankruptcy – it was not automatic after two years, as it is in these palmier days. To the press, Wilfred said he and his wife Mabel vowed to pay back every penny, and had worked and saved until they could. Oh yes? My father was a creditor, having been the guarantor at the bank, and when Wilfred asked him if he would forgo that part of the debt owed by Fred, Arthur said no, he wanted the lot. Yorkshire businessmen do not give much away, even to those close to them.

7

It would be churlish of me to mention the actors in the Pickles family and omit our daughter Carolyn. Like her brothers, Roger and Simon, she has had the advantage of a good, loving, kind mother – the nicest woman I ever met. Sheila was seventeen and I was sixteen when we met. The boys are like their mother and deservedly popular, though they have no aspirations to abandon modesty and take to the boards. Carolyn has more of me – the tempestuous side – though she is kind and thoughtful like her mother, from whom she has also inherited acting talent. Since she was about eleven, we have watched Carolyn act. She played the title role in *Mother Courage* at Manchester University, where she read drama. Then she went through the agonies of earning her Equity card, played Miss Bluebell, founder of the legendary troupe of dancers, in the TV series *Bluebell*, and was later Detective Chief Inspector Kim Reid in *The Bill*. Carolyn has two delightful daughters, who benefit from a good mother's influence. Our two sons each have two children. And so it goes on – family life getting better with each generation.

What made me what I am? My family and my northern background.

2

Was all the agony of the Bar worthwhile?

I have talked about some of the influences that directed me towards the Bar. So how did I become a barrister, and how did I fare?

First I should perhaps explain what a barrister is. The legal profession in England consists in fact of two separate professions – barristers and solicitors. Barristers, or counsel, specialise in presenting cases in court and advising on difficult points of law or fact. They receive their work from solicitors. The latter do the preliminary work of collecting evidence by interviewing witnesses, obtaining statements from them and gathering documents. Barristers operate in sets of 'chambers': they are not partners, as they do not share profits, but they share expenses such as rent, typists' wages and telephone bills.

The first step for a would-be barrister is to join one of the four Inns of Court – Inner Temple, Middle Temple, Lincoln's Inn and Gray's Inn – in London. They are all medieval in origin. The first two lie between Fleet Street and the Thames, divided from each other by Middle Temple Lane. Lincoln's Inn is in Chancery Lane, and Gray's Inn in Holborn near the top of Chancery Lane.

I joined the Inner Temple by mistake. When I was a law student my father took me to Leeds to see a barrister he knew. He recommended the Middle Temple, saying that Inner tended to have more public school/Oxbridge products, but I mixed them up. Not a very good start in the profession, one might say. It has made not a ha'porth of difference, as at the Bar and on the Bench I was rarely in London. When I was, I hardly ever lunched or dined at the Inn, though when I was a pupil at the Temple for a year I had done so, as regulations require. It must be twenty years since I went to the Inner Temple, except to walk through its ancient court-yards and quiet gardens.

The Inns of Court are independent of the state, though ultimately under the control of the High Court judges as 'visitors'. There are three sets of members: students, barris-ters and benchers. The last-named consist of barristers or QCs, and are a self-perpetuating body. They never elect a mere circuit judge as a bencher. Not that I fancy that sort of position – too in-bred, too incestuous. I am not clubbable enough for it, though the table talk may have some attrac-tion. On the whole I find many of those people wearying to talk to, as they seem to 'orate' most of the time.

In the Middle Ages the Inns were like universities – young men went there to stay and study. All that is left of that now is the need to 'keep terms' by dining in hall three times a term; there are four dining terms a year. So twenty-four dinners have to be paid for and eaten. There is this to be said for the system: it is good to meet fellow students, some of whom will be one's colleagues and competitors, and to get the idea of both the camaraderie and the cut-and-thrust of the Bar.

I have the notion that, according to George Bernard Shaw, a profession is a conspiracy against the public. (If he did not write that, he should have.) The young barrister, eager to get his foot on the ladder and join the conspiracy, first finds it directed against himself. Once he joins it – if he is ever able to – he will as eagerly try to prevent others joining. This unjust situation, in which members of a pro-fession can prevent their would-be competitors from competing, is unique to the Bar. It arises from the pupillage and chambers system.

Pupillage is a system whereby young intending barristers

spend twelve months in chambers working with a junior barrister (that is, not a QC), who is called their pupil-master. It is now compulsory, though in my time it was not. To obtain a place in chambers as a pupil a candidate needs to have a law degree and to have passed the finals of the Bar examinations.

Until he has been in pupillage for six months, the pupil is not allowed to appear in court. Instead he daily reads his master's briefs for appearing in court and instructions for advising, attends his conferences with solicitors and lay clients (as they are often known, to distinguish them from the barrister's other client, the solicitor), and sits behind him in court, giving what help he can in looking up the law and making notes.

After the twelve months' pupillage is over, the aim is to find a place in chambers – preferably the same chambers, since the pupil will already have been making useful contacts there among solicitors. The snag is that a set of chambers, especially in London, may have four or five pupils. But the existing members (there could be about twenty of them) may feel they only have room to offer permanent member-ship of the chambers to maybe two of these pupils. The others are allowed to 'squat'; hang on, loosely attached to the chambers, receiving a few scraps of briefs as they des-perately write around to heads of chambers asking for a tenancy or even a further pupillage. Having been rejected by their original chambers does not help.

Some barristers go into industry where there are various openings for those possessing legal qualifications, without ever having had the chance to show what they can do. They have been successfully kept out by practising barristers more fortunate than themselves. There are English people practis-ing law in New York who could not get into chambers in their own country.

The Bar Council – the regulatory body of the Bar, composed entirely of barristers – decided recently that pupils must be paid £6000 a year. This is good in principle but on balance it may be counter-productive, as some sets of chambers will reduce the number of pupils they take.

Most heads of chambers in London have the public school/Oxbridge stamp, so beginners who are also in that category do not find it hard to get into good chambers. Here is the first reason why the Bench is dominated by such people. A beginner with a brilliant academic record has an advantage when seeking pupillage, if he is personable and does not try to eat peas with his knife. The son or daughter of a solicitor with a litigation practice – one who acts for people going to court – should have no problem. The off-spring of a judge or QC has the door open and a desk waiting before he is ready.

My pupillage was arranged by my law tutor at Oxford, S. N. Grant-Bailey, a small, thin, eccentric man with an un-shaven spot on his top lip. During tutorials he thought very deeply and spoke very slowly, as if going into a trance, and twisted his legs like inspired pipe-cleaners. He apparently had a small practice at the Bar in writing opinions for solicitors on matters of law. This practice was conducted from chambers in Gray's Inn, where I think he lived; they were also the registered office of a restaurant. As a tutor he was not outstanding – though very kind – but he had extensive contacts with judges and QCs for 'moots' (debates by law students on legal points) and pupillage.

Grant-Bailey arranged for me to go into the chambers of Gerald Slade QC, at 1 Brick Court in the Temple, as a pupil to Neville Faulks. My pupil-master was a classicist with a quick brain and a breezy, informal manner, introducing himself as 'Faulks – like the old folks at home'. He had had several lean years at the Bar before the Second World War, and after service in the army was building a practice. When I went to him in 1948 he was forty and recently married.

In London, counsel's chambers specialise, whereas this tends not to be so in the provinces. Slade's chambers did high-class civil work with the accent on libel and slander; Slade, and Faulks later, edited a textbook on the subjects. As an advocate my pupil-master was urbane, smooth and concise, though not always meticulous.

On the High Court Bench, to which he was in due course elevated, Mr Justice Faulks was quick and informal if a little slapdash and aloof. The first time you appeared before him could be disconcerting; you looked up and the judge's chair would be empty – he frequently walked about to ease some medical condition. It was said that when trying one case at Leeds he went behind a curtain at the side of the Bench, saying, 'Carry on, I'm listening', while cigarette smoke curled slowly into court.

Whatever I learned in my pupillage it was not how to speak on my feet. My total of briefs comprised three unde-fended divorces which I did with awful nervousness, draining me. The first was unpaid – one of the last under the poor persons' procedure whereby people without means were allowed the services of a solicitor and barrister free in civil actions. Under legal aid, its successor, clients are means-tested and make a contribution if it is considered they can afford to do so. My second brief was a paid one from the solicitor who had sent the first. The third was a return of Faulks's – a brief passed from one barrister to another by the chambers clerk. It is done with the solicitor's agreement and is a good way for young barristers to start to get known and make their way. The member of chambers who shared our room and had very little work reacted jealously when this brief was handed to me.

The only criminal work Faulks did was prosecuting for the Board of Trade. When I suggested to the chambers' clerk, Edward Love, that I might watch some of the cases at the Old Bailey, he said, 'For goodness sake don't get mixed up with that lot down there.' He was referring to some of the barristers, and especially those like the one in John Morti-mer's play *Dock Brief*; down-and-out and briefless, such ageing counsel haunted the Old Bailey, hoping to be picked by a judge for off-the-cuff legal aid defences and dock briefs. I heard of one who collapsed through malnutrition, and the soles of his feet could be seen through the soles of his shoes as he was carried away.

Edward Love was a quick-witted Londoner who had started work in the Temple at about sixteen; a clever illusionist, especially with cards, he was a member of the Magic Circle. He wrote a book on card tricks, which he exchanged for *A Book for Brides* in which I had written a section on the legal aspects of matrimony. I was hankering to write, though with scant success. Love dealt with pupils like a sergeant-major with recruits. We were not permitted to have coffee in the morning or tea in the afternoon when members of chambers had theirs brought, so we went out to a Lyons coffee bar and chatted.

Gerald Slade QC was tall, courteous and dignified – not pompous, though ponderous. He was kind and helped students by presiding at moots. He once said to me that he had received so much help when young that he was only too happy to help others, and I have tried to remember that. A stern sniffy teetotaller, Slade devoted his days to the law, his wife and four daughters, and tennis. In court he had a slow, trenchant, painstaking manner, but he ground out results impressively and participated in some celebrated cases. He always refused to appear before the cantankerous Mr Justice Hallett – whom we shall encounter again – preferring to return his brief.

Slade defended William Joyce, alias 'Lord Haw-Haw'. A sneering fascist who broadcast from Hamburg in English during the Second World War, he was charged with treason soon after the war ended. Slade told me that, if he had put Joyce into the witness-box to say that he had destroyed his British passport, that might have saved him from the gallows. Joyce's connections were with Eire and the USA, and the only proof that he was a British subject, and therefore guilty of treason, was that he had once obtained a British passport. He had no real duty of allegiance to Britain, and to hang him was spiteful. When I said so to Judge Openshaw, while sitting with him at Preston Crown Court, he said that for such a remark I deserved the same fate as Joyce (I don't think he meant it).

Sadly, Openshaw's career and life were cut short by a madman's knife in the judge's own garage; the man had followed and harassed him for years because of a sentence Openshaw had passed on him. When sentenced to life imprisonment the murderer threatened that judge with the same fate. Perhaps we should be surprised that more judges are not attacked; many defendants must have felt venomous towards me after being sentenced, but the venom presumably evaporated as they realised I had a job to do, and they were not as guiltless as they had said in court.

Another of Slade's famous cases was the libel action brought by Harold Laski, professor of political economy at the London School of Economics and a leading member of and theorist for the Labour Party. Before Lord Chief Justice Goddard and a jury he sued the *Newark Advertiser* over its report of a speech he had made during the 1945 general election campaign. The newspaper reported Laski as saying that if Labour did not get power by consent they would get it by revolution. The professor's version: if Labour did not win there would *be* a revolution. On this nice distinction hung the reputation of a vain, tedious pedant and thousands of pounds in costs.

Slade appeared for Laski, and Sir Patrick Hastings QC for the newspaper. The two had very different styles. Hastings left Charterhouse public school early and could not afford to go on to university. He was never a pupil, but persuaded a QC to let him attend his chambers and 'devil' (look up the law and make notes for cases). Hastings had a short but unhappy career in politics, becoming Attorney-General (and so knighted) in the 1924 Labour Government; it was his decision to drop the prosecution of John Ross Campbell, a left-wing editor, for sedition that led to the downfall of that government.

Hastings was perhaps the most formidable advocate I ever saw in action. He was concise, incisive, biting, sarcastic, self-deprecating. He believed there was always one point in a case, and if you found it and went for it you would win – though not, of course, if you picked the wrong point. In his autobiography (Heinemann, 1948), Hastings described the cross-examination of Laski as one of his most difficult: he was crossing swords with a fencing-master who was a leader in his field, political theory. But in the end Patrick Hastings dominated and destroyed Harold Laski. The jubilant *Daily Express*, who would have been sued next and had to pay damages if Laski had won, published the full transcript, which I used to lend to pupils as an example of how to cross-examine (if any of them still has the book, I would like it back!). Labour supporters raised a fund to pay the professor's costs, and he was said to have been left with a profit, but he died not long afterwards – worn out, some said, by that case.

Halfway through my pupillage Gerald Slade was appointed a High Court judge, and Love, devoted to Slade, went with him on to the Bench as judge's clerk. Slade supplemented his meagre civil service salary.

The role of a barrister's clerk is an odd one. He – or increasingly in these days, she – can be likened to a boxer's manager who arranges fights, fixes fees and gets a percentage of the 'take'. It can be a love/hate relationship in the law or in the ring. Both spheres, though different in many respects, involve aggression between gladiatorial figures, with the clerk or manager looking on, greasing others' palms and holding out their own for the resultant shekels.

In my early days a clerk was unqualified except by experience, and that is still largely so, though the clerks' association organises training of some kind, which is not compulsory. Barristers' clerks usually began as junior clerks (especially in London), as solicitors' clerks or as civil servants working in the court service. Clerks work for barristers, who are 'qualified', have status and often come from higher up the social ladder. Yet the clerk can direct work to or away from a member of his chambers, especially the beginners; he can make or break them, almost. Although touting for briefs is forbidden, it goes on in ways that have shades of subtlety; a clerk who gets on well with solicitors can nudge work to his chambers. The Love/Slade barrister/clerk relationship was not love/hate, but based on Love's admiration and Slade's confidence. A bad relationship can make life hard for a barrister, and sadly that would later become my lot, as will be seen.

Clerks were paid on the basis of what was called a bob-on-the-guinea (one shilling – 5p – in every twenty-one – £1.05) and every brief had a small additional fee for the clerk. After decimalisation this became, more prosaically, 10 per cent of gross fees. A clerk in prosperous chambers could earn a colossal amount – more than, say, the Lord Chancellor and more than most of his barristers. Some clerks owned racehorses and had yachts in the south of France. Sir Valentine Holmes QC, one of the leading post-war silks (after the material from which QCs' gowns are made), owned and ran greyhounds in partnership with his clerk; they went everywhere together.

I heard a true story about another leading QC, Sir Gilbert Beyfus, travelling first-class on a cruise liner; in the tourist class (surprisingly) were two clerks from the Temple. Beyfus was a large man with a facial twitch; big in reputation, in court and in head. One morning he strolled down the steps from the first-class quarters dressed in his white suit and passed the two clerks, who said, 'Good morning, Sir Gilbert.' They thought the great man had ignored them, as he went by without a word.

'That will cost Sir Gilbert Beyfus a thousand guineas,' said one to the other.

'Two thousand,' remarked the other.

Junior barristers in chambers are asked by solicitors to recommend a QC to lead them in a particular case. Beyfus would in future be passed by without a word.

The only enduring mark I made during my pupillage was to have my notes for one of Faulks's cases printed in the law report by mistake. The case was Beeken v. Beeken 1948 P302. When the law reporter borrowed the brief after the hearing, my notes were inside and he assumed they had been used in addressing the Court of Appeal. Apart from that, my twelve months in the Temple left few traces either on others or on me, though I must have learnt some things.

The chief one was that the Temple, especially in high-class civil chambers, was no place for a barrister from the north who had no pull in London and virtually no cash anywhere. I did have a loyal, charming, understanding wife – we had married in August 1948 – but few other assets. Despite all my attempts at public speaking at the Oxford Union and elsewhere, I was hesitant and nervous on my feet. But I had hopes and aspirations as I took the road back to the north.

Hawkins, my London clerk, spoke to a clerk in the Temple whose barristers did most of their work on the north-eastern circuit – one of the six geographical regions into which the country is divided for legal purposes. There was a vacancy in the Bradford chambers of J. Stanley Snowden.

Stanley Snowden had taken over these chambers in 1930 without becoming anyone's pupil, and he had had it hard at the start. We knew which year he had begun, as there was a ten-year gap in our law reports after the volumes he had inherited ran out and before he could afford to start buying them himself. Like me, he had had to economise in his early years; although, also like me, he had a businessman father to whom he could go in emergencies.

Snowden's back was bent with curvature of the spine, but

18

his character could not have been more upright; he was a forthright man of principle who never dissimulated or deceived. Despite his background (he had been to Sedbergh, a northern public school, and Cambridge) he spoke and behaved like the solid northerner that he was. Before a jury he was a first-class advocate, though not an outstanding lawyer – advocates in the criminal courts are actors rather than lawyers, and points of law arise rarely. Snowden's stooped back, deep voice and frowning face made him a frightening figure to a dishonest witness, whom he would demolish doggedly.

His trenchant style was effective whether he prosecuted or defended, though it was not one to model oneself on completely. When prosecuting he did not make a note for his opening speech, preferring to thumb and stumble through the witness statements. He made spidery (illegible to me, if I was on his side in a case) notes when an opposing witness gave evidence but did not appear to use them. It was all in his head, as it should be – and is, when confidence based on experience has battened down one's nerves.

Stanley's technique was based on a shrewd knowledge of people and bulldog grit. He could sense when part of a witness's story did not fit, feel for the joins and strip the tale apart, piece by piece, question by question, until the witness stood naked. No one ever fought harder for a defendant than Stanley Snowden. He liked to find a grievance, to convince the jury that his client had not had fair play. In one case, debris from a blown-up safe had travelled in the same police car as the accused. 'If you convict my client, he will always believe those traces from the safe got on to his clothes in the car!' The jury did not convict.

Although a Liberal in politics, Stanley Snowden was in other areas the most conservative of men. He had an addiction to the past and a reluctance to change that was comical to others. He genuinely believed the cinema had never been the same since the talkies came in, and that golf had been ruined when the steel shaft replaced hickory; television was a debasement of radio and he would not have a set in the house – though he did eventually, for his wife. They had no children but doted on a bull terrier called Bill, proudly showing the latest photographs of it and arranging to have it beautified.

Our chambers in Bradford were in Martin's (later Barclay's) Bank Chambers in Tyrrel Street – a building that had once been a department store. The three upper floors, reached by a groaning lift – which had a groaning attendant, Chris, until modern technology sent him groaning into retirement – had balconies arranged around a well, at the bottom of which bank employees scratched pens under a greenhouse roof. If anyone had jumped off a balcony they would have cleared desks of cheques, replacing them with shards of glass and startling rows of poorly paid clerks. None of us did jump, although I felt tempted at times in the years it took me to find my financial feet.

We had two rooms on the first floor. The clerk's room had a window, but an adjoining building blocked out most of the daylight; partitioned off was a section we called the snug, although it wasn't very. It had no daylight, ventilation or sound-proofing, but it was the place for conferences with solicitors and the lay clients they brought.

Two new pupils soon joined, decisions on such matters being made solely by Snowden and Leslie Gardner, our clerk. They were John Cotton, now a circuit judge in Sheffield, and David Loy, now a stipendiary magistrate in Leeds. When I became head of chambers I tried to organise and modernise, and even introduced the hitherto unknown principle of one-person-one-vote in matters such as whether to take another pupil or whether to give a pupil a tenancy.

These were the Dickensian chambers where I spent twenty-seven years of my life dreaming my dreams; planning my victories; binding my wounds; clashing from time to time with others, and especially Gardner; getting tangled in the old boy net; clashing with old boy judges in court; waiting day after day with little to do except gossip and write plays, most of which were doomed to rejection; and always believing – except in the bleakest moments – that any day the tide could sweep into our Bradford backwater, surging me to success. It never did, but the tide levels did rise over a period. I never drowned, though sometimes I lay soaked and gasping on the shore, wondering if I was in the right job.

I kept records of my cases and fees, though Gardner resented that. At first he would not even let me see the fee-books which he kept meticulously and with the scrupulous aggressive honesty that invested all he did. My gross income from the Bar for the first five years, from 1949 to 1953 respectively, was: £262, £440, £425, £677 and £6l6. Even bearing in mind that I am talking about the money values of forty years ago, I was by no means well off. Crime was burgeoning but not booming, and it was poorly paid on the defence side. Almost all defendants who were represented had legal aid, and a mitigation on a plea of guilty brought three guineas (£3.15), or five (£5.25) if the plea was not guilty, however long the case lasted. A prosecution brief on a plea of guilty attracted three guineas, though some local authorities only paid two for a committal for sentence by the magistrates to quarter sessions; pleas of not guilty were better paid. Eventually both sides' barristers were paid more or less the same in criminal cases, but it took years for this to come about.

We youngsters sat in court at quarter sessions and assizes day after briefless day, watching other counsel in action and learning more from the incompetent than from the competent: the former's mistakes are easy to fathom, whereas the latter make it all look deceptively easy. We sat there eager to learn and hopefully to earn: a legal aid or a dock brief could arise at any time, as in a soup kitchen where the opening hours were unknown until they happened, so if you wanted soup you had to wait at the gate. In those days a defendant who was granted legal aid on the day was allotted by the judge one of the young barristers sitting in court. Also any accused person who was unrepresented had the right to a dock brief provided he had one guinea – later two. He could point to any counsel in court except the prosecutor, and the one chosen had to do the case for him, however long it lasted.

I spent weeks preparing my first brief in a criminal case. It was usual to start your career with pleas of guilty, but I began several rungs up the ladder with a defence to attempted rape. Even after forty years I remember some of my phrases, and the indulgence of Mr Justice Streatfeild; in his summing-up he quoted with a smile my reference to a 'late but learned judge'. Streatfeild knew it was my first case and, as with a maiden speech in the House of Commons, it is usual to give the beginner an easy ride. My client was acquitted, and Snowden penned me a kind note. The brief had been sent by a solicitor whose father sat on Halifax Council with my own father; he sent me several more cases until he learned that I was then in the Labour Party, whereupon he announced: 'He'll get no more bloody work from me!'

My immediate colleagues had other non-Establishment blemishes, Geoffrey Baker being Jewish and John Cotton a Roman Catholic. A really ambitious and far-sighted parent who aims for his child's success in the law makes him – in fact or appearance – white, Anglo-Saxon and Church of England, with an in-built mental computer geared to saying the right things to the right people. There are many such computed products at the Bar, a fair number of whom soon rise silently to the top. Being a 'socialist' in those days was a real handicap to a professional man – I had been elected as a Labour councillor in 1956 – and it still is to some extent. A woman who did housework for us had a son who was coming up at quarter sessions and she asked the solicitor, a Tory member on the same council, to send the brief to me. It was his duty to comply, but the brief never came.

WAS ALL THE AGONY OF THE BAR WORTHWHILE?

When assizes and quarter sessions – since amalgamated into crown court – were not in session I went into chambers day after fruitless day, reading law reports, preparing the evening lectures that I gave on two or three evenings a week to banking students and the like, or writing plays – two were broadcast by BBC Northern Region in about 1952 and enabled me to buy our first television set.

A familiar figure at Bradford quarter sessions was James Wicksted Perkins. Let aspiring barristers take heed. As a young man Perkins was a well-known tennis player and a partner in a prosperous firm of Bradford solicitors. He could have become affluent and respected, retiring to Morecambe or Scarborough with a pension; but, despite warnings about the hazards, he fancied himself as a barrister and in the mid-thirties he changed over. At first Jimmy Perkins received briefs from his old firm and other Bradford solicitors, but there are limits to loyalty and friendship, set by the duty to clients. When I first met him, Perkins was senile, impoverished and unkempt, and wore an old suit and dirty, screwed-up bands (the white tabs which barristers, judges and some clerics wear around their necks). Perkins had virtually no work and no private means; his marriage to a younger woman had ended; he was reduced to sleeping in the barristers' robing room at Leeds Town Hall, where he kept a small spirit-lamp in his locker. Eventually the civic authorities forbade this nocturnal use of the premises, and Perkins was helped by the Barristers' Benevolent Association.

During the day Jimmy scribbled for hours on scraps of paper, writing what he said was to be a book containing all the combinations of facts a lawyer might have to deal with! He wheedled two guineas out of several QCs as advance payment for a copy of the great work when published. Gardner, our clerk, said that if Perkins had not been a barrister he would have been done for false pretences.

Jimmy used to trundle along to Bradford quarter sessions

wearing his scruffy old suit and carrying an even older suit-case; out of charity the prosecuting solicitor's clerk kept two briefs for him in cases of little importance, such as petty theft. The recorder was Frank Beverley, who had long since retired from the Bar. He did not say much because he did not know much. He sat up there blinking like a bewildered owl, and used to interrupt prosecuting counsel who started to 'open' the facts in a guilty plea by saying, 'I've read the depositions. Call the officer.' On one occasion, contrary to his practice, Beverley said to Perkins as he shambled to his feet, 'I haven't read the depositions in this case.' Of course neither had Perkins, who was nonplussed by such an unusual requirement.

Neither Charles Dickens nor John Mortimer could have done full justice to the scene that day in the Gothic stone court in Bradford Town Hall, as blinking Beverley and pathetic Perkins looked at each other, both open-mouthed. When Perkins died, his obituary in the *Yorkshire Post* read well: former solicitor, noted tennis player and so on. I sup-pose my own obituary may not read too badly: the regard for truth which inspires some journalists tends not to extend to those who pen obituaries.

There used to be some absurd rules of legal etiquette. They show how antiquated the Bar was then, as it is still to a large extent, though most of the rules I am about to relate have gone. If a junior counsel became a QC he had to undertake to practise only from chambers in London. No one was certain why; it may have been originally because Queen's Counsel acted for the Crown and had to be near the royal court. Rudolph Lyons QC used to travel from his Leeds home to London for a conference; on the same train could be his Leeds solicitor and client, who also lived in Yorkshire! Another strange regulation was that a clerk to London chambers was not allowed to reside within our circuit. A barrister was not allowed to join an organisation such as the Rotary Club, which in those days required a member to wear a badge stating his occupation. Buying a solicitor a drink or even meeting him socially by intent were contrary to etiquette, as was going to a solicitor's office except on one's own personal business.

Any publicity for a barrister had to be avoided, except for the reporting of his cases. I recall the shame and guilt I was made to feel when, having appeared at Sheffield quarter sessions for the first time and been asked by a reporter if I was related to Wilfred Pickles, the resultant press cutting was sent by the barrister's clerk in Sheffield to my clerk, censoriously. The circuit mess had disciplinary powers over its members, in theory, and there was one barrister (later disbarred) who was 'tried' for seeking and obtaining publicity for himself and his cases in the press through a woman journalist he knew: we acquitted him.

Although touting is still forbidden, it has always gone on. When I was head of chambers we noticed we were not receiving many briefs from the Bradford prosecuting solicitor, although ours were the only chambers in the city. The clerk who handed out the briefs was being 'treated' in pubs and other places by members of a set of chambers in Leeds, and most of the briefs were going there. I spoke to the head of the Leeds chambers, later a circuit judge, but he pooh-poohed the matter.

I then took the drastic and easily misunderstood step of going to see the prosecuting solicitor himself, pointing out that I had no wish to tout, but that we were trying to provide a service and if we were failing in some way I would like to put things right. I did not tell him about his clerk being 'entertained'. The solicitor came back to me, saying he had not realised where the briefs were going – he left that to his clerk – but had directed that, in future, briefs must be shared equally between the two sets of chambers.

It is fair to concede that I then discovered that Gardner, our clerk, had lent the prosecution's clerk some money, forgetting – if he ever knew – that, as Shakespeare wrote in

25

Hamlet 'loan oft loseth both itself and friend'. I must further concede that the previous clerk to the prosecution in Bradford had been Gardner's personal friend, and he came over to us for morning coffee and afternoon tea almost daily!

Our clerk, Leslie Gardner, was burly in body; his round, puffy face was heavily creased; his thinning, plastered-down hair was cut in Prussian style; and he was a martinet. He had been in the RAF police during the Second World War, and those whom he arrested must have suffered as we did. His first wife held the fort in chambers during the war and then deserted, going off with and marrying Gardner's friend from RAF days. Like many highly sensitive people, Gardner was insensitive about the injury he did to others; in fact he went out of his way to do hurt as compensation for the hurt that had been done to him. Liking nothing better than a grievance to gnaw upon, he wanted to be injured – and relished the wound when he was.

Almost from the start, Gardner and I clashed; we remained in that uneasy relationship until I was senior enough to deal with him. But the blame must have been mine as much as his. It began in this way: every quarter he gave us each a chit with details of what we owed for rent, bobs-on-the-guineas and so on. I happened to ask him what the item 'P. cash' was for. The answer, which I might have anticipated, was 'petty cash', but he thought I was accusing him of trying to cheat me in some way. He complained to Snowden, said he did not want to act for me and refused to speak to me for a time. He made sure I paid for my crime by diverting any spare briefs to others; when he did hand any in my direction he made sure I realised how forgiving he was.

He and I never really got over that first misunderstanding. Gardner upset every pupil who arrived, and some of their wives as well. When one of my pupils came on his first day, Gardner's greeting was, 'Have you brought your cheque-book?' (Although no fee was then payable to the pupil-master, it was still usual to pay ten guineas (£10.50)

26

to the clerk.)

When Snowden retired in 1972 and I succeeded him, the final confrontation between Gardner and me was already on the way. There were two main causes: his persistent rudeness to solicitors and their clerks; and remuneration. When decimalisation abolished guineas, barristers had to alter the financial arrangements with their clerks. In our new agreements with Gardner we undertook to pay him 10 per cent of gross fees, but I insisted on a clause that, if we decided to take on a junior clerk also, the 10 per cent should be open to renegotiation. Soon after that, since Gardner was then in his early sixties, we decided to take on a junior clerk: the amount of work justified it, and we wanted to provide for continuity when Gardner retired in two or three years' time.

There was bitterness; there were wrangling meetings; members of chambers were divided on how to deal with the man on whom, in a sense, some were imprinted. I said I had had enough, and it was him or me. That must have reached him: some of my colleagues were close to him and they visited socially (he once came to my house, to a party, but I never went to his). Then he played what he thought was his ace: he gave us all three months' written notice, the wording varying in accordance with his feelings towards us – my notice being curt. He must have thought he was indispensable and that we would never find a successor in the tight, small world of barristers' clerks. He intended to stay, happy to see me go.

I approached a junior Bar clerk in Leeds and a solicitor's clerk in Bradford, but after speaking to Gardner they turned the job down. I wrote to the Barristers' Clerks' Association in London, and a young clerk in the Temple came twice, the second time with his wife; I showed them round local residential areas. I was offering 7 per cent, and he was on the point of accepting when, he said, for family reasons he could not move north. Gardner was rubbing his hands confidently. A Bar clerk predicted that our chambers would break up, and one member did leave to join other chambers. Time was ticking by, and my less robust companions suggested we ask Gardner to stay for a time; but I set my face against that.

Then I heard about Mrs Peggy Maud, who worked as a secretary in Leeds chambers. We met her and, to my colleagues' surprise, I decided at the last minute to offer her 5 per cent of gross fees, which she accepted.

Peggy was a very pleasant woman: warm, kind, friendly and conscientious, but firm when necessary. There was a three-week overlap before Gardner left: I warned Peggy he would make it hell for her, and he did, although I pointed out to him that she would have to collect and pay to him his dues for past work. The first time he took her to the barristers' clerks' room in Leeds Town Hall, none of them spoke a word to her all day. I told her that if she was pleasant to them – and she could not be anything else – they would not keep it up, and I was right. She was ousting Gardner, as they saw it, and setting a dangerous precedent by accepting 5 per cent when they were on 10.

But she was soon popular with them, with solicitors and with us. The other clerks told Peggy how Gardner had sabotaged my practice by agreeing that my cases could go into court lists even when I had other work elsewhere, yet telling me that the judge's insistence was the cause. Our chambers survived, and today prosper. Peggy went with me to the House of Lords in July 1976, with my parents, wife and three children, when I was sworn in as a judge by Lord Chancellor Elwyn-Jones.

Looking back from retirement, what impressions of life at the Bar detain my eye? The early years were ones of comparative penury. Sheila and I never went short of food, but we did of drink – and were none the worse for that. A year or so after we married we were invited out to dinner and had wine – an unthinkable luxury for us. What a grand life our friends must live, we thought. We did not have smart furniture in our large Victorian terraced house, which we bought for £1000 in 1949 on a 2½ per cent mortgage at £4 15s 5d (£4.77) a month, and it was so under-heated that you could see your breath in the hall in winter. If you wanted more coal for the lounge fire there was a bell to ring: no one answered it except ourselves, as the maid class had gone and the cellars and attics no longer buzzed to their quiet chatter. Women in service such as my grandmother and her mother had given way to a generation – mine – that stood on its feet and refused to bow the knee to anyone, and a good thing too.

For years I economised on weekdays by eating cheap lunches in railway refreshment rooms (they do not seem cheap there nowadays). When we lunched at the department store near our chambers – then a family business, but since House-of-Frasered – I did without coffee or a sweet, and not because I had a weight problem in those days. Taking a taxi was as likely then as my going by Concorde now, and I still prefer to walk half a mile than hail a cab: early habits are not easily shrugged off. In court I heard of young people, even the unemployed, taking a taxi; on some occasions house burglars took the loot home in one.

I had a pair of brown shoes which I dyed black so I could wear them in court. As we sat in Leeds assize court one day Geoffrey Baker said he could smell polish, and wondered whether it was coming from the table (on which we would have laid our briefs, if we had had any). I did not tell him, and he will only learn the truth if he reads this book. I can look back and smile at my early deprivations – they were trivial compared to many people's. I am sure those thin days were good for Sheila and me and our three children – none of whom has been spoilt by having too much too soon. It is good to have to climb the rock of life handhold by handhold, with no tools save effort, thrift and ingenuity.

Life in chambers was good. At the Bar one lives with the lively, the generous, the erudite and the profound (they do not all have all of that) and one's colleagues were always there to go to for advice on points of law, amount of damages or etiquette. I enjoyed attending the meetings and dinners in Leeds of the Bar mess – a local barristers' society-cum-dining club which every area has. There I met counsel from other chambers on friendly, social terms. There were small mess dinners and larger ones on special occasions, such as 'judges' nights' when the High Court judges sitting in Leeds came to us with studied condescension. Witty speeches, some impromptu, were made on such occasions, hair was let down and home truths were told. Alcohol flowed – too freely at times. A barrister who later became a Cabinet minister, and his friend who later rose to the High Court Bench, were driving home together after Bar mess when they were stopped by a policeman for having no lights. As the officer opened the passenger door the future minister fell into the gutter. The officer, who recognised him, said 'Good evening, gentlemen', helped the passenger back into his seat and with a 'Goodnight, gentlemen,' they were on their fortunate way.

Women barristers were not allowed to join the mess or attend any of its dinners or meetings. There was only a handful of women, and only one expressed any interest in joining when I raised the matter in about 1960. I did so because it did not seem right to exclude women. When my motion was debated, there was strong opposition, from men who instinctively thought that what was must be right, and that any change must be wrong. Some said we would have to guard our tongues and the character of mess would be debased. Others said the women should start their own mess (all six or so of them!). Yet others said High Court judges would object to speaking in the presence of women (in those days there were no women on the High Court Bench itself). My motion was defeated. In 1965, after moves at national level, women were admitted to mess by a motion passed unanimously. The antique creature known as the Bar was slowly slithering from its prehistoric slime and trundling on to firmer ground.

There was a moment that comes back when I awake in sweating terror some nights – though worse things terrify me more. The first day of Leeds assizes, in about 1950, was a splendid occasion, finding us once great British at our ceremonial best. We were no longer the workshop of the world and were becoming the toyshop of the world. No nation could dress up and play-act as we did and do. We had forgotten how to work and remembered only how to play. Three liveried trumpeters, paid for by the High Sheriff out of his own deep pocket, trumpeted in the judges. His scarlet-and-ermined lordship and his brother lordship robed in civil black, step by step and in step with each other, slowly climbed the steps of Leeds Town Hall.

Number one court was full. Everybody was there. The sheriff stood unruffled in his ruffle and buckled in his elegant shoes that did not buckle to, but were for decoration; resplendent in black silk tights and knee-breeches, a man from the eighteenth century. There was the sheriff's chaplain on the Bench, ready to pray when his lordship's clerk put the 'black cap' – a piece of black cloth in reality – on top of the high judicial wig, but not that day. Civic leaders were there to welcome His Majesty's judges, as were the chief constable and his chief cohorts. Local magistrates had come, proud to be part of it all, and – last but most prominent – bobbing rows of bewigged barristers, with wigless solicitors sitting behind the briefed – who could not easily be distinguished from the briefless, except by other barristers.

All stood, as their lordships and the Bench party entered and bowed. The judge's clerk spoke: 'My lords the King's justices do strictly charge and command all persons present to keep silent, on pain of imprisonment, while His Majesty's commission is read.' You could have heard a brief drop – though none did – as the clerk of assize, a former barrister who prospered in his new role better than in his old one, then read the anciently worded document: 'To our well-beloved and trusted cousin [not related really] and those of our counsel learned in the law [QCs] . . . greeting. Know ye by these presents [not gifts] that this shall be a commission of oyer and terminer [Norman French for 'hear' and 'determine'] and general gaol delivery . . . Saving unto us the amerciments [fines] from thence to us accruing . . . ' When the names of the two judges were read out the judge concerned bowed, placed a black tricorn hat fleetingly on top of his wig, and sat, leaving all the rest standing and some gaping.

The ancient ceremony over, the modern one began. The court was still packed as the first case was called on – mine! I was there to do a plea in mitigation for some miserable miscreant, before a liverish little judge, his face creased by pitiless arrogance. I briefly cross-examined the police officer, suggesting my client could not read or write, and the witness agreed. 'How do you know – because he says he can't?' was his lordship's tart riposte. I forget the term of imprisonment, which my client long since completed, and by now both men may share the same extra-terrestrial environment. I wonder what they say to each other.

No monster in the judicial jungle was more monstrous than Mr Justice Hugh Imbert Periam ('Hippy') Hallett. He was attached to ('adorned' would not be the *mot juste*) our circuit, though he was rarely seen there before his elevation to the Bench in 1939, Lord Chancellor Maugham having been impressed by him when he heard him do cases in the Judicial Committee of the Privy Council. Hallett was the most talkative and difficult of tribunals. Tall, massive, with a stoop and a high-pitched voice, he peered down at the inferior world through pince-nez spectacles. He used to whisper to his clerk, looking down at the ones in wigs, 'Who shall we do today?' and he did me more than once, though I make no complaint – I came through, shaking away the sweat. All young counsel were fair game. Hippy had no kind word for anyone, and none had one for him – except to his face. Far from adorning the Bench, he blemished it, combining controlled venom with uncontrolled malice as few judges did even then.

I recall an ice cream salesman charged with rape. The evidence was marginal but Hallett was bent on getting him and did, awarding seven years – and there was in those days no parole, only the possibility of a remission of one-third of the sentence for good behaviour. The purveyor of ice cream – not a client of mine – had a large slice of his life purveyed into prison.

John Cobb, later for a tragically brief period a High Court judge, told me a true story about Hallett that highlights his character. Cobb was at one time Hallett's marshal – a young barrister who goes with the judge on circuit for several weeks, living in the judges' 'lodgings' (a mansion in reality) and acting as a sort of poorly paid secretary, as when he swears-in witnesses. Hippy Hallett had a purse, and every day before breakfast he checked its contents. One morning he announced there was a penny missing and they must find it. Etiquette demanded that no one could start breakfast before Hallett, being the senior judge in residence. Eventually Cobb, on his knees by the skirting board and hungry, discreetly took out a penny of his own and said the missing coin had been found. 'Splendid, marshal, splendid,' said the judge, tucking into his cornflakes and devouring the *Times*. Later that morning, as they sat in court, Hallett took out his purse during one of the boring periods that every contested case has, and counted his money again. There was a penny too much. 'Marshal,' he hissed at Cobb, 'you've cheated me!'

Mr Justice Hallett had a good brain: he had mastered his law, as he had Latin and Greek. No judge used his tongue so dextrously or so frequently, and in the end he tripped over it and fell to his (generally acclaimed) doom. Lord Denning deals with this in his book *The Due Process of Law*. He writes of Hallett: 'He started his judicial career quietly enough but – as often happens – as his experience grew so did his loquacity. He got so interested in every case that he dived deep into every detail of it.'

The climax came in Jones v. National Coal Board 1957 2 QB 55. Hippy asked more questions than those of both counsel added together, and his judgement was set aside by the Court of Appeal, Lord Denning presiding. He said: 'A judge of acute perception, acknowledged learning and actuated by the best of motives, has nevertheless himself intervened so much in the case that one of the parties – nay, each of them – has come away complaining that he was not able properly to put his case; and these complaints are, we think, justified.'

I feel a certain sympathy for Hallett; I know the temptation and I have not always avoided it. Soon after that case Lord Chancellor Kilmuir persuaded Mr Justice Hallett to retire – he had qualified for a full pension, having served for seventeen years. A barrister told me that the last time he saw Hallett, the retired judge was sitting on a beach in the south of France dressed in a dark suit and reading ancient Greek.

When I joined the north-eastern circuit in 1949 the other High Court judge from that circuit was Mr Justice Geoffrey Hugh Benbow Streatfeild. He was present at Carr Manor, the judges' lodgings in Leeds, to which kind Mr Justice Slade invited me when he heard I had come to work in the north. That evening opened a door into a world I knew little about – the world of top people, the gentry, who do some things differently, such as eating fruit with knife and fork, not hands and teeth. When we stood at the end of the meal and the nicely spoken women withdrew, I nearly followed them, though by the time I heard 'Shall we join the ladies?' I was cottoning on. I was always a bit ill-at-ease when I lunched at Carr Manor, even though in later years I was usually the oldest judge there.

Geoffrey Streatfeild was the 'godfather' of the north-eastern circuit, influential with the Lord Chancellor's office in London on the matter of who should be QCs and judges or any area where 'they' wanted to know about 'us'. The impression that remains in my mind is of tall, dignified Streatfeild speaking with slow deliberation; of dignity maturing into pomposity. This may seem unkind of me. Streatfeild could be kind to others, as he was to me in court, but his kindness was dispensed in a patronising way. A man in his position – garlanded with power, larded with patronage and inflated by flattery – has to be rare to remain simple and modest, even if he began like that.

Here is a slight instance of Streatfeild's manner, about which I may be too sensitive. As he and I talked before that dinner, he cut me off mid-sentence to say we must go in to eat. For all my faults I hope I would never do that to anyone. The lower on the ladder of life a person is, the more important is it to consider their feelings. The public often assume that the Bench is bubbling with brains but at any level below the highest this is a fallacy. Even a High Court judge does not need a high intellect. If he is courteous and careful and has common sense he will get by, lauded and liked by all including the Court of Appeal.

In 1961 the recordership of Leeds, the highest judicial post on the circuit for a practising barrister, was vacant. In those days every large town had a recorder, a QC or junior barrister who sat there for a few days or weeks a year, practising at the Bar for the rest of the time. The candidates for the Leeds post were Rudolph Lyons QC and George Waller QC. They were similar in seniority, with Lyons ahead by a whisker – when he was not appointed he was disappointed, though he got the post later. But anyone who understands how the legal Establishment works could have no doubt who would be preferred. They were of similar ability at the Bar; I would have preferred Lyons to lead me, especially when defending in a criminal case. But he was

Jewish, from a grammar school and a provincial university. How could he hope to be chosen against Waller – a Church of England, Oundle and Cambridge rugby blue and England trialist who had married the daughter of Lord Hacking, one-time chairman of the Conservative Party?

Furthermore George Waller had played his cards perfectly. I have known him from the days before he took silk, and observed him as a QC and High Court judge; when he retired he had reached the Court of Appeal. At Bar mess meetings George never ventured a toe into any controversial area (the Lord Chancellor's office do not like controversial QCs). When any subject was discussed he spoke as if giving judgement on the Bench, saying 'on the one hand' and 'on the other hand', so that it was difficult to know what he did think. He is tall and handsome with a soft, well-modulated voice, exquisite manners and a charming manner, and those who meet him find him delightful. Those who appeared in court with or before him did not notice an outstanding intellect but, as I have said, that is not essential equipment for a QC or judge.

George Waller has been careful in everything he has done, and it has taken him high. If you know him well, as I do not, you may possibly find him cold at the centre. He was said to have lost his temper in court only once, over some sort of model brought into court during a civil action in which he was counsel. I once went to see him when he was a presiding judge of the circuit. I had been trying to get in touch with Mr Justice Cumming-Bruce to ask if he would sponsor me for silk, which he eventually did, and thought Waller might be able to assist.

Mr Justice Waller sat in his room fully robed with his wig still in place, looking at me through large lenses, his eyes like two fish gaping through their glass bowls. I said I could not very well ring a High Court judge. George Waller was ready to help: if he had to ring Cumming-Bruce about something else, he would mention me to him, but he would not ring specially. (Why on earth not? I asked myself.)

Waller has always been tepid, hesitant to commit himself; his early fear of compromising his prospects has most likely become part of his personality, so he is unaware of it. Let me make it clear that in my view Sir George Waller has no malice and no enemies, and is deservedly popular. He is a very proper English gentleman. His son Mark's appointment as a High Court judge surprised neither those who knew him nor those who did not.

Excellence at games is a splendid asset for a barrister, especially if he has ambitions for the Bench. A friend of mine was an Oxford cricket blue, and he was embarrassed at the scholarship interview at his Inn of Court by the interest shown not in him but in the number of runs he had made in the varsity match. He got the scholarship, and when the time comes for his elevation to the Bench his blue will be on his curriculum vitae – better than the black marks that were on mine!

Carl Aarvold was a celebrated rugby player, a Cambridge blue who also played on the wing for England. He did not fly as high or as fast at the Bar as he had done on the playing field; he never took silk. But he is affable, and I am sure he did well as a judge in the ancient, prestigious posts at the Old Bailey – common sergeant and then recorder of London. He also presided over the Lawn Tennis Association. Once described as the best after-dinner speaker in London – a rare accolade in a city not short of that breed – Carl Aarvold has talent beyond the fields of law and sport. With every respect to a nice man, however (we have not met since mess dinners in my early days at the Bar), would he have sailed so grandly on the judicial high seas if he had not been so fleet on the wing?

Two of the most formidable men I met in the law – Geoffrey Walter Wrangham and Harry Hylton-Foster QC – were products of Eton and Oxford. Education at that great school – founded originally for scholars of limited means but now filled mainly by the sons of the rich – is undoubtedly ideal for an intending barrister. Self-confidence is vital. A certain detachment, arrogance, indifference to the feelings of others is also useful at the Bar and on the Bench: I record that with a sigh. I must also record that not all Old Etonians are like that.

Wrangham's career at Eton was touched on in *Enemies of Promise* by his school contemporary Cyril Connolly. Chapter 20 is entitled 'Dark Ages' and deals with the beatings then – but not now – administered by boy to boy. The Sixth Form had supper in their own room and a special fag, 'Senior', was sent from there to fetch the 'wanted' fag.

'Connolly, you're wanted.'

'Who by?'

'Wrangham.'

'That's all right,' Connolly writes that he replied, 'he won't beat me, only tick me off. He's my fag master.'

'He's going to beat someone. He's got the chair out.' The chair was only put in place for beatings, and sometimes the fag was sent beforehand to fetch the cane for his own chastisement.

Punishment did not always immediately follow the offence. Connolly used to pray in the chapel, 'Please God, may Wrangham not "want" me, please please God may Wrangham not "want" me or may he forget about it by tomorrow and I will clean my teeth. Amen!' According to Connolly, sometimes all the fags were beaten at once.

We knelt on the chair bottoms outwards and gripped the bottom bar with our hands, stretching towards it over the back. Looking round under the chair we could see a monster rushing towards us with a cane in his hand, his face upside down and distorted – the frowning mask of the Captain of the School or the hideous little Wrangham. The pain was acute . . . The Captain of the School, Marjoribanks, who afterwards committed suicide, was a passionate beater like his bloody-minded successors Wrangham and Cliffe.

The name of Wrangham went on to chill the hearts of many, including me in my early years at the Bar. He could not beat me physically, of course, but he took it out of me in court at times when he was on the bench. Wrangham had followed his scholarship to Eton with a classical scholarship at Balliol College, Oxford, where he won a double first. The one academic hurdle he failed to clear was the last one – a fellowship at All Souls' College, Oxford, which represents the blue riband of the academic world. Lord Hailsham is a member, as is William Waldegrave. Lord Denning failed, attributing that to the way that he, a grammar school boy, spoke Latin, and despite his first-class honours in mathematics and law at Oxford. I suspect that if Denning had been to Eton, All Souls would have accepted him.

The only occasion on which I recall Wrangham speaking to me off-guard was after an appeal, heard by recorder Frank Beverley at Bradford quarter sessions, by a licensee convicted of permitting betting on the premises. There was ample evidence from undercover police officers of betting slips flying around, yet the recorder (the director of a brewery) allowed the appeal. Wrangham had lost, and as he left court he said to me, 'There is no other court in England where such a decision would have been made.' He was right; he usually was.

I learned much by watching Wrangham in action. He was brilliant at speeches in mitigation of sentence after a guilty plea: not a surplus word. He marshalled his points like a battle commander disposing his troops, compelling the judge to leniency by logic and conviction. He had a deep voice, a severe manner and formidable power. I cannot say I liked Wrangham, but I admired him, and if I had been in trouble with the law I would have gone to him before any other counsel on the circuit. He did not like me; I doubt if he liked any of his colleagues, but he had degrees of dislike. He probably thought I was an upstart who needed suppressing, and he was probably correct.

Harry Hylton-Foster was the best all-round advocate I ever saw in action. Like the great Irish lawyer and statesman of the early twentieth century Edward Carson QC – Lord Carson who said: 'Ulster will fight and Ulster will be right' – he was equally at home whether appearing before magistrates, cross-examining in front of a jury or disentangling complex legal points in the House of Lords. Hylton, as everyone knew him, was tall with an aquiline nose and clear, piercing eyes. In court he stood erect and still, his feet riveted at attention, as he had schooled himself. He was a gentleman and thought of himself as one. Whatever Wrangham thought of himself, he was a bruiser when compared with the elegant Hylton.

I recollect Hylton at a meeting of the circuit's 'grand court', a festive occasion when specially composed songs are sung after dinner and home truths told about colleagues. A favourite song was – and perhaps still is – 'The Night-Soil Man', a reference to the poor unfortunate who before the days of modern plumbing used to empty earth closets:

> *The night-soil man,*
> *Shovelling shite in the middle of the night,*
> *He does what he can,*
> *As his balls go clang, clang, clang.*

After fifteen years, I cannot vouch for word-for-word accuracy. But I do recall Hylton leading a line of barristers, who had dined well, as they marched round the room singing the song; Hylton was clenching a daffodil between his teeth. I cannot imagine Wrangham relaxing that far – though if he thought it expected of him he would most likely have willed himself, with Roman fortitude.

Harry Hylton-Foster's career swung off-track. He had

political ambitions, and his talent should have taken him to the Woolsack, but he was diverted by duty and died disappointed. Elected as Tory MP for York in 1950, at first he still did cases at Leeds Assizes, sometimes going by train to vote in the Commons in the evening and returning by sleeper; the Labour Government had only a tiny majority. In the 1951 Conservative Government he was Solicitor-General, the junior of the two Law Officer posts in the Government. By seniority in Parliament – there can have been no other reason – Reggie Manningham-Buller (also Eton and Oxford) was made Attorney-General. If it had been the other way round Hylton would presumably have become Lord Chancellor when Reggie got the job in 1957, as Lord Dilhorne. Manningham-Buller – known as 'Bullying-Manner' – was said to have been bullied at Eton and after that to have taken it out on others. He was one of those whose education passed him off as abler than he was: polished rather than bright.

When Hylton became Speaker of the Commons in 1959 the north-eastern circuit gave him a dinner in celebration. As we were being told where to stand for the official photographs I heard him murmur, 'I always do as I am told.' He had taken the Speaker's job out of duty, and he was said never to have been comfortable in it. I was saddened when I heard in 1965 that Hylton had dropped dead in the street at the age of sixty. With a whimper, one felt. As with many, the wheel of chance won less for him than his high talent deserved.

As a young barrister, I found that appearing before High Court judges could be terrifying. You had to 'screw your courage to the sticking-place', as Lady Macbeth says. I did my first defended divorce before Mr Justice Hubert Wallington. He was in his late seventies when I first encountered him at Leeds assizes: a sonorous, inflexible, difficult old man. While my client, the wife, was in the box the judge asked her some questions. When I thought he had finished, I

41

asked her one. But the judge tapped his pencil on the desk – his favourite gesture of admonition. 'Mr Pickles, it is most discourteous to intervene whilst the witness is in the hands of the court.' So after that I left long gaps after he had apparently finished his interventions.

In cross-examining the husband I suggested that he had inconsiderately fathered too many children on to his wife. Tap, tap with the pencil. 'Doesn't God come into it?' intoned his lordship. My instructing solicitor hastily scribbled me a note, 'He is a Catholic.' As he did not believe in divorce, Wallington may not have been the most suitable judge to try cases between parties who did believe in it. In that case there was ample evidence of cruelty, but in dismissing the wife's petition Hubert Wallington gave the parties a homily on the sanctity of marriage and I went home feeling cheated, as my client must have.

In another case Ernest Ould, a down-to-earth Yorkshire counsel who knew little law but had an effective nose for relevant facts and later became a county court judge, said to his client in the box, 'Tell us what happened next, Mr Jones.' Tap, tap.

'Who are "us", Mr Ould?' asked Wallington.

'Oh, you and me and my learned friend, my lord,' said Ould, with the breezy manner which he may have inherited from his bookmaker father. He was happily unaware, and perhaps unconcerned, that he should have said: 'Tell his lordship.'

One day I went into Wallington's court to 'mention' a case for my colleague Geoffrey Baker: to have the case taken out of the list or to have a date fixed. The judge asked what the issues were, and since I happened to have looked at the brief I told him that the adultery alleged by the respondent was admitted in the client's 'discretion statement' (details of his own adultery). Tap, tap, tap. 'Mr Pickles, I have always understood that it is most improper to disclose the contents of one's client's discretion statement until it is placed before the court.' I tried to explain and must have shown irritation – I did that with judges at times – and he then said, 'Will you come and see me in my room at 1 p.m.?'

'Certainly, my lord,' I replied.

It looked to those in court – and one is never unobserved – that he was going to remove his wig and give me a wigging.

But before the appointed hour Wallington's clerk came to me and said, 'Don't be too hard on the old boy. He's nearly eighty. He wants to apologise.' I thought to myself that Sir Hubert Wallington was not the sort of man to apologise to anybody, and that if he did wish to, why couldn't he do it in the hearing of those who had heard the previous exchange?

When I entered the judge's room his opening question sounded ominous. 'Which Inn is yours, Pickles?' I thought he was to report me to my benchers.

'Inner Temple, my lord.'

'I'm in Gray's.'

'Look, my lord, what I was trying to say this morning – and I'm sorry if I – '

'Oh, don't think you're on the carpet, Pickles. On the contrary, I am.'

He went on to tell me how he had addressed the Birmingham Law Society on discretion statements (hardly the most riveting of topics, especially as expounded by Wallington). The aged judge then said that if ever I thought of this incident in the future, he hoped I would look on it in the nicest possible way. I began to feel sorry for him; he was doddering and trying to be nice to me, but not finding it easy. I never saw him again.

It was said that not long afterwards Lord Merriman, the President of the Divorce Division, sent for Wallington. They were both about eighty and there was then no compulsory retiring age for judges of the High Court or above (the great Lord Denning was the last of that breed). 'They are trying to get rid of us, Hubert, but we're not going, are we?' was the presidential statement. But before long they had both been eased out.

Life at the Bar had unexpected hazards for the young. I knew a homosexual High Court judge; he was not from our circuit, but came round it. He was a courteous, sensitive, cultivated man and an able lawyer with a subtle mind. I did a case before him at Leeds, and after it had ended his clerk said that his lordship invited me to dine at the judges' lodgings that very evening. When I arrived at Carr Manor, dinner-jacketed, for my second evening there, the judge – who was a bachelor and whom I had never met out of court – welcomed me, and I referred to my wife. He seemed to lose interest in me then, as I look back – I did not know of him then all that I later learned.

A young member of the circuit, from the same top public school as that judge, went to stay for the weekend at his house but left prematurely, saying, 'Mr Justice X is an evil man, and his butler is worse!' He declined to say more – not wanting to let the old school down, perhaps. I did a buggery case before the same judge, who showed great interest in a remark my client had made to the police, 'When I see a man's prick, it's like gold.' The defendant was sentenced to eight years for his attentions to boys, so the judge did not let his private predilection interfere with his public duty – or was he in some way punishing his own guilty self by such a sentence?

As an advocate I was good on some days, bad on others. I was temperamental. I could be eloquent; I could be tongue-tied – the words could flow; or the stream be dammed. I could cross-examine incisively; I could examine crossly and indecisively. There have been times when the engine of my mind has almost seized up, and I have barely been able to coax it along.

At other times it has run ahead of me and I have found it hard to keep up. I sometimes fell out with judges in court. I did not find it easy to be ingratiating all the time with them and with solicitors, as an ambitious barrister has to be. I do not mean he has to get on his knees, but he should tread carefully and be wary where he puts his feet. As an advocate and as a judge, I was too often tense when I should have relaxed. The ideal is relaxed power, like a jaguar or Jaguar. It is better to be easy and pleasant with people, using power and position gently but firmly and never becoming angry – that spells inadequacy and failure. No one should ever lose their temper in any circumstances: there is no need, and it achieves nothing but hostility and ill-will in others, and wasted emotion in oneself.

Power, the ability to thrust and paralyse with words, should be kept in reserve, for the occasions when it is needed. To use it too soon is to fire away before the enemy has arrived on the field. I am too emotional; I feel things too strongly, even passionately at times, and that can be dangerous for an advocate. For a judge, strong feelings are surplus baggage; he should be calm and consider everything carefully, objectively. I tried to do that, not always successfully. Can we change our own characters? Obviously not. We are stuck with what we have inherited and experienced. But the mature person, certainly the mature judge, should be able to stand back, moderate his attitudes and restrain his words. A judge, and also an advocate, has so many aces and the parties and witnesses so few cards at all. They must not leave court feeling the game was loaded against them, the process unfair.

There were drawbacks to life at the Bar. Not being allowed to form partnerships with other barristers was wasteful. I had to purport to cover an enormous field of law. It was easy with criminal work; the law is simple and most cases are completed without anyone looking at our 'bible', *Archbold's Criminal Pleading and Practice*. Most cases in the crown court, which is where criminal cases are dealt with, turn on the evidence – can it be proved they did it? But I did civil work too, including divorce, damages for personal injuries (the Factories Acts have complex regulations), hire purchase, property cases including landlord and tenant, and occasionally easements such as rights of way. I did conveyancing in the Bar final examination, but I have never mastered that arcane art. I even gave an occasional opinion on libel or slander, though happily none ever got to court: the technicalities are a lawyer's dream or, in my case, a nightmare. It would have been easier for us in chambers, and for solicitors who briefed us, if we could have specialised in different fields. It must be conceded, however, that solicitors have partners, and the senior ones tend to do less and less yet draw more and more. Barristers have no partners to lean on and have an incentive to keep on their toes.

Would I suggest the Bar as a career to a youngster? No. But if a young person feels he or she must try for it, I would say, 'Go on, you *have* to.' If you have been to the right school and university and have the right parents, you will get a head start in the law – but even then you may fail. It is possible to succeed without those aids. Try to get into good, busy chambers, work hard, master details, be patient. You may have to wait before you earn; there will be frustration and failure along the way. Desperate frugality will do you no harm, but strengthen you. You will be in the hands of solicitors, your clerk and judges; some of these people will be narrow in outlook and overbearing in attitude. But you should be as pleasant to people as you can. If people *like* you, that is half the battle. If you are able too, you are near victory. But never grovel or be sycophantic – others will not respect you for it and you will not respect yourself.

Be firm and stand up to judges when it is necessary, but only then. Curb your aggression and use it sparingly, against frauds, perjurers and unjust judges – but never against witnesses who are honest and doing their best.

After having too little work you will find at times that you have too much, and have to sit up some nights preparing for the next day. You will have to do it, and should feel guilty if you know you have not done your best. You will at times feel frustration and humiliation at the hands of some judges like me. But they are not all like me. There will be compensations. You will give help to clients who desperately need it and look to you for it. Speak up, speak clearly and concisely. Do not repeat yourself with a judge unless he is dim, and most are not. Repetition to jurors can be forgiven, but they are not all dim – collectively they usually show common sense and even wisdom. At times the words will flow and soar, moving even jejune jurors and jaundiced judges. You may one day wave wands, move minds, play a blinder and go home feeling great. But do not expect to do that with your first few cases. There are good people in the law at every level, people of integrity, charm and learning whom you would not find in such profusion in any other trade or profession, and they will compensate for those less given to goodness. Stick at it, and good luck to you.

So was all the agony of the Bar worthwhile? Er, yes, probably it was in the end – but not in the beginning.

3

Why did I join the Bench and
how did I fit in?

When I was called to the Bar in 1948 by the Treasurer of the Inner Temple, ex-Lord Chancellor Simon (a great man in his day, but who remembers him now?), I had not the vaguest ambition or intention to become a judge. I wanted to follow the likes of Simon and combine the Bar with politics, using the former as a stepping-stone. I had met Simon when he came to speak to the Oxford University Law Society while I was president. He was as vain and self-important then as he had always been. To be fair, he had good reasons for vanity if there ever are any: double first in Greats at Oxford, President of the Union, Solicitor-General at thirty-three and holder of the Great Seal as Lord Chancellor.

When I was a student, politics obsessed me. Getting into Parliament as soon as possible and combining that with writing was more important than anything the law seemed to offer, long-term. But, as an Oxford tutor said to me, 'Life is full of frustration and disappointment.' Things turned out very differently from my early hopes. I was far too idealistic and impractical ever to succeed in politics, and I did not succeed.

I may have gained my interest in politics from my father. When I was six he was elected to Halifax Council as a Liberal. He was thirty-one, the age at which I too became a councillor, and later, in 1950, he was elected Mayor of Halifax. My political life, if it can be called that, began in

1943, when I was an eighteen-year-old student declared medically unfit to serve in the forces because of a childhood accident to my right hand.

People's thoughts were turning to what would happen after the war, and a political party called Common Wealth was formed by the writer J. B. Priestley and a landowner (until he gave it away) Sir Richard Acland. I joined with naive enthusiasm. We in Common Wealth wanted a new start, based on bright-eyed socialism, with everybody sharing and working joyously together – like those colourful, mendacious films of Soviet workers and peasants marching across sunny wheatfields, arm in arm.

Someone in Whitehall thought we in Common Wealth were subversive, and two plain-clothes policemen came to our public meetings. They showed more interest than the public as a whole did. I learned years later, from a woman who had typed for the local police, that reports about me were sent regularly to the Home Office. But the notion that we constituted any sort of threat was about as sensible as the idea that Josef Stalin was a saint – though millions thought he was. Sincerity seeped from every pore in our earnest bodies. Students, schoolteachers, one or two manual workers and a bankrupt businessman who led us, locally we were about a dozen strong.

Common Wealth won one or two by-elections, but when the war ended so did the truce between the main political parties – and so did Common Wealth. After that I wavered between Labour and Liberal and at Oxford was active in the Liberal Club, becoming its treasurer.

In a 1951 local election, aged twenty-six, I stood for Labour in the ward where I lived, but lost. The publicity given to my membership of that party did not improve such practice as I had at the Bar. Most solicitors are Conservative and almost all conservative. Five years later I was elected to the council in Brighouse, then a cosy little non-county borough with a population of thirty thousand.

One of the things I learned as a councillor is how strong is vanity. I have as much as the next man, but vanity takes different forms. I never wanted what seemed to obsess most of my colleagues – to be mayor. I wanted to get things done. The mayor was only a figurehead, but, especially to those who worked at a factory bench or office desk, it meant something to be addressed as 'His Worship the Mayor', to wear the fur-trimmed gown and follow the mace-bearer. In the Mayor's Parlour you were Somebody, and important people – even your own boss – looked up to you.

None of that pomp was for me, but I did take myself too seriously in other ways. In 1959 I left the Labour Party, because I could not reconcile my own views with certain of the party's policies. I then joined the Liberals, which had no lines that were hard to toe, and stood for Brighouse and Spenborough in the 1964 general election. I enjoyed making speeches and sending them to the press, and twisting the tails of the two big parties. We just managed to retain the deposit, thanks to the 6411 electors, including myself, who voted for me. The big moment came when Jo Grimond, the party leader, was persuaded to stop for a few minutes and be photographed with me on his way from Huddersfield to Bradford.

After 1964 I slid out of active politics. I was thirty-nine and my political career was ending before it had really got going; my idealistic fervour had melted under the searching sun of experience. If I had stayed with Labour, I would probably have got into Parliament and then been thrown out of the party for not doing as I was told. I realise now that my interest in politics was romantic and impractical.

How do I, a failed politician, sum up politics and politicians? In any political party, idealism exists in the ranks of supporters – those who knock on doors, hand out pamphlets and man committee rooms. Why else would they do it? A politician who wants to make a career of it is in a different position. He has to be ready to throw his ideals overboard –

not all at once, though, or he will be thrown overboard by his rivals. He must be ready to say things he doesn't believe, passing off bad policies as if they were good. The concept of an honest politician is almost a contradiction in terms. Neil Kinnock, basically a well-intentioned man, has thrown out his left-wing beliefs in order to get Labour elected and himself into No. 10 Downing Street.

Most of us are basically selfish; we have to be, to survive and prosper. A professional politician is driven by two desires: to express his ego and to get his probing fingers into the bran-tub. By ego I mean the need to be and feel important, influential, with one's hands on the levers of power. And by bran-tub I mean money from directorships, books and articles, flying about the world at others' expense – and sex. Politicians talk a lot about serving the public, but deep down the majority of them are in it for what they can get out of it.

Most large organised groups are run mainly in the interest of those who run them. This applies to public companies, the papacy, political parties, the Kremlin and the English judiciary. Find me a judge who wants to improve anything beyond his own position, and I will find you fifty who do not. I know High Court judges who make more fuss about waiting five minutes for their coffee than about the five years litigants have waited for their cases to come on. The coffee affects judges personally; the delays do not. The main aim of those who run a political party is to get or keep political power for themselves.

There was another reason for my abandoning politics after the 1964 election. Out of the blue, in September 1963 I had been asked to sit on the Bench. I had been at the Bar for fifteen years, but I had not expected to hold any sort of judicial office.

At that time the lowest rung on the judicial ladder for a barrister was to sit at quarter sessions as an assistant recorder. When a recorder left for promotion to a more senior recordership, a full-time judgeship, or retired or died, there was a shuffling-up of the various recorderships.

In 1963 Henry Suddards, the recorder of Middlesbrough, became a county court judge. Another member of our chambers, Geoffrey Baker, had been his assistant recorder. He became deputy recorder pending a new appointment, and as the next in seniority – 'Buggins' turn' is an essential feature of British public life – I was asked by Baker to be his assistant. The new permanent recorder, Douglas Forrester-Paton, then asked me to stay on as his assistant.

My judicial career was launched unceremoniously and almost by accident. I had received no training at all for the Bench – it did not exist; the Judicial Studies Board, which now runs courses for those who sit on the Bench, lay in the future. My appointment had to be approved by an official in the Lord Chancellor's office but that consisted of a perfunctory phone call to Suddards. I had no black mark against me then – though I was known to be a bit of a rebel.

I had, for instance, agitated for more democracy in the way things were decided in chambers – such as the rents paid by the various members. So that beginners were cushioned for their first seven years, I introduced a sliding scale. I had proposed at the circuit Bar mess that women should be allowed to join. That failed at the time but I successfully supported the motion that they should be allowed to attend the dinners given by the circuit to its members who became High Court judges. These were usually held in the Middle Temple Hall in London, white tie and tails being obligatory. Now the dinners take place in York or Leeds and we wear black ties. Let no one say the Bar never progresses.

Although it was strange at first – everything seemed the wrong way round – I soon enjoyed sitting on the Bench, albeit for £27 a day or whatever it was. And no expenses were allowed against income: the Inland Revenue said that in theory we were supposed to live in the area where we were recorders. I was not a recorder and I did not live in Middlesbrough, but such facts are easily ignored.

The reasons why I liked sitting at quarter sessions are the key to my eventually opting to become a full-time circuit judge. The uncertainties of life at the Bar may be looked on as attractive – you never know when your big chance will come. When young you do not complain about sitting up all night to read a brief that was delivered late, then standing up in court all next day, hammering away for an elegant victory and perhaps gaining a new client.

But those uncertainties do not remain attractive. As the years pass, your juniors – even your own ex-pupils – start to pass you. Sitting up all night is too tiring even to think about. Dealing pleasantly with unpleasant people, such as some solicitors and High Court judges, becomes less easy. A youngster is eager for the clash of newly forged swords, but less so the older man with his rusty blunted weapon. He has done it all before. He knows every move. Nothing is fresh. The middle-aged counsel knows the ploys of every crook. Most defendants in criminal cases are guilty and everyone involved, except the jurors, knows it. This causes a certain cynicism. A trial is a game with intricate rules, watched with fascination by the person in the dock at the centre of it all.

As for civil actions for damages arising out of injuries sustained in accidents at work or on the road, I never liked them. They are expensive exercises with intricate rules, the only certain winners being the lawyers. In these games of ploy and counter-ploy, clever lawyers can defeat just claims.

On the Bench you are above all that. The game is the same, but instead of rolling in the mud you merely follow the play and your referee's garb stays clean. You have responsibility, but you feel it less. You do not feel blamed if you lose; the judge cannot lose. You are not beholden to others, such as solicitors or a barrister's clerk. As a judge I did not work long or uncertain hours. I arrived at court, the work was put before me, I did it and went home. If the work ended before lunch, I lunched at home. I never had to sit up through the night preparing a case. In fact there is no need to prepare it at all, however complex it is. Counsel or solicitors must explain it all in court. The summing-up in a criminal case, or the judgement in a civil action, can be prepared, if it is prepared at all, in court during the case. I hardly ever took work home. However, some judges did, and High Court judges work harder than circuit judges like me.

A barrister is essentially partisan. He has to do all he can, within the rules, to win for his client. There can be a certain grubbiness in this. Securing the acquittal of a plainly guilty defendant satisfies one part of an advocate, but the process lacks – how shall I put it? – nobility. A judge strives not for any client, but for justice, and this can be noble. It can be satisfying if a judge has done his best and feels he got the right answer. The media may hound him or the Court of Appeal overrule him, but if he really did his best he has no need to worry. And most of his decisions will reach neither the press nor the Court of Appeal.

Not long before his death Mr Justice 'Roddie' Smith was heavily criticised by the press and the public because he had imprisoned two young women for the manslaughter of their brutal father, whom they had stabbed to death with knives. The judge became so depressed that he could not work for several weeks, and some said that it contributed to his early death – he was younger than me. A judge should be able to batten the hatches and ride through such waves of hostility. 'Do what you think right and forget it' is the best attitude; worry about the case beforehand, but not afterwards.

There is a certain status in sitting on the Bench, even on the lowest rung, and much more as a full-time judge. People defer to you, whether or not they mean it. I hope I was no more vain than the next judge, and perhaps less. I am not for pomp, as opposed to dignity, which the solemn process of deciding important matters in others' lives must have. I do not favour cringing deference, in myself to others or in others to myself. Judicial office and all its power should not go to the holder's head – though there is a natural tendency for that to happen, and I did not avoid it completely.

I enjoyed going to sit at Middlesbrough quarter sessions, even in its inadequate old town hall. Douglas Forrester-Paton and I stayed at the Royal Oak in the pleasant village of Great Ayton. We went for brief walks in the Cleveland Hills before the rigours of the day. Later I sat as assistant recorder at other quarter sessions, mainly Leeds. This inevitably harmed my practice at the Bar. I was too often unavailable in the Bradford chambers where Leslie Gardner was 'looking after my affairs'.

After centuries, the Courts Act 1971 abolished courts of assize and quarters. Not before time, in my opinion – though not in that of most of the Bar and Bench. Their members are never eager for change, as Lord Chancellor Mackay has discovered, though it cannot have surprised that wise man. The crown court now sits in most of the towns that formerly had quarter sessions. Recorders and their assistants – including a few solicitors – are not attached to any one town, but can be moved about as the administrators choose, though they do it tactfully and with deference.

Assizes and quarter sessions used to be run by a handful of administrators, only a few of them civil servants; at certain quarter sessions some of the organisers were in outside firms of solicitors. The work has indeed multiplied in the last twenty years, but the number of administrators has mushroomed like a nuclear explosion. Functions are divided and subdivided, everyone having a neat label. At one crown court where I sat I asked what number two in the hierarchy actually did; all he *seemed* to do was ask me where I wanted a new telephone put and the like. Number two was supposed to be responsible for listing cases for trial – a very exacting job – but he had no experience in listing; this senior executive officer had been moved from his previous post, and had to be slotted in somewhere. In fairness, although when I raised the matter at a meeting the circuit administrator purported to defend what had happened, the man was moved on before long.

I have no wish to decry the work done by court clerks and other administrators, nor to suggest that they are adequately recompensed – they are grossly underpaid. There is a continual drain of staff to solicitors and other employers who pay more. Against that there is security of employment. A civil servant cannot suddenly be made redundant, except for 'limited efficiency', and there is a complex and fair system of tribunals for such a situation.

When the first list of crown court recorders came out in December 1971, I was not on it. With several others who had also served for years as assistant recorders I had been passed over, because the late Mr Justice Raymond Hinchcliffe, the senior presiding judge of the circuit, did not like us on personal grounds. He and I had clashed in court and I had stood up to him. I went to see Hinchcliffe in his room at court in Leeds and confronted him about my omission. He lied to me, but soon I was appointed a recorder and sat for several years in Manchester Crown Court. If that was exile, no one said it was, and I was never sure.

In 1975 I applied for a full-time circuit judgeship. I have already explained some of the reasons for preferring the Bench to the Bar. Although I was never ambitious to be a judge or thought myself likely to achieve it, I was driven in that direction like a rudderless yacht. I was fifty, then the best age at which to apply. Now it seems to be forty-five: judges qualify for a pension after fifteen years if they are then sixty-five, and the Treasury naturally prefers to get twenty years' service rather than fifteen.

Then there was the question of security. Most people go for that, though not necessarily when young, or as the main object in life. Half-pay as a pension, a tax-free lump sum on retirement equivalent to one year's gross salary: these things spell security, as does the rule that a serving judge can be ill for up to six months without a reduction in salary. One circuit judge I know had a triple by-pass operation not long after his appointment. If he had still been at the Bar that would have meant financial hardship.

There are two types of judges 'of first instance' – that is, excluding those in the Court of Appeal and the House of Lords as the final appellate court. They are called circuit judges and High Court judges, and the public sometimes mixes up the two types. I was a circuit judge, and my principal court was Huddersfield Crown Court. We were not allowed to claim travelling expenses for going to our principal court from home and back. But if I sat at, say, Leeds, I was paid whichever was less – the cost of travelling from home to Leeds or Huddersfield to Leeds. The other crown court at which I regularly sat until my retirement was Wakefield, while in county courts I sat at Bradford, Keighley and Skipton.

I had no secretary or clerk who travelled with me; there are different court clerks at each court. I drove my own car and carried my own robes. My title was 'His Honour'. I did not try the most serious criminal or civil cases: not murder, manslaughter or even rape, though I did deal with robbery, burglary and causing grievous bodily harm with intent.

There are just over four hundred circuit judges; some are QCs but most are not. In 1990 90 per cent were ex-barristers; the rest were solicitors. Sixty-three per cent went to public schools; 25 per cent attended state schools; and the balance were educated abroad or were too shy to reveal all in *Who's Who*. At the time of writing there is one black circuit judge, Mota Singh, who sits at Southwark Crown Court in London. A former Kenyan international cricketer, he came to Britain in 1965 and took silk in 1978. I met him while sitting in London, which I did for two or three weeks a year for several years, in order to help them out and to help myself to variety, the delights of the Big City and the generous expenses which the Lord Chancellor's department (surprisingly) allowed. That system has been stopped now, and circuit judges stay on their own circuit.

High Court judges, on the other hand, travel regularly round all six circuits in England and Wales, a practice that has gone on since the time of Henry II (1154-89); they used to sit at the assizes. Every High Court Judge receives an automatic knighthood – he could refuse it but none ever has. Each has his own clerk, a sort of secretary, who probably cannot type but acts as a liaison officer. If a barrister or anyone else wishes to see the judge, they go through his clerk. The only persons more pompous and self-important than some High Court judges are some of their clerks. They use the royal 'we': 'Sorry, sir, we can't take your case today, but we may be able to tomorrow.'

While visiting cities like Leeds or Newcastle their lordships stay at judges' lodgings: palatial houses in extensive grounds, with a permanent staff – butler and cook and possibly one other. If a judge has a marshal with him, he has the privilege of dining with the judges; but the clerks eat separately.

High Court judges travel to court from their lodgings in big posh cars – Rolls-Royces, or in these days of economy more likely a Mercedes or even a vehicle lower down the pecking order. They are escorted by flashing blue-lighted police cars and/or motorcyclists which even stop other motorists when the traffic lights are in their favour. (While travelling to the lodgings for lunch as a guest – their lordships could not eat in the building with circuit judges, which would dilute their dignity – I used to imagine the scene in court after an accident on such an occasion leading to a civil claim: against the sheriff, I suppose, as the judges' host on behalf of Her Majesty.)

At the time of writing, of the eighty-two High Court

judges 79 per cent went to public schools and 13 per cent were educated by the state; the rest say nothing on the subject in *Who's Who*. Eighty-four per cent went to Oxbridge. Almost all were QCs at the Bar, and they did not apply to join the Bench, as aspirants to the circuit Bench must: the Lord Chancellor asked *them*.

Whereas at the Bar most circuit judges had a humdrum, knockabout practice – nothing flashy and rarely headlining – not so a High Court judge. Typically, he worked fanatically hard from prep school, through public school to Oxbridge, where he gained a good though not necessarily a first-class degree. After pupillage in good, busy chambers – which he had no difficulty in obtaining – he was given a place there. He always kept his nose not only clean but firmly applied to the grindstone, and his tongue well controlled. He never said a wrong word to those in authority.

Our typical High Court judge took silk at about forty, and since he had always been nice to his colleagues – now his juniors – they recommended his name to lead them in big cases. His ultra-polite, patrician style was liked by solicitors, who felt flattered to be able to brief him. He knew his law, and night after night polished his briefs. He was a hard, careful worker. He rarely if ever fell out with judges, in or out of court, and avoided controversy. There were no black marks of any kind on his record. And so, worn out with work, all the originality and spontaneity drained from him, he was sent for by the Lord Chancellor. Now at last came the request he had worked for all his conscious life: to join the High Court Bench, wear the scarlet and ermine, live among the élite. Then, of course, the effort for promotion to the Court of Appeal as one of the twenty-seven 'Right Honourable Lord Justices'. And for the really clever who really endeavour – a Law Lord (eleven in number) and a place in the upper House of Parliament.

It should not surprise anyone that, whatever the list of qualities your typical High Court judge may have, modesty is unlikely to be at the top of it. They represent the Queen in a special sense. After attending a local law society dinner as an official guest one High Court judge wrote to his hosts to say it was quite wrong that he and his colleague had had to queue with everyone else to use the toilet. A special one should have been set aside for their use; they represented Her Majesty. In that case, quipped one wag who heard about it, they should have used the ladies!

Whereas a High Court judge may achieve further promotion, a circuit judge is unlikely to rise further – though a few have. Roddie Smith, a nice, able man whom I knew, was promoted from the circuit Bench to the High Court but, separated from his family in Newcastle upon Tyne, found the life miserable. He had to spend half the year sitting in London, and the other half going round the circuits. When he died he had been enquiring whether he could return to the circuit Bench. The answer would almost certainly have been 'No'. It is a one-way road, and it also carries an anomalous pensions penalty. A circuit judge who gets promoted has to start earning his pension again – the earlier years do not count. The same applies to a stipendiary magistrate who becomes a circuit judge. This injustice could easily be rectified; there is no reason for keeping the rule – except official lethargy.

When I applied to the Lord Chancellor for a circuit judgeship, I was asked to provide the names of two or three judges as sponsors. I cited Judge Henry Scott QC and Mr (later Lord Justice) Roualeyn Cumming-Bruce, who as the junior presiding judge of the north-eastern circuit in 1971 had admired my stand against Mr Justice Hinchcliffe. Then came the sort of chance on which a career can turn.

As head of the local chambers I was invited to the centenary dinner of the Bradford Law Society. Lord 'Tom' Denning was to have been the main speaker, but Lord Justice 'Fred' Lawton came instead. When introduced to me he said he knew of me, having tried appeals in criminal cases for years, and that he approved of my ideas on sentencing. At the dinner, Judge Raymond Dean QC and Gilbert Gray QC told me that Fred Lawton was a supporter of mine. I asked them if he would support my application for a judgeship, and the answer came that he would if I wrote to him. In his reply he said that, though he did not know me personally, he had read many transcripts of cases I had tried as assistant recorder or recorder and had noted me years ago 'as a very considerable performer indeed'.

This was manna from heaven: most judges knew me only as an advocate, but here was one who could speak of my performance on the Bench. Without that, would I have been appointed? Who can say? The process is as secretive as so much in public life.

I have met Sir Frederick Lawton several times recently. He lives in retirement near York, next door to his solicitor son. Fred Lawton was my sort of judge: a robust, impressive man. His father was a prison governor and he himself went to a grammar school. His diction is clear, his mind sharp and his power of recall remarkable. He can give intricate details of a case he was involved in decades ago. We need more people like him on the Bench, but where are they to be found? Most QCs are not at all like him, being smoother, softer, more patrician.

And so, having been supported by Fred Lawton, early in 1976 I went to the House of Lords to be interviewed. I was seen by civil servants numbers two and three in the Lord Chancellor's office, Wilfrid Bourne and Derek Oulton, both later to be permanent secretaries to the Lord Chancellor, with the 'KCB QC' which goes automatically with that position. All honours are suspect in my eyes, but automatic honours should be regarded as absurd when seen through any sensible person's eyes. As for making a permanent secretary a QC when he probably only practised at the Bar for a few years and left to become a civil servant – it is as absurd as the snobbish gradation in honours: BEM for the worker at his Bench, an MBE for someone higher up the social scale.

As for titles, they are an even stronger indictment of our nation as effete in attitude and insular in outlook. I would scrap the whole medieval system. Does this mean that I would also sweep away royalty? Logically, that must follow. But not sweep away in any revolutionary sense. I would prefer the monarchy and its hangers-on to wither away till they have all become commoners like the rest of us. 'Mister' is a good enough title. But such changes are unlikely to take place soon.

A title is a name, a word, and to attribute to it – especially if it was inherited – virtue or superiority requiring deference goes against my grain. People bowed to me in court, and I bowed back during all those years. It was part of the procedure. Having joined the club, I obeyed its rules – well, most of them! But I feel there is no need to bow today. To stand, yes, as the judge comes into and goes out of court: dignity is required when decisions are being made about people's lives and fortunes – for the judge to stand up and go out while the court went on chatting would not do under any system. But standing up in silence should be enough. Such deference is not to the judge personally, but to him as a symbol of the law. And in 1976 I was about to become that symbol.

At my House of Lords interview there was general chat about such things as Oxford. Bourne and I had been there at the same time, though we had never met before the interview. Oulton, being a Cambridge man, was slightly at a disadvantage at that point.

About six months later I received a letter from Bourne offering me a circuit judgeship based in Sheffield. The process of selection was no more probing or detailed than I have described, though a fair number of judges and QCs may have been consulted for all I know. I did not have to appear before a selection board or committee. Having read my file, containing in particular what my sponsoring judges said about me, and having conducted that interview, Wilfrid Bourne put my name before Lord Chancellor Elwyn-Jones, a pleasant Welshman who met me for the first time – and then only for a few minutes – when I was sworn-in in his room in the House of Lords in July 1976.

His knee-breeches and silk stockings indicated that he had taken time off from the Woolsack, the traditional seat in the House of Lords where a Lord Chancellor spends much of his life. He is too busy to devote much time to selecting circuit judges – though he must give more to High Court appointments and more still to vacancies in the Court of Appeal and House of Lords, and to the key posts of Lord Chief Justice and Master of the Rolls, who are responsible for the criminal and civil courts respectively. The Prime Minister is said to have a hand in those two appointments and possibly others. It is all very vague. Nothing is written down. No statute defines these areas, except that the Queen makes the appointments on the advice of the Lord Chancellor. That means in practice that many of the decisions are taken by civil servants and then rubber-stamped.

There are so many judicial appointments. In addition to those I have mentioned there are hundreds of lay (unpaid) magistrates – a system that goes back to 1264, and whose members, though not legally trained, are selected by virtue of their background and standing. Then there are sixty stipendiary (paid) magistrates, who have formerly been barristers or solicitors. And there is a network of tribunals – not courts of law, though similar – which decide such questions as whether an employee has been wrongly dismissed or whether a claimant is entitled to certain state benefits. At the time of writing, of the full-time chairmen of tribunals, twenty-nine are barristers and thirty solicitors. There are ninety-one part-time chairmen, all practising lawyers. The chairman and two lay people make up a tribunal;

no wigs or gowns are worn. Finally there are district judges – until recently called registrars – who sit in county courts, trying small civil cases and arbitrations and deciding preliminary matters in High Court civil claims. In London 'masters' do a similar job in the High Court. All these posts are filled by the Lord Chancellor, nominally – though he can know little about most of the candidates, merely scrawling his signature or initials against names put before him.

I have agitated for a fairer system of appointment, and there have been recent signs that changes are slowly being made. Applicants for recorderships and assistant recorderships are now vetted, not only by civil servants but also by a panel of QCs. There are about seven hundred recorders, forming a corps from whom judges of both types come. Recent information on 478 recorders revealed that 92.5 per cent are barristers and 95 per cent are men. Sixty-nine per cent of those whose education was known went to public schools, and 90 per cent to Oxbridge. This hardly makes them representative of the public as a whole. It is one of the chief indictments of the judiciary. How can a judge understand litigants whose lives are so different from his own?

The way in which Lord Chancellor Hailsham summarily ended the career of recorder Manus Nunan, and dealt with his protests even more unjudicially (see pp. 190–1), demonstrate the need for a new system of appointment, promotion and control. The unfettered discretion of the Lord Chancellor – a politician – has led to some bad appointments in the past. Lord Kilmuir indulged in political nepotism when he chose sixty-four-year-old Harrovian and ex-Tory MP Gerald Howard as a High Court judge. I appeared before Howard frequently: he was idle, bad-tempered and a generally poor judge. Eyebrows were raised when Lord Hailsham promoted the sister of the then Attorney-General, Sir Michael Havers QC (later Lord Chancellor for four pension-earning months). She leaped from registrar to the High Court, missing out circuit judge level. No one else has done that before or since.

Lord Justice Butler-Sloss, as she now is, is said to be a good judge (I have never met her); and able, experienced women candidates for the Bench are rare. But whispers of nepotism were inevitable, and would have been avoided if she had been appointed or recommended by a board or committee consisting of lay people as well as lawyers. Until such a procedure is introduced, there are bound to be complaints and criticisms of our élitist system and the arrogance and remoteness of judges from privileged backgrounds. Judicial candidates should be subject to the same scrutiny and assessment that civil servants and many in industry have to undergo. I look to Lord Chancellor Mackay to do more in this area, and I have confidence that he will. He is no Hailsham or Havers.

I have told of how I arrived on the circuit Bench. Was I fit for the job? How did I find it? First, what are the ideal qualities in a judge?

Lord Scarman has said: 'The judge's job is to listen. Witnesses should be given every opportunity to settle down and say what they have to say in the way they want to say it.' That is correct, so far as it goes. The parties should feel confident that a judge is willing and able to reach a fair decision in a fair manner – contrary to what the public sometimes think, a judge sits alone, without a jury, in most civil cases and in criminal cases where the defendant pleads guilty. Qualities that are necessary in the Court of Appeal and the House of Lords are largely superfluous to circuit judges, who do not often deal with difficult points of law. We deal directly with the public, and in most of our cases points of law arise rarely. The dispute is not about the law, but about the facts. What did happen? Is it proved the defendant was the man who did it, or who had the necessary intention? Who was at fault when the cars collided? What was the agreement when the work was arranged? Was it done properly? Is the child better with the mother than with the father? In all those disputes someone is going to win and someone to lose, but both sides ought to leave court feeling the judge understood their case, listened patiently to their evidence and decided the matter fairly, impartially.

A judge should be courteous, pleasant, patient; in charge but not dictatorially. He should keep quiet except when it is necessary to intervene. The advocates and witnesses should do most of the talking. One difficulty is that under the English legal system judges are mostly chosen from the ranks of barristers, and the requirements for the two jobs are not the same. An advocate has to present his case incisively, delve into the other side's witnesses by cross-examination, get to the facts by analysis and persistence. A judge who has spent twenty-five years doing that may not find it easy to sit back and let others do it. I confess that at times I did not sufficiently curb and moderate myself on the Bench, especially in the beginning – I was too impatient and not relaxed enough. I hope I improved – I certainly tried.

No one trained me to be a judge, apart from one day's training on sentencing before I was appointed a judge in 1976. Since then I have, in 1977 and 1985, attended five-day residential seminars relating to crown court work. I have from time to time taken part in sentencing exercises – discussing disguised cases and saying what sentences we would pass: the main lesson there is what a lottery sentencing is! You can have ten judges sitting in a crown court building, and no two would pass the same sentence. There could be a variation between, say, probation for two years to prison for two years. No two judges are alike in their early experiences, family influences or attitudes drawn from a thousand events.

For myself, I liked to look for merit, to reward those who, though disadvantaged, had done their best to pull themselves from the pit. Those who had had advantages – such as a good, comfortable, caring home – but squandered them did not receive the same sympathy. I did not like to see the strong and unscrupulous impose themselves on the weak and vulnerable. Nor did I favour those who had claimed every state benefit for so long that they had become incapable of standing on their own feet. I regarded sane adults as capable of making their own decisions, and answerable when they chose to harm others. When a defendant said: 'Think of my wife and family if I go to prison,' I replied 'No. They are your responsibility, not mine. You knew what would happen to them if you were caught. They are your victims, not mine.'

What was my relationship with other judges? In later years I did not have any contact with most of them. The life of a judge, as opposed to that of a barrister, is solitary, though I chose to make it more so than was strictly necessary. In the county courts where I sat I was the only judge in the building and I lunched alone, usually just eating fruit from home, although the usher would go out to buy a sandwich when asked. In some crown courts, such as Huddersfield, I was also the only judge. At Wakefield there was another judge or recorder, but though we met for a chat at times we did not lunch together; there were no dining facilities. At Leeds there could be a dozen judges or more in the building which housed both crown and county courts, but I did not often lunch in the judges' dining room. This was partly because I was watching my weight, but also because I had noticed a certain awkwardness – reticence – peeping through my colleagues' politeness. They did not tell me what they thought about my media work, except for the occasional barbed comment, but most must have disapproved to some extent and some probably denounced me unreservedly when I was not there.

I gave up going to judges' meetings, which are held twice or three times a year on the north-eastern circuit. I had referred to some of those meetings, and what had or had not happened there, in my earlier book *Straight from the Bench*, and the other judges would understandably have felt embarrassed if I had continued to attend. 'Can we have an assurance that Judge Pickles will regard our discussion as confidential?' someone would have asked, inevitably and understandably. (No one can be more 'private' and 'confidential' than judges and the top civil servants who deal with them.)

Did I let the side down? Some of my colleagues must have mouthed that public school cry when discussing me, though I had the impression that a few judges and barristers – especially the state-educated ones – were neutral or even favourable towards me. Happily there are now more of the latter than ever, though the high-fliers, the really ambitious ones who aim for judicial heights and reach them, still tend to come from the select élite that has attended the top public schools and the smarter Oxbridge colleges.

If I had been to Eton, I would have been better educated than at my own minor public school. I would most likely also have been more Establishment-minded. When I went to address the Eton College Law Society recently, I was courteously received despite my having previously used words in public that were less than flattering to their school. It was a very interesting experience to see the school that in some ways embodies much that I dislike about Britain, yet that has produced so many leaders in all spheres including the law.

A thought worried me at times: did I as a judge seem to young counsel as that formidable Old Etonian Geoffrey Walter Wrangham had seemed to me? I do not refer to mental equipment – Wrangham was way above me in that – but the manner in which he treated some counsel in court, including me. On the Bench I tried to make allowance for youth and inexperience – but I am sure I 'did a Wrangham' at times, and that was inexcusable. What was easy for me up there on the Bench may not have been for counsel. The judge holds all the aces, calls the shots, dictates the play. He can ask counsel or a witness to repeat something or declare an adjournment, and no one can stop or fault him – not in that court, though there is the restraining influence of the Court of Appeal looking over his shoulder.

But even if at times I unconsciously emulated Wrangham's manner I did not share his background, and have always gone my own way. I have paid a price for independence, and been prepared to. After my elevation to the Bench, the Establishment gave me only what it was obliged to. I did not complain; I would have done the same if I had been in its shoes. I did not even achieve the lowest rung on the extra-duties ladder – liaison judge to a Bench of magistrates. This is an unpaid post, and its duties involve keeping in touch with the magistrates – addressing them on sentencing, attending their sentencing conferences and passing on complaints or suggestions to the circuits' presiding (High Court) judges. I did give speeches to magistrates in various parts of the country, at meetings or after dinner, but the invitations came direct from them. They seemed to feel frustrated by weak Home Office policies arising out of prison overcrowding, and they looked to me, and no doubt to others too, to support their firmer attitude towards offenders. Judges and magistrates, working in the trenches, grapple daily with criminals and see things differently from those at 'Staff HQ', who prefer to pore over statistics. We tend to be ethical in our approach and 'they' to be logistical.

Some circuit judges are asked to do High Court work, such as civil actions, custody or wardship, and to try rape or even murder cases. I was never once asked to do any of that. I understand why that was – I was not regarded as a reliable, 'OK chap'. But I was happier retaining my independence.

The job of a circuit judge is an easy one. It is demanding neither upon your intellect (if you have one) nor upon your time. Difficult questions of law rarely arise. Weeks went by without anyone in my court quoting from a law book. A barrister or solicitor who walked into court bearing a pile of reference books was squinted at as if he were in a Bateman cartoon. In the crown court almost everything turns on the facts and evidence, and little on the law; similarly in most county court cases.

In both crown court and county court work, it was rare for me to take work home. Almost all my effort was applied in the court building, and most of it during the court hearing itself. It was unnecessary to look at any of the paperwork before a case: counsel would explain everything in court. I did, however, scan the pleadings before starting to hear most civil actions if they were likely to remain contested. Many were 'settled' on the day of the meeting, after both parties, their lawyers and witnesses had assembled for the first time and the moment of truth was imminent. It is often better to agree the result rather than to throw it all into the lap of the judge. You have some control over a compromise but no control over the judge, except by arguments which he may not accept.

With criminal cases I usually glanced at the files beforehand, but not in detail. You can get the feel of a case by scanning the prosecution statements; the list of the defendant's previous convictions, if any; and the social inquiry report, if there is one (only in cases where a plea of guilty is indicated beforehand to the probation service). It can also be useful to trip through the questions and answers recorded at the police interview of the accused. Details can be grasped in court.

There is no excuse for a judge getting the summing-up wrong in a criminal case, though most judges do from time to time. There are guidelines, approved by the Lord Chief Justice, setting out model forms of directions to the jury: for the functions of judge and jury, the burden of proof, a child's criminal responsibility, the effect of a plea of guilty on a co-accused, intention, recklessness, alibi, self-defence and many more. It is all there neatly set out for the simplest of sitters, the most jejune of judges, to read to the jury.

I always summed up on the same pattern, which I commend to others:

1. Law for me, facts for the jury.
2. Burden of proof, explained simply once, and not repeated or embroidered – the wrong word here can end in a conviction being quashed, by the Court of Appeal.
3. Jury must be unanimous. If the time comes for a direction about 10:2 or 11:1 verdicts (after not less than two hours ten minutes' deliberation by the jury), there would be a further direction about that.
4. Jury must choose a foreman or woman when they retire, to preside over them and then speak for them in court.
5. Jury must consider all the evidence, including any parts I do not now remind them of.
6. Charges in the indictment explained simply, once, together with other points of law such as self-defence.

I then outlined the evidence on both sides as neutrally as possible, refraining from comments except for the occasional (deadly?) aside, such as, 'The prosecution allege with some force, you may think, members of the jury, that if he is telling the truth the defendant would have . . . ' I used to write out a summary of the evidence: this made the summing-up much shorter and neater. Inevitably I became less conscientious, in this respect, towards the end of my career, and often used my longhand notes of the witnesses' evidence. It must seem odd to some people that an English judge still takes a note of the evidence in longhand. In some countries and occasionally here, as in a long, important planning appeal, the shorthand or taped record of the evidence is transcribed daily before the next day starts, so that the tribunal can sit and listen. But this approach, although useful, would be very expensive.

71

There are other areas where we could improve things without great expense. Witnesses are often left standing, although there is usually a seat for them. They should always be told that they can sit or stand as they choose. And in every court I have ever been in, the witness-box is in the wrong place. A witness should sit facing the court, as the judge does, but to one side and at a slightly lower level. And there should be an unobtrusive amplification system. 'Do speak up, please. We all have to hear you. Address your answer to the back row of the jury.' These words outnumber all others spoken in our courts, and a little thought and expense would make things so much easier. We have not advanced far from the days of quill-pens and candles.

As to sentencing, I often formed a preliminary view when looking at the file before the case started, or during the case. But defending counsel's efforts could reduce the sentence in perhaps 10 per cent of cases. It must not be thought that lawyers are all useless or that their words are not noticed.

On about half of my days on the Bench, I did less than a full day's work. A full day for me was 10.30 a.m. to about 1 p.m. and 2 p.m. to 4.30 p.m. One county court judge sat at 9 a.m. sometimes – he was a keen golfer – but that was 'not on' in my book. After all, counsel and others may have to travel a long way, and then confer, before going into court. Some judges sit at 10 a.m. in the county court, sometimes because it fits in with taking their children to school, but I had a rule not to sit before 10.30 except for bail applications which I had in chambers two or three days a week in an average crown court stint. Three hours is too long to keep up one's concentration.

Where there were jurors, I usually had a quarter of an hour break mid-morning and mid-afternoon. But not enough care was taken to see that tea or coffee were available, by hand or machine. Judges and administrators do not always pay attention to such simple things. If I had raised matters like that at a meeting of HM Council of Circuit

Judges they would have wondered what bee I had in my bonnet before going on to discuss judges' salaries, expenses and pensions.

I always took at least an hour for lunch, though some heedless judges who had brought lunch to eat in their room sometimes took as little as twenty minutes. That is unfair to court staff, who are too diffident to complain. A clerk may have shopping to do during the lunch break. I took this up through the circuit administrator, asking that all judges sitting on the circuit be reminded of this inconvenience. I do not know what happened about it. (Perhaps it was disposed of as 'Another of Judge Pickles' ideas. File it.' But I am probably being unjust.) There is a strong tradition that every judge controls his own court in his own way in such matters. That tradition is taken too far, however.

A civil servant in the court service (or elsewhere) works set hours, albeit with flexi-time. A judge can go home when the court finishes, even if that is at 11 a.m., as has happened to me on more than a few occasions. Exit before lunch was frequent. In the county court a case listed for three days can be settled before the first day's hearing begins. A defendant who is expected to plead not guilty, meaning that time has to be spent hearing witnesses, is free to change his mind at any time. There are so many variables – including last-minute applications for adjournments because a witness is unavailable or one side is unready for some reason. Some judicial days inevitably go short, yet some cases are listed but not reached. This is not all due to inefficiency: listing officers work hard and efficiently within archaic traditions.

Crown court work could be organised much more efficiently, and expense and delays reduced, if judges sat for longer periods at one court and if cases were allotted to judges instead of judges to cases. I rarely sat in the same court for longer than three weeks at a time, cases being put before me each week on each day, shortly before they were due to be tried. It would have been much better if I had sat at a crown court for at least six months, a list of cases being given to me as soon as they arrived from the magistrates' court. They would have remained my cases, unless I transferred a particular case to another judge.

A clerk would have been attached to me for the whole period, instead of my being given different clerks each week or even each day. We could then have kept a constant check on the progress of the cases, in liaison with the listing office for that building.

This system would also block the defendant who pleads not guilty before judge A in the hope of getting the more lenient judges B or C next time. If his case was in judge A's list he would get judge A, so he might as well plead guilty now.

At present, listing officers are too much in the hands of solicitors and barristers' clerks, and do not have sufficient authority to insist, for example, that a case should go into the list for hearing even though the defending counsel selected will be involved in another case for the next two or three months. My attitude was that the show must go on, and that Mr X is not the only suitable counsel.

To give an idea of a circuit judge's life in the county court, here are details of an actual week I spent in June 1990:
MONDAY I had eleven 'children's appointments' in chambers (my retiring room): I had to decide whether I was satisfied with the arrangements for children under sixteen, or under eighteen if undergoing full-time education, of divorced parents. I sat as usual with a probation officer in his or her capacity as divorce court welfare officer. I understand that some judges refuse to do that, or used to. In one of today's cases the officer went with the parties to sort out access: that is the main way in which welfare officers can assist at these hearings.

There was one application to dismiss a claim by a deceased wife, which she had made before she died, to set aside an award of a lump sum as between her and her husband. I adjourned this matter for further argument as only twenty minutes had been set aside today and both parties' solicitors are going to provide written submissions to the court. I shall not mind if another judge gets this: it looks tricky.

I then went into open court, and there was one application for a person to be ordered to provide evidence about his means, a judgement having been given against him. As he had filled in the form already, that was easy: he left without penalty. If he hadn't come I would have ordered seven days' imprisonment. They usually comply before they reach prison.

There was an application for possession of a house, and by agreement I made a suspended order for possession and the payment of the arrears of rent. If he keeps up the payments he will stay in the house.

There was an agreed judgement against a husband by a building society, and I adjourned the claim against the husband's absent wife who had apparently forged a mortgage in her husband's name.

Then I resumed a case that had been part-heard from February this year, in which the plaintiffs are house-owners who engaged the defendant, a young joiner, to erect a conservatory which, say the plaintiffs, turned out to let in damp. Even today the case will not finish. One of the plaintiff's witnesses, a builder who was to give evidence about the cost of remedial work, was not here. The defendant's counsel has a meeting over in Manchester with a High Court judge at 5 p.m. and I therefore adjourned the case to yet another hearing.

I rose at 3.45 p.m. (At a later hearing I gave judgement for the defendant joiner.)

TUESDAY At 10.30 a.m. I had only one application in chambers, and that was to adjourn an accident case which had been fixed for July; one side had not supplied the further and better particulars which had been asked for in

March. I said the case had to be tried – I could not allow the adjournment. I ordered the side which had not produced the further and better particulars to do so within seven days or their claim would be stayed (prevented from proceeding).

In open court at 11 a.m. I had a case where a man had failed to fill in a form as to his means – he is a judgement debtor (one who has been ordered by the court to pay a certain sum of money). He was prepared to fill it up and then be orally examined, so he was soon on his way.

I made an agreed suspended committal order in favour of a Collector of Taxes against a taxpayer: twenty-eight days' imprisonment suspended on his paying the judgement by monthly instalments. (Imprisonment for debt has been abolished – except where tax is owed.)

There was then a possession case in which the woman landlord was not represented, and the defendant was represented by John Martin, a barrister who works for a minimal salary at the Bradford Law Centre. He is an expert on landlord and tenant law but fair with landlords. I told the plaintiff that the law is very complicated as to landlord and tenant, and a landlord has to get the forms and notices correct or he loses. On my suggestion she had a word with Mr Martin, and then they came back and she agreed to withdraw her claim without any order as to costs. I told her that if she did decide to start again, she ought to get advice at least as to the legal position and as to the notices that she needs. She could manage the case herself in court when she had got the documents right. (Law centres run on shoestring budgets, but do a good job in cases like the one cited, immigration cases and those involving employment – unfair dismissal and so on.)

There was then a Landlord and Tenant Act matter: an agreed order for the grant of a new lease of business premises.

Next I had a case arising out of an accident. It took place thirty months ago when the plaintiff was driving her Ford

Fiesta along a narrow lane, and collided with a lorry driven in the opposite direction by the defendants' employee, the defendants being a county council. I found for the plaintiff, as she seemed to me to be telling the truth. In particular I did not believe the defendants' employees, who stated that when giving her a lift afterwards she said she was in a hurry to get to her next appointment. In fact she was a teacher, and at 11.15 a.m., when the accident took place, had just come from a teaching appointment and did not have another until the late afternoon. I also found that her evidence about being close to the nearside when the accident took place – there being room for both vehicles to pass – was accurate. There was evidence from her husband that later the same day he measured the distance between the marks left by the nearside wheels of his wife's car and the wall at eight inches.

Cases like this almost always turn on which side's witnesses seem to have told the truth. That depends on the impression one has of them, and implications such as that of the teacher not being in a hurry.

WEDNESDAY Today everything was in chambers except the pronouncement of the decrees absolute of divorce. It was a pity that I had to put on my robes just for that formal few seconds' announcement. In fact I forgot to put my wig on, but nobody seemed to notice.

As on Monday, I had several 'satisfaction' hearings concerning children. And there was one custody matter which was resolved until Friday by the intervention of the probation officer, who said there was no reason why the children should not stay where they are until then.

The main case – concerning custody – lasted for most of the day. I rose at about 3.45 p.m. Unusually I gave custody to the husband. The wife, with whom the children had been living, was plainly far gone in drink and had been banned from five pubs for that reason; there was also ample evidence that she neglected the children, abused neighbours and was completely out of control. On two occasions she had allowed a baby of about eighteen months to roll along the street in a push-chair. The other child is seven. The husband works as a chef and so he will not be able to look after the children himself, but his mother, who has brought up five children and impressed me as a very good person, will do that.

THURSDAY I had two adoptions. The children were brother and sister, the mother had remarried and she and her second husband were adopting them. The first husband had consented. Adoption had the effect of cutting legal ties and obligations for him, including the payment of maintenance for the children.

There was an application to return children who had been kept after an access visit by the husband. They had in fact been returned, but since there was an access dispute, instead of spending three months and a lot of public money (up to £1000) on a report I suggested that the welfare officer, who was in the building, should see the parties. I accepted his suggestions for interim arrangements for access, which will be reviewed again in three months.

Next there was an application for a non-molestation injunction by a wife, but the husband gave an undertaking on the basis of which the application for the injunction was adjourned indefinitely. (An undertaking or promise has the same effect as an injunction, in that breach of either is contempt of court and can be a reason for imprisonment.)

After that there was an application by a husband for custody of a five-year-old child. His former wife wanted to take the child to Germany since she had just married a British soldier stationed there. I made suggestions, which avoided a ninety-minute hearing (the estimated time if it had remained contested). There was no point in having a report made on the stability of the marriage to the soldier: they had only just married. Almost certainly any report about the husband by the army would indicate that he was a good soldier. It was agreed in the end that the mother should have leave to take the child to Germany, upon undertaking that she and her second husband would bring the child to the UK three times a year for the natural father to see him. In any event the soldier is only going to Germany for a maximum of eighteen months and British troops are being withdrawn from the country. So the situation should not last for long.

All the above cases today were in chambers. There were two cases in open court where defendant judgement debtors had not given details on oath of their means. There was also a case where a local council had claimed possession against two squatters, but they had already gone by the time the case came up.

Then I had an application to adjourn a civil action fixed for July. It was not the first time I had had such an application in that case. One of the issues is whether documents were forged. A handwriting expert is not available for the trial in July, but I ordered that the case should go on; the handwriting evidence can be heard on a later day. Where there are several parties (there are three parties in this case on the defence side, and the plaintiff), problems can arise. If you adjourn a case to another date, by the time it comes around there may be some other reason to adjourn. The previous adjournment application was on the basis of the unavailability of another expert witness.

Then for most of the day from soon after noon until 4.30 p.m. I dealt with the first part of an interesting case in which the plaintiff, a police sergeant, is suing the defendant, a landscape gardener, over an agreement for the replacement of a garden on three levels by paving stones. There is a preliminary issue, which I have yet to resolve, as to whether the parties agreed to a compromise through the agency of the trading standards officer. The plaintiff claims, perhaps a bit optimistically, that he should not pay for any of the work that was done in his garden, and that he should have damages for the difference between the cost of the rectification work and the contract price. He also wants damages for the inconvenience involved in the interim. It is thirty months since the work was done.

The plaintiff's and defendant's costs must add up to several thousands. The costs of a further hearing, which is to take place at the end of July, will come to another £1000 at least. Today when I suggested that the parties might compromise, and I hinted what it should be, I was told that unfortunately negotiations had fallen down on the question of who should pay the costs! I decided that there had not been a binding compromise. (After further hearings, the damages on the claim and counter-claim were roughly equal, and I ordered both sides to pay their own costs. No one gained except the lawyers.)

FRIDAY In chambers I had the Guardianship of Minors case which I adjourned last Wednesday. The wife, who recently came out of a mental hospital, had applied for custody of the two children who are with the husband and his mother. The wife has since had a further breakdown, is now actually back with the husband and is talking about a reconciliation. In those circumstances her application was withdrawn. Instead of the case taking ninety minutes, which had been estimated, it took about five.

I had a case where the wife petitioner in maintenance proceedings asked for the committal to prison of the respondent husband for failure to file an affidavit as to his means. The respondent did not come and, after the solicitor had given formal evidence, I ordered a fourteen-day prison sentence suspended for one week; this will give the husband one last chance to do what the court had ordered him to do. If a person is told to do something by a court and refuses, in the end there is only one penalty that is applicable: gaol.

Finally this week I had an application to commit a husband to prison for breach of an undertaking which he gave in May this year. The parties were married in February and then lived together for less than a month. The wife was pregnant by another man, although she did not know this at the time of the marriage; she thought she was pregnant by her husband. When he discovered the truth the husband was violent to her – though his feelings were understandable, his actions were not justifiable – and they had been parted since March.

On 24 June, in an alleged breach of his undertaking, the wife says that he followed her into two pubs. Then, outside a club to which he had been refused entry because it was known the wife was inside and that there had been some previous trouble between them, he did £650 worth of damage to her car by smashing the headlamps and all the windows except one. The car, which was only worth £400, was therefore a write-off. She now has no vehicle and cannot take her child to and from school. The club doorman gave cogent evidence that it was the husband who did the damage.

I sentenced the man to four months' imprisonment and made an injunction whereby for twelve months he is not to assault, molest, interfere with or approach or communicate with the petitioner, and not for that same period to go to her house or any address at which she may from time to time reside. (After a few weeks the husband applied to me to 'purge his contempt'. His father had the money to pay for the damage to the car, so I released the husband on condition that money was paid. Justice seemed to have been done – in my eyes and, I hope, in that of the parties.)

So how did life on the Bench match up to my expectations? I went there for security and tranquillity, but at times it guaranteed neither.

4

Was I too hard on solicitors
and barristers?

During my time on the Bench I certainly criticised solicitors more than any other profession or group. Was this because I saw more of them than any others? I encountered them and their work daily. On some county court days spent hearing civil cases I never saw a barrister – only solicitors or their clerks.

Were my strictures justified? Do solicitors serve the public as they should? Is the public protected properly from their inefficiency? Should solicitors' wings be clipped further (they have already rightly lost their monopoly of conveyancing)? Or should their wings be extended by allowing them to become partners with barristers, estate agents or accountants? Should the door have been opened, as it has been, to solicitors by letting them apply to be advocates in the High Court and be eligible for judgeships there? Do some of the present problems come from the division between barristers and solicitors, and should there be only one legal profession?

It would be wrong to condemn all solicitors, as I have obviously not met all 56,000 in England and Wales. And I did not see those who did only conveyancing, company work or probate. Those whose work I did observe varied in ability from average to poor, with a few who were excellent and more than a few who were awful.

The most common sin was delay. No one who has bought

or sold a house needs to be told about the dilatory ways of solicitors; nor anyone who has been in a civil action, where even a simple case can take several years to get to court. There is no reason for this save tradition and a lack of incentive to get on with matters. Although I knew solicitors who acted promptly, especially if prodded by me in court, as a profession they generally worked at two speeds: slow and stop.

Take one case I tried and the Bradford solicitors' reaction to my criticisms. I do not say these practitioners were worse than those in other courts, though as a group they may have been more complacent. On 15 May 1984 the Bradford Law Society wrote to Lord Chancellor Hailsham, complaining about the remarks I had made concerning solicitors since I had started to sit at Bradford County Court in September 1983. They enclosed several press cuttings, including one from the *Yorkshire Post* dated 24 May 1984 which read as follows:

A judge apologised yesterday to a motorist who took one of the biggest house-building firms to court and had to wait nearly four-and-a-half years for justice.

Judge Pickles, sitting at Bradford County Court, had been told that Mr J. T. had his Mini-van written off in December 1979, when he drove over a protruding manhole cover in an estate being built by B. Developments.

Judge Pickles said: 'This is a case of a little man caught in the wheels of bureaucracy. He has been bewildered. He has waited year after year for his claim to be settled and no one has helped him.'

While hearing the evidence Judge Pickles repeatedly commented that the delay had made it difficult for witnesses to remember the facts. He said: 'People cannot remember things for years. It makes the legal system farcical. People are not getting a proper service from the complacent, inefficient profession known as solicitors . . .

Someone has to take the solicitors' branch of the profession by the scruff of the neck and shake them.'

At the end of the case he asked Mr T. what he had thought about his experience. Mr T. replied: 'I am not very happy about it.'

In reply to a request for my comments, I sent the Lord Chancellor's office a paper about court delays which I had written for my fellow judges on the north-eastern circuit. I do not know what Lord Hailsham's office wrote to the Bradford Law Society; in fairness, surely I should have been sent a copy? The same society complained again in September 1985 about further remarks of mine on delays. On neither occasion did I receive a word of rebuke from London. Lord Hailsham did, however, set up a Civil Justice Review body to examine court delays and related problems. I wondered whether my document had triggered this off; certainly they would never have admitted it. If it had, it would not have been the only occasion on which words of mine bore some fruit. Not all did: many fell stonily to the ground, and properly.

I sent a copy of my document on delays to the Bradford Law Society, but it was never acknowledged. Was the society concerned about wounds to its own esteem and not about the effects of delays on its clients? I had no complaints from Bradford solicitors via London or direct after 1985, although I did not relent in my public comments whenever I thought they were called for.

The way the Bradford Law Society handled those complaints made me doubt its shrewdness – a quality which all lawyers need. Why did it not take the matter up with me? What did it hope to prove by writing to London – my dismissal? Not a hope! A snotty letter from Lord Hailsham? One never came – not this time, anyway. Maybe its members thought I would be resentful and hostile. That didn't happen either. I continued to treat them in the same way –

pleasantries for the pleasant, barbs for the barbarous, and a wary eye for all.

But whatever the various parties' attitudes, delays undeniably do occur.

It was in February 1985 that Lord Hailsham set up his Review Body on Civil Justice. Its report, published in June 1988, showed that the average time taken in personal injury cases between the accident (on the road or in the factory, usually) and proceedings being commenced was nineteen months in the London High Court and eighteen months in the provinces; and fourteen months in the county court. The time between advice from a solicitor to proceedings being started was ten to twelve months in the High Court and nine months in the county court. In 65 per cent of cases, proceedings had not started within a year of the accident. In the High Court it took nineteen months from the start of proceedings to asking the court for a trial date; in the county court, thirteen months. In both categories, half the actions took longer than the average period I have quoted. It took ten months in the High Court between asking for a trial date and the trial itself. The end result in the High Court was that it took an average of at least four years between proceedings being started and the trial itself.

The report stated:

Delay on the scale found by the review undermines justice. It reduces the availability of evidence and erodes the reliability of that which is available, denies compensation to those who are entitled to it until long after it is most needed, tends to legitimise inefficiency in the offices of lawyers and in the courts, and crucially saps public confidence in the capacity of the courts to do justice. Delay causes continuing personal stress, anxiety and financial hardship to ordinary people and their families. It may induce economically weaker people to accept unfair settlements. It also frustrates the efficient conduct of commerce and industry.

Procedure should be streamlined. Delays caused by shortage of judges, staff and buildings can be cured by money. But the most important step in reducing delays is to take hold of solicitors, shake them and make them get on with things. A solicitor consulted by a client injured in an accident – and possibly in other types of case too – should have to report to the Law Society every six months, giving reasons why the case has not been started, or reporting progress. Once proceedings are under way the plaintiff's solicitor should have to go before the district judge (formerly called the registrar) every six months to explain any delay, with financial penalties if he has dragged his feet without good reason.

Apart from the problem of delays, I found myself frequently having to point out to solicitors a lesser but still irritating inadequacy: their spelling and grammatical mistakes, which were much too numerous for a supposedly educated profession. Even in affidavits (documents verified on oath and so requiring care) such errors proliferated. When one Bradford solicitor came into my chambers with an affidavit in a domestic violence case, I pointed out at least eight spelling mistakes.

'But we have to do them in a hurry, your honour,' I was told.

'And you have to do them correctly. You should have checked it,' I replied (perhaps he had).

Because he continued to argue, I disallowed his costs for preparing the affidavit. I was told he left my room mouthing things about me. Underneath he might have a heart of gold, but at that moment I was more concerned with the problems he brought to his clients instead of solving those they already had.

At one time I had an usher who had been a businessman. I said he must be appalled at the inefficient way we ran the crown court, and he agreed. The average businessman would not survive long if his standards were like ours. We have no competitors. Perhaps courts could be privatised, with cases going in preference to the more efficient ones, and judges and court officials being paid according to output!

Much of the inefficiency in the crown court is caused by solicitors. The north-eastern circuit has a listing information form for defending solicitors to complete and send to the crown court listing officer. In about 10 per cent of cases the form was never sent in. About half were completed in a rather slapdash manner. Admittedly the form is inadequate. About seven years ago I suggested to the then senior presiding judge how it could be improved. He replied that there were plans to design a form to be used nationally. I was still waiting for it when I retired.

Two questions on the document which cause problems are: 'is there a reasonable possibility that the case will proceed as a plea of guilty?' and 'Is a pre-trial review (PTR) likely to assist in the expeditious and efficient disposal of the case?' In answer to the first, solicitors often put 'Possibly', 'Probably' or 'Perhaps to a lesser charge'. They will obtain the defendant's statement (for some reason it is called proof of evidence) but may not have received it when they fill in the form. In many cases they cannot be sure what the defendant will plead until they have conferred with him and counsel.

Difficulties created here would not occur if we had a single unified legal profession. It is not easy for a busy counsel to arrange a conference with solicitors and defendants, and if he can postpone it until the day of the court hearing, he does – with the connivance and support of his clerk. If the defendant is in prison it is even more difficult to arrange a conference, bearing in mind the distances that often have to be travelled and prison restrictions on available times. It is tempting, therefore, for solicitors to think they will sort it out on the day of the hearing when everyone is present. That is why solicitors often put 'Yes' to the question of whether a PTR will assist. A PTR involves the defendant and both side's counsel appearing in open court at a cost of £150 or more to the taxpayer. If the defendant pleads not guilty, all that can be done by the court is to ask the defence for a list of the prosecution's witnesses they require to attend at the trial, and for counsel to estimate the number of days the trial will take.

If defending solicitors caused an unnecessary PTR by the careless way they filled in the form, I usually penalised them by depriving them of payment under legal aid for preparing the PTR case. Sometimes I also made them pay both counsels' fees for that day. The only way to make solicitors sit up and improve is to hit their pocket: exhortations tend to be ignored. I was only one judge; I was not there all the time. Why should they change the ways of generations merely for cantankerous, eccentric Judge Pickles?

There are further angles. A busy barrister has a file of briefs on his desk and he knows he will not be able to do them all – some will be returned to other counsel. So it is pointless to read a brief in advance unless the solicitor asks him to and tells him why in a covering letter. Thus important advice which occurs to the barrister when he does look at a brief, probably on the evening before the court hearing, may come too late to be acted on. Evidence may be needed – a letter from an employer, for example; its absence may cause a defendant who intends to plead guilty to say not guilty until his next appearance in court in several weeks' or even months' time.

Again, the barrister who attends the PTR may not be the one who will finally do the case. He may have attended merely to hold the brief and go through the motions. He has no authority to make decisions such as trying to negotiate with the prosecution a plea of guilty to a lesser charge.

In the crown and county courts elementary mistakes by solicitors came to light all the time. They failed to warn a witness to attend. Or they wrote to the defendant telling him the trial date and asking him to confirm having received the letter; but then they failed to follow the matter up after hearing nothing in response. Hence, no defendant on the day of the trial. The police have to be radioed to go to his house or workplace. Meanwhile everybody waits: jurors, witnesses, lawyers. The case may have to be adjourned.

All that could have been avoided with a little foresight by the defending solicitor. But – and this is the nub – the partners in the firm know nothing about it until a rocket comes roaring from the judge. Legal aid work on behalf of those with limited or no means is not well paid – increasing numbers of firms are refusing to do it for this reason – and so many cases are handled by young, inexperienced clerks. Law students are sometimes employed to go to court to 'instruct' counsel, although they are ignorant about the case. Even solicitors sometimes told me, dolefully, that this was not their case – they had just been handed the file and had rushed to court, without having time to read it.

Photographs were often placed before me in court loose, captionless and unnumbered. Or the numberings on copies of the same picture was inconsistent. It was like a game of cards with counsel, judge and witness shuffling their own packs – but the various packs did not contain identical cards. Letters and documents were frequently produced piece-meal, instead of in an agreed bundle in date order, every sheet being given a separate number, starting at the top. Time after time after time I had to tell solicitors how to do their work in such matters. I felt I was trying to educate the ineducable. Any competent employee in any business office would have done better.

Not long ago there was a PTR before me at which the defence said it required the tapes of the interviews between the police and the defendant. A letter followed from the crown prosecuting solicitor, saying the tapes were available at the local police station. When the case came before me for trial, the defence applied for an adjournment as they had not received the tapes. The solicitors had never bothered to telephone or call at the station for them; they had done nothing but sit there, waiting for something to happen. Whether my words of exasperation, which were reported in the press, had any effect I do not know. I doubt it.

The Germans and Japanese are better than us at making and selling things in a number of industries. Their 'secret' is no secret at all: it is planning and attention to detail. Our national socks need pulling up before overseas rivals finally take our trousers down and tan the hide off us.

Women solicitors are often better than men. They tend to dress more smartly and do their homework. But one woman applied to me in chambers to take a case out of the list for a day about two weeks ahead as her expert witness would be on holiday. 'Where is he going?' is a question even a child would surely have asked. But not this woman. I asked her to go and phone the man. She soon returned and said all was well: the expert would only be in the Lake District and would drive to Bradford for the hearing, albeit without enthusiasm. A little forethought would have avoided the waste of the solicitor's time – and costs, presumably – as well as court time.

Counsel can be just as unthinking. One man applied to me to take a criminal case, set to be heard the next week, out of the list. He said a consultant surgeon would have to be called and he was operating on the day in question. I asked for the information that should have been available already. Was it really necessary to call the surgeon? Why could his statement not be agreed with the prosecution, amended if necessary, and put before the jury without calling the man himself? Doctors are busy people doing vital work, and expensive to call as witnesses – yet so many are called unnecessarily. When precisely would the consultant be operating? As we would not require him on the first day of the trial, could he come on the second day, if necessary at a time to be agreed with him, and we would work round that?

Counsel's instructing solicitor wrote down my questions – rather wearily – and before long counsel thanked me and said in fact all was well: the witness would be able to attend without difficulty (at the trial his statement was read). How much public money did that application to me cost? £100, maybe slightly less.

I could reel off dozens of similar instances, but one more example will be quite enough to make the point. A three-day case was due to be heard by me in five days' time when the defending counsel applied for it to be taken out of the list, and the prosecution agreed. I went into the 'difficulties' one by one.

The counsel who was briefed for the trial itself would be sitting as a recorder (public duty is a ground for taking a barrister's case out of a list). That turned out to be inaccurate.

The defence wanted to examine a car that was an exhibit in the case. 'Where is it?' I asked, not unreasonably. Counsel did not know. 'Somebody must know. A phone call by the prosecution will find it,' I said.

'But our expert will then have to examine it and it will take three weeks to get his report.'

My response – as in all such cases – was: 'It will only take three weeks if we give him three weeks. He'll have three days – ample time.'

'But it's a complicated case,' pleaded counsel, acting as advocate for himself. 'It looks as though *I'll* have to do it, and look how thick the bundle of statements is.'

'Mr Smith, you have four days before the case starts. You may have to work at the weekend or late into the night, as I used to. But the show must go on. This case has been listed after careful consideration. If I unlist it, next time there will be some other problem – a witness on holiday, say. It is already a year since these offences were allegedly committed.'

Then the prosecution explained its difficulties – well, that is what they called them. They had witnesses to find and interview, and statements to take. So what was my reaction? Not couched in the most judicial language, perhaps, 'You know who they are and where they were last known to live. They're unlikely to have taken off for outer space. If they refuse to give statements, serve them with witness summonses to come here.'

There was a further problem, both counsel solemnly agreed. There were lengthy tape-recorded interviews, and the transcripts would have to be edited (prejudicial or irrelevant parts erased) before the final versions could be copied.

'You're both here today. Do it now,' I suggested.

However, I relented. I was anxious to be reasonable (I did not always have that attitude). I would adjourn the application until 2 p.m. the next day, when all the matters raised should have been clarified. But twenty-four hours later there was still some rumbling opposition from both sides, though less audible than the day before. I gave a final concession after consulting the listings' officer. The case would be marked not to start before 2 p.m. on the trial day. So the case went on.

Should it have been necessary for me to expend all that mental effort, to say nothing of court time and public money? The defence had not got down to things. There were too many difficulties from their angle. The case was too complex to master easily. As for the prosecution, the Crown Prosecution Service is under-funded and consequently its staff are stretched. They have so many cases going through that it is cosy and easy for both sides to agree on an adjournment at the expense of others, of course, not forgetting the patient, weary defendant. But since I insisted, the case did actually start on the due day.

Another barrier to efficiency in the law is the fact that some solicitors try to cover too wide a field. A client goes to them for conveyancing, and then almost automatically for any further legal services such as an accident claim. One person can hardly be an expert in all the various fields such as conveyancing, probate, companies, divorce, civil actions, crime, and landlord and tenant; in addition there are other even more specialised areas like town planning, tax and patents. Yet one-man firms still exist, or try to. A few years ago a survey was done which showed that in Bristol there were seven one-man firms and in Oxford there were two. The number of firms with two-and-a-half partners were twenty-one and five respectively. For six to ten partners, both cities had five; and for eleven to fifteen it was five and one. In large cities there are much bigger firms: London for instance, has huge law firms.

When I was at the Bar a solicitor running a one-man firm asked me to advise on the amount of damages his client should receive for an injury. I said £800. When he instructed me to draft the statement of claim I asked to see the writ. He looked at me blankly. He had not issued one. But the accident had happened more than three years earlier and so any action was barred by statute from being brought to court. The solicitor had thought the period was still six years, as it had been at one time, and he was not insured against claims for negligence. He should have paid the lay client £800, but did he? Or did he tell her that counsel said she had no case? I never knew.

Clients like that plaintiff have no 'clout'. They know nothing of their rights and are easily fobbed off with excuses. They usually obtain legal aid, and feel diffident about pushing things with their solicitor. And so years pass and good cases go off, as evidence becomes more difficult to obtain and witnesses die, disappear, disperse or simply forget. At the Bar I had one solicitor client who confessed he had simply filed a case away and forgotten about it. Sometimes I had to explain delays to judges by saying that a solicitors' clerk had had a nervous breakdown or gone elsewhere, leaving the papers in his drawer.

*

Would changes to the solicitors' branch of the profession and, in particular, a fusion with the Bar end the inefficiencies I have referred to? First, a historical note. Today's legal professions emerged gradually over centuries. Only in the 1600s did the shape we know now start to evolve. The control of attorneys-at-law and solicitors-in-equity by the courts was already established. Solicitors were and still are regarded as 'officers of the court', the significance of which in practice has never been clear to me. It does enable solicitors to sound important, however, and to try to justify the unjustifiable. 'But I am officer of the court, your honour.'

Barristers have never been so regarded. They are not concerned with the administrative work involved in legal proceedings, and do not deal with court officials, except fleetingly during a hearing. Barristers have traditionally come from the privileged sections of society – sons of the wealthy. This still applies, though less so than formerly.

Attorneys and solicitors were finally excluded from the four Inns of Court in 1793: the two professions were then separated, and have remained so.

In 1739 attorneys and solicitors together formed the Society of Gentlemen Practicers in the Courts of Law and Equity – the forerunner of the Law Society, which was founded in 1825, receiving its royal charter twenty years later. At that time, most attorneys were also solicitors. The former name died out; it was thought to be associated with shady activities. Since a statute of 1873, all practitioners in the profession's 'lower' branch have been known as solicitors. This is unfortunate. To me 'attorney', which we only preserve in the title of the Attorney-General but is generally used in America, is preferable to 'solicitor', which imputes a certain grubbiness. After all, the usual use of 'soliciting' refers to an older profession than the law – and a more useful one, some would say.

In contrast, there was no body representing barristers

until the Bar Committee was set up by the General Council of the Bar in 1895. The Bar Council, as it is known, is elected by barristers; it is empowered to deal with all matters affecting the profession and to take such action as may be expedient. The Inns of Court remain responsible for the education of Bar students and calls to the Bar.

To be admitted to the roll of solicitors it is necessary to pass the Law Society exams (not easy – some never get through) and be articled to a solicitor for five years, or two years if you have a requisite law degree. Membership of the (national) Law Society is not essential. It allows a solicitor to use its London facilities such as the reading- and dining-rooms and library. A solicitor who handles a client's money has to have a practising certificate, which costs about £400 a year.

There are about 127 local law societies, all autonomous and proud of their independence. Solicitors in their areas are entitled to join. An annual dinner is held; I have addressed several of these. On a more mundane level, law societies exchange information with members and act together to solve local problems, say with a particular estate agent – or judge!

Many people feel aggrieved by the service they get – or, more likely, they do not get – from their solicitor. Some wrote to me, hoping I had a magic wand to wave in order to rectify matters. But I felt uneasy about correspondents who said their solicitors had let them down. I had insufficient means to assess their situation, and all I could do was to write back and say, 'Sorry, I can do nothing.' Sometimes I would tell them of the Solicitors' Complaints Bureau; some replied, saying that they had tried it and it was as useless as their solicitor had been.

The Law Society set up the Bureau in 1986. It has adjudication and investigation committees, but its powers are limited to the investigation of complaints of misconduct and inadequate professional services, and it cannot investigate complaints of negligence on the part of solicitors. The adjudication committee can call for a solicitor's file, and it has powers varying from issuing a rebuke to instituting proceedings before the Disciplinary Tribunal – a statutory body independent of the Law Society whose members are appointed by the Master of the Rolls. It has a majority of solicitors, as opposed to lay members. Most of its cases are referred to it by the Law Society. It can strike a solicitor from the roll, suspend him, fine him up to £3000 or order him to pay a client's costs.

In 1989 the Law Society allocated £7.3 million to the Complaints Bureau which dealt with 20,951 matters, of which 14 per cent were non-complaints such as requests for advice. And 84 per cent of the complaints were resolved by the staff without reference to the adjudication committee. The chief areas of clients' complaints are delays (what a surprise!), poor communications and negligent or inadequate services. Unfortunately, to add insult to injury, there is further delay in the investigations of delay: it can take up to three years for the Bureau to deal with a complaint. There is nothing odd about that: why should the solicitors who investigate be more expeditious than those whom they investigate?

The Legal Services Ombudsman was appointed under the 1990 Courts and Legal Services Act. He is a kind of court of last resort for complaints against solicitors, barristers and licensed conveyancers. A non-lawyer – to counter the suspicion that dog is reluctant to eat dog – for complaints against solicitors he replaces the Lay Observer, who had a similar role.

But the Ombudsman is toothless; he can only make recommendations. The professional body concerned must inform him within three months what they have done and intend to do about the matter. If the answer is nothing, the Ombudsman can draw himself to his full statutory height

. . . and do what? He can require the body to publish its reasons for rejecting his recommendations. No more than that.

The 1989 Lay Observer's report told of the continuing rise in complaints, bringing the system close to breakdown. A total of 613 were received that year, an increase of 18 per cent on the previous year. He reported one case where it took six years for solicitors to get a claim to a court hearing. The Complaints Bureau staff had decided to take no further action, even though on the solicitor's own account unexplained delays totalled three years!

The disciplinary procedure does have teeth. It may be some consolation for aggrieved clients to know that in 1990 forty-eight solicitors were struck from the roll, thirty-one suspended from practice, seventy-nine fined between £250 and £3000 and ten reprimanded.

I have not noticed any pulling up of socks during the four years the complaints procedure has been grinding away. In matters large and small, there is still too much shoddiness.

In May 1991 Lord Chancellor Mackay lamented that the cost of the judicial system was forecast to rise to £1200 million within three years. Legal aid had more than trebled in the previous decade, to £705 million. He suggested that, in order to limit such expenditure, the courts might have to be by-passed in some types of cases. Other options included arbitration or mediation, insurance or limited no-fault compensation schemes. All but the poorest should be expected to make some payment towards their legal aid. Applicants could be asked why they considered it necessary to pursue the litigation. These ideas should be pursued and discussed. As one would expect, Lord Mackay is bringing fresh thinking to this area.

No area of civil law needs more reform and receives less than the 'fault' system; at the Bar I found it distasteful and unjust. Changes would reduce solicitors' and barristers' incomes in this lush field, so they oppose them. To win damages arising out of an accident, a plaintiff has to prove the other side was at fault – 'negligence': it means the same. Absurdities and injustices proliferate. The late Mr Justice Stable tried two civil actions arising out of the same road collision. For some reason the cases were not tried together: the judge held one driver negligent in one case, and the other driver in the other, though the evidence was the same in both. Actions stemming from factory accidents also have a large element of lottery in them.

Most claims are settled, but in others the plaintiffs have to surmount a series of hurdles and defendants' insurance companies understandably exploit the system, dragging out the process, taking every procedural point and concealing relevant facts until compelled to reveal them. After years of waiting, some plaintiffs accept less than they should. If a defendant pays money into court as an offer of settlement, and the plaintiff refuses to accept it but the judge awards less than that sum in court, the plaintiff has to pay the defendant's costs incurred after the payment-in. So he may recover nothing, or even owe money to the defendant. No wonder many plaintiffs dare not take the risk, and settle out of court unfavourably to themselves.

Australia and New Zealand have 'no-fault' systems: an injured person receives damages without having to prove negligence – unless the injuries were self-inflicted. Our system puts money into the pockets of lawyers and insurance companies and takes it from those injured. Despite the recommendations of the Pearson Committee on Civil Liability and Compensation for Personal Injury in 1978, lawyers have successfully opposed reform.

I represented a bus conductress whose driver had done an emergency stop, throwing her into seats and injuring her neck. The driver said he had to brake because a dog followed by two young boys was about to run into the road. To succeed we had to prove he was wrong to brake so hard.

Reported cases pointed to his being wrong if there was only a dog – he should have put his passengers' safety before the animal's; but he was right to brake as he did if it was the only apparent means of avoiding the children. My client could throw no light on all that: she was upstairs collecting the fares at the time. Three independent witnesses gave slightly different versions, though all said there was a dog on the pavement and at least one child. But was the child about to run on to the road?

The case came to me for an opinion to put before the legal aid committee; if I said she had reasonable prospects of success they would finance her claim – she could not afford to do so herself and she had no trade union to back her. I only had the witnesses' statements and would first see them in person, except for the plaintiff, if and when they gave evidence in two or three years' time. No one could predict which judge would try the case, and judges differ in their attitudes. After much thought I advised the case should go ahead 'until the close of the pleadings' – in other words until both sides had put their cases on paper, when the prospects of success could be looked at afresh. I drafted a request for further and better particulars of the defence, and the claim looked slightly better when the replies arrived. We obtained a consulting engineer's report, and it looked better still; nevertheless it remained marginal, speculative. Legal aid was extended.

At the trial the case went better than I expected, and the plaintiff was awarded £6000 because the driver should have sounded his horn to warn the children. The defendants appealed to the Court of Appeal and the decision was over-turned: on the facts as found by the trial judge, if the driver had sounded his horn it would have been too late to warn the children. So after that lengthy process the plaintiff received nothing, although she had undoubtedly been injured in an accident that was in no respect her fault. If the trial judge had found the facts differently, his judgement would have been upheld.

A further unpredictable element when counsel advises on a claim is that there are 'plaintiff's judges' and 'defendant's judges'; others are neutral. One judge, who later served in the Court of Appeal, as a trial judge was never known to decide for a wife in a divorce matter or for the plaintiff in a factory accident claim. That judge even contrived to find against a workman on whom something was dropped from above while he was on the factory floor!

The financially ruinous legal costs which litigation can involve are well known. Only the poor, who receive free legal aid, and the rich can afford to go to law. Rights are trampled on, while good claims are not pursued or are settled out of court disadvantageously. I tried cases in the county court where the costs mushroomed out of proportion to the damages claimed. The Civil Review report in June 1988 stated: 'The legal costs of both parties often equal or exceed the damages recovered. It can cost a total on each side of £5000 in legal fees to win or lose a damage claim for £5000.' A study of plaintiffs' costs in 232 bills taxed in 1984 revealed that costs in a London High Court case averaged £6830 and in a county court action £1540.

Actress Charlotte Cornwell sued journalist Nina Myskow for libelling her as a 'middle-aged actress with a big bum'. The plaintiff won £10,000 plus costs, but the judge had made an error and the Court of Appeal ordered a retrial. Miss Cornwell had to pay the costs of both hearings. Although she was awarded £10,000 plus costs at the retrial, she was so out of pocket on balance that I believe she had to sell her house. She must have wished she had turned the other cheek.

There are various ways in which lawyers can be paid properly, while parties bring or defend civil cases, without ruin threatening. One way is the contingency fee, whereby a plaintiff's lawyer takes an agreed percentage of the damages if he wins but nothing if he loses. This is widespread in

America and exists to a limited extent in Scotland. One of Lord Mackay's Green Papers dealt with this subject in January 1989, and favoured a restricted scheme. I agree: let us try it.

It is possible to obtain insurance to cover legal costs. Relatively new to Britain, such insurance is well known in the USA and Germany. One policy available in late 1991 has an annual premium of £42, and covers personal injury, consumer, neighbourhood and home rights. The latter covered a claim where variations in the electricity supply resulted in appliances being ruined. The electricity board denied liability, but after intervention by the legal protection insurers they agreed to replace all the items. A comprehensive household policy could have this type of cover as a relatively inexpensive option.

At present both barristers and solicitors are forbidden to form partnerships with members of other professions. Lord Mackay's Green Paper, entitled *The Work and Organisation of the Legal Profession*, proposed that those rules should be abolished in the interest of the client. I agree. Accountants, surveyors, engineers and architects are allowed to have members of other professions as partners. This would be healthy for solicitors, enabling them to serve the public better and open their eyes to the more businesslike way that other professions are conducted. Lord Mackay would also allow partnerships between barristers, and between barristers and other professions. I doubt whether barristers would wish to take non-barristers as partners; certainly they would not immediately do anything so revolutionary. But a firm made up of barristers, solicitors and consulting engineers could be useful in civil claims arising out of accidents.

At present a barrister employed by the Crown Prosecution Service can appear in the magistrates' courts as an advocate; he cannot appear in the crown court. Nor can a barrister who works for a company as a salaried employee act in court for that firm. Those barristers cannot remain members of their chambers. They are no longer practising at the Bar as such.

Should a barrister be allowed to be a partner in a firm of solicitors? At present he would have to be disbarred and qualify as a solicitor after passing more exams. If he were allowed to remain a barrister, join a firm of solicitors and appear for them in any court, this would threaten the existence of an independent Bar and lead to a fusion between the two legal professions: so the Bar say in their strenuous opposition to such proposals.

In the evidence I sent to the Benson Commission on Legal Services I was against fusion – as was the Commission, which reported complacently in 1979 that things were all right as they were. I have since revised my view. The antagonism between barristers and solicitors concerning the areas which each can and cannot enter has gone on for too long. It is based on selfishness, not on concern for clients. The existence of two separate professions is regarded by their members as being in their own interests, but may not be in the public interest.

In 1896 E. B. V. Christian wrote these words in *A Short History of Solicitors*: 'It seems certain that the twentieth century will begin and it may end with barristers in sole possession of the right of audience in the supreme courts and solicitors still sitting, as Charles Dickens said, silent like truth at the bottom of the well.' Solicitors have pushed the frontier forward since then and will soon be able to plead in the High Court and become judges there, though the judicial hurdle they have to get over is high. They must pass through a consultative process with the Lord Chief Justice, the Master of the Rolls and the heads of the High Court's Chancery and Family Divisions. When the Green Paper came out, Lord Chief Justice Lane dubbed it 'one of the most sinister documents ever to emanate from Government'. He called a protest meeting of Supreme Court judges, to be held during court time, though public criticism led to it being switched to a Saturday morning. The Lord Chief Justice then snubbed the Lord Chancellor, an unprecedented action. Lord Mackay should have led a formal procession of judges, QCs and recorders at a ceremony to mark the beginning of the legal year on 2 October 1989. But the judges called it off. Lane refused to speak to Mackay unless he had to: while Lord Donaldson, the Master of the Rolls, said to Lord Mackay: 'Get your tanks off my lawn!'

The strength of the Bar's opposition to the encroachment by solicitors on its territory is indicated by the £1 million they raised in order to employ Saatchi and Saatchi to fight Lord Mackay. These moves by Bench and Bar illustrated as vividly as anything could the diehard conservatism that opposes reforms affecting them.

Will solicitors rush to rival barristers as advocates? Not many, initially. Since 1972 solicitors have been able to appear in the Crown Court in appeals if they did the case in the magistrates' court. But I have noticed that hardly any take advantage of this. At some crown courts, solicitors have full rights of audience by ancient custom going back to quarter sessions days. Doncaster is such a court; I used to sit there, but saw very few solicitors appearing as advocates.

The problem is wider than mere rights to appear in court. Behind it lies the ultimate question: should the two professions be fused into one? If it is so advantageous to have two separate legal professions, why do so few countries have them? Outside the United Kingdom and Eire, I know only of three states in Australia where the practitioners are compulsorily divided. When the High Court of Australia heard the UK Government's application to suppress *Spycatcher*, solicitor Michael Turnbull appeared for Peter Wright – and won. In Canada there are solicitors, barristers and QCs, but all are permitted to be partners in one firm. In no country which has any kind of unified legal profession is there any movement for separation. Apart from any other considerations, it must surely be cheaper for the client to pay one

103

set of fees instead of two.

There are other real disadvantages in our present arrangements. In my early years at the Bar I spent plenty of time doing nothing but waiting for briefs that rarely came. If I had been an advocate member of a firm that would not have happened. I could not specialise in one or two fields of law only, but had to purport to cover several, as did the other members of my Chambers. We were not partners and could not allot different fields to our members. Some specialisation did and does occur, but not officially. If a barrister likes civil cases, for instance, and solicitors regard him as good at them he may be able to drop criminal work.

Sometimes a client falls into the gap between solicitor and barrister. When I was practising at the Bar cases used to come to me which had already been wholly or partially ruined by the solicitor, through delay or the failure to take obvious steps. I used to feel that, if I could have handled a case from the start and throughout, the client would have been served better.

I was once, for example, handed a brief on the day before the hearing in the High Court. I had known nothing of the case previously. The woman plaintiff had opened a lavatory door in premises such as a store, to be immediately confronted by a step up of which there was no notice and which was not coloured to make it stand out. She fell and was injured. The defendants had made an ex-gratia offer which the solicitor had rejected without consulting the barrister who was then acting. The solicitor had not asked counsel to advise on evidence, or taken any measures to obtain expert evidence. The other side had an expert who gave evidence that there was no negligence, although he did not feel happy about it (so I was later told by counsel for the other side). The plaintiff lost and had to pay what for her was a fairly substantial amount towards her legal aid costs. She had been grievously let down by a divided legal profession. The solicitor was in practice on his own and was known for his addiction to drink. However, I doubt if any complaint about him would have got anywhere – certainly not in those days when the Law Society was more of a solicitors' protection society than it is now.

Bar Council Chairman Anthony Scrivener QC wrote to every judge on 26 March 1991, setting out the Bar's arguments on the extended rights of audience for solicitors. The arguments are those which, with others, are used against fusion. Scrivener, who has a refreshingly unpompous manner on TV, says that grants of new rights of audience to solicitors should meet the following criteria:

1. 'A high-quality service should be available to all irrespective of means. There must be no second-class service for those on legal aid.'

The document goes on to say that the same quality of advocacy must be available to those who require legal aid as to the wealthy, large companies, the Government and the prosecution. The inference is that those on legal aid get the same service as the wealthy at present. Come off it, Scrivener! Let someone on legal aid ask for George Carman QC or one in his class.

2. 'All advocates must be under duty to exercise independent judgement.'

The inference is that a barrister is free to decide whether a case should proceed or not. Scrivener may be in that position for all I know. Ask the average barrister if he takes that attitude with the Crown Prosecution Service. If he gets a lot of work from it, he cannot possibly exercise theoretical independence. I know: I prosecuted in thousands of cases.

3. 'The client must have freedom of choice and be able to make an informed choice as to representation.'

This again is Scrivener's scribbling, divorced from what happens in practice. He states that the client's freedom of choice should not be taken away by a 'tying-in' requirement that, before any legal services are provided, the client must agree only to use a particular advocate. Large companies are free to brief counsel of their choice. But in 99 per cent of criminal defences the solicitor chooses counsel, and goes only to one or two sets of chambers. The defendant has whichever counsel he is given – though he may ask for the same one he has had before from the chambers his solicitor briefs. In nearly all civil cases, the solicitor and not the client selects the barrister when one is required.

4. 'There must be a wide choice from a pool of specialist advocates available to all and sufficiently large to meet demand.'

According to 'Tony', as he signed the letter sent to us all, 'the Bar provides a pool of expert advocates who are available to every solicitor throughout the country and thereby to the public'. We are back to George Carman QC. No doubt he is sought by solicitors nationwide – though he can only do one case at a time. It is very rare for barristers to go out of their own area in criminal cases, and fairly rare in civil ones. Those in London chambers do get about more than those in the provinces, but they did not come before me very often. Local work is done by local barristers. Although the standard of advocacy is very high at the top end of the Bar, say the top 10 per cent, the average barrister is mediocre and a fair proportion are poor; no better than the average solicitor, and much worse than the best. It is true, however, that there are specialist fields such as tax, companies, planning, patents and property rights (Chancery) where almost all the specialists are in London.

5. 'All advocates must be subject to enforceable rules which provide for proper and appropriate conduct in all aspects of advocacy.'

Our worthy advocate for his own case goes on: 'The structure of the Bar and its existing rules of conduct contain all that is necessary to meet those criteria.' He is saying that solicitors who wish to be High Court advocates ought to accept the Bar's rules. He does not go so far as to say that they should become barristers, but I think he probably would, if pressed.

There are some formidable advocates in the higher echelons of the Bar who will use all their powers to hold the line against solicitors and maintain its privileged positions. Not long after I was appointed a judge in 1976, I attended a meeting of HM Council of Circuit Judges in London. It had been called so that we could discuss our evidence to be sent to the Royal Commission on Legal Services. Fusion was the main topic.

The High Court judges had prepared their document and we had a separate one. As I remarked to a colleague: 'When the Commission reads the documents, it will realise why they are High Court judges and we are not.' Their document was superbly written, as one would expect. All the arguments against fusion were analysed and marshalled cogently. I was more impressed with it then, however, than I am now.

Incidentally, our meeting was a shambles. In the chair was a circuit judge – chosen, of course, on the basis of seniority. For some reason, the civil servant who was secretary to the Commission had been invited to attend; he probably only came because he did not know how to decline politely. During the discussion one judge, well known at the Old Bailey, was on his eloquent feet discussing our document while the rest of us thought he was discussing the other. The clarity of thought and incisiveness which the public might expect from a large gaggle of judges was not evident. It was a disorganised ramble around the subject. I vowed never to attend another meeting of HM Council of Circuit Judges and I never did, though I paid my subscription loyally – well, I paid it.

When Hailsham was Lord Chancellor the Bar had no need

for concern: he was its strongest supporter and defender. Lord Mackay is made of different stuff. He is courageous enough not simply to conserve what is, but to look at what should be. I would not like to see the Bar with all its history and traditions disappear as a distinct group. Its high standards must be maintained. Barristers specialising in advocacy and legal learning are bound to outdistance solicitors at the higher reaches. But the present separation of the legal profession into two distinct branches must not be allowed to remain as it is.

How do I view the way ahead? I foresee an independent Bar operating in its chambers as now. Changes should be introduced gradually, so that their effects can be gauged. The guiding principle should be freedom of choice. Barristers should be free to form partnerships with others, or with solicitors. If a barrister joins a firm of solicitors he should be free to act only for that firm and in any court, or to do work for other firms of solicitors. He would remain a member of his Inn. A barrister should also be free to join a non-legal firm or company, acting for them as he would now if briefed via a solicitor.

If the Crown Prosecution Service wish to employ barristers at a salary, to appear in any court as advocate, that should be allowed. If when I was judge I had ten guilty pleas and appeals against sentence in a day's list, there might have been eight or ten counsel appearing for prosecution and defence. This was, and is, unnecessarily wasteful. Two or three barristers could do all the day's work. The prosecution would still brief an 'independent' barrister for difficult cases.

On the defence side, solicitors who did not have a member of the firm (a barrister or solicitor) specialising in or prepared to do advocacy, would go to counsel's chambers as now. Under legal aid such a defending barrister would not be paid a separate fee for each case, but one fee based on the total work done that day.

My proposals would inevitably lead to a smaller Bar, but would that matter? Many barristers have no idea how to analyse and present clearly. They try to ask improper questions which are really comments. Repeatedly I had to tell counsel that a question should elicit facts within the knowledge of the witness. I do not know what is taught at law school these days – I received no instruction in advocacy – but it seems that many barristers learned very little. The loss of 80 per cent of the existing Bar as independent practitioners would be no real loss. They would be better employed in other areas, with firms of solicitors or other businesses, using such legal expertise as they have for a salary.

The corps of independent counsel that remained would be an élite. They would be specialists, paid well in fees. The senior judicial appointments would go to them, but others to barristers and solicitors, regardless of whether they had salaried jobs.

My proposals will be understandably condemned by those who see threats to their independence, income and prospects. But I believe the public would have a more efficient and less expensive service from lawyers, and that should be the chief test. I further believe that the thinking behind what I have written accords generally with Lord Chancellor Mackay's. If so, I am happy to support that great and good man.

So my response to the question posed at the head of this chapter is: I may have been too hard on some barristers and solicitors at times. But others deserved more stick than I gave them. Whether with stick or carrot, the legal profession urgently needs reform.

5

Was I too easy on the police?

Life without the police would be unthinkable; we all rush to them when we are in real trouble. Yet our organised police force is relatively new. How did people manage in the old days? Why do large sections of society now distrust and even loathe the police? Is police misbehaviour the reason, or the only reason? Are there enough safeguards against it? Are judges, including me when I was one, partly to blame because we are seen as pro-police and let them get away with things?

First, let's take a look at the history of keeping law and order in this country, and how it's organised today.

In medieval days, the feudal lords' retainers collected their dues and carried out rough justice between man and man. During Edward I's reign (1272–1307) the 'hue and cry' was devised. Any person who saw or heard an offence had to shout out the miscreant's name or identity and give chase immediately. When the hue and cry was raised, every male over sixteen had a duty to join in pursuit. Anyone who failed to do so was treated as an associate of the felon and liable to suffer the same punishment. Yet in the fourteenth century, 'murder, rape, beating and robbery by violence were everyday incidents', according to G. M. Trevelyan's *English Social History*.

In the 1500s, the office of constable was established: he was elected annually but received no pay. If a parish failed to elect one, a statute of 1665 empowered the local justices of the peace (lay magistrates) to make an appointment. In a borough, watchmen supplemented or acted in place of parish constables. Stationed at the gates of a town during the night were a body of men whose members were recruited by an early form of conscription among the middle classes. Any man who refused this duty could be put in the stocks and ridiculed by the populace.

In the 1600s every parish in England was given police duties, with a parish constable who was paid a fee by the justices. Charles II gave permission to justices to appoint constables on a permanent basis with fixed remuneration, and the power to appoint special constables. The early specials were called 'bell men' because of the bell and pike they carried; they were more familiarly known as 'Charlies' after Charles II.

In 1749 the novelist Henry Fielding, London's first stipendiary (paid) magistrate, chose six volunteers whose number was quickly expanded; as 'thief takers' they were ancestors of the Metropolitan Police. At first they worked only for rewards after successful prosecutions, but then they were paid a guinea a week. Soon there were sixty mounted and one hundred foot patrols in London, with their headquarters in Bow Street.

In 1829 the Home Secretary, Sir Robert Peel, set up the Metropolitan Police. It was under the direct control of the Home Secretary, who appointed a commissioner as its head; this is still the system. The new force, known as 'Peelers' or 'Bobbies', after their founder, wore blue tail-coats and tall hats to show they were civilians and not soldiers: there were unfounded suspicions of a plot to destroy public liberty through military tyranny. One result of the new force was the migration of criminals from London. By a statute of 1838 every borough had to appoint a police force, and this applied to counties from 1856.

In 1946, the separate forces of non-county boroughs which shared local government functions with county councils were abolished, though the independent boroughs retained theirs.

The need for further amalgamation is highlighted by an episode which does no credit to myself.

In the mid-sixties, I ran into the back of another car that had stopped and was waiting to turn right. Momentary inattention was the only explanation I could have given the local Bench, if I had been done for careless driving as I should have been. But I happened to live opposite the Chief Constable of Halifax. He was reluctant to prosecute local people, and there was a reason for that. A pleasant, handsome man, he had had a close shave when, soon after the Second World War, the Watch Committee voted to sack him. The charges, as I remember, were misuse of civil defence equipment of a trivial value – it was at his home – and kissing a policewoman on the back of her neck. Presumably it was not the place on her that mattered, but the place where he did it – the police station.

The chief appealed to the Home Office, who rightly reinstated him – probably advising him to 'watch it'. It was well known, though not the subject of a charge, that he had also had an affair with the daughter of a prominent citizen, and as both lovers were married to others there was gossip. After that, our chief constable tried to keep in with Halifax people, at whose hands he had almost tasted disaster.

The chief and I were not close friends. We met socially a couple of times and I used to see him at Halifax quarter sessions. One day as I was washing my car he sauntered across and said he had some papers on his desk concerning my car accident. 'My chief superintendent wants to prosecute you. He says we let you off that speeding.' I said nothing. 'Insurance companies expect us to go ahead in this sort of case, so it's a bit difficult. But I'll tell you what I'll do. I'll wait until the super goes on holiday and then mark it "no action".' He added: 'I help you and you help me.' I still do not know what that meant, but I did not feel I should insist on being prosecuted.

That instance pointed the need to amalgamate small

police forces and to move superior officers around, as happens now. When Halifax lost its separate force in 1968 some officers resented it, but policing has to be done over wide areas: crooks do not respect boundaries, and a small force cannot afford specialist services such as a fingerprint department.

In 1911 the population of Halifax was 101,000 and the police force numbered 101. In 1968 the population had fallen to 95,450 but police numbers had increased to 207. Today 170 cover the same area. In 1990 there were 39 forces in England, including the Met, the City of London and four in Wales. England had, to the nearest hundred, 114,200 officers, including 24,500 in the Met and 800 in the City. Wales had 6400. Of those in England and Wales about eleven thousand were women.

But should there now be a national police force? The Government sees no need for one, or even for larger regional forces, and I agree. This is not because liberty would be threatened – that is an illusion. A final amalgamation, while possibly leading to greater efficiency, would reduce the links with local communities which police committees provide. And though bigger can spell better, it can also spell more bureaucratic. A national force might become as remote from ordinary people as the army. Regional crime squads have been set up to combat crime which crosses boundaries. The National Drugs Intelligence Unit was established to co-ordinate the information available to police and customs officers. A National Crime Intelligence Unit is being set up.

There is an odd tripartite system for administering the police service: the Home Secretary, the local police authority and the chief constable. The authority has a statutory duty to maintain 'an adequate and efficient' police force. Yet it cannot hire or fire the chief constable without the Home Secretary's approval. Because the Home Office provides half the funds for the force, it holds the whip hand if, for example, the authority wants to reduce police numbers under the pressure of Community Charge capping. This is a typical British muddle. Constitutionally, the constabulary is answerable to no one – not the police authority, the Home Secretary, or even Parliament; but to the law alone. During the 1984–5 miners' strike the Home Secretary was not accountable to Parliament for police actions.

Year by year since the mid-fifties I have observed crime rising; the reason is that people's attitudes have gradually changed. Most offences are committed by males aged between fifteen and twenty-five, one in three of whom acquires a criminal record. They think and behave differently from their parents and grandparents. In today's society God no longer looks over our shoulders, inhibiting such sins as theft. The sin now is not in the deed, but in the discovery. And people have greater expectations. They want to enjoy the good things of life, and if they cannot afford them by means of their earnings or handouts, some help themselves to others' goods and care nothing about the harm they do.

The 'common people' no longer want to be looked on as 'common'. They feel as good as anybody else, and I sympathise with that feeling – though not with what it can lead to. Most criminals are created in the home, where neglect and bad example breed wrong values. The exhortations I heard when I was young are not heard now: 'Work and save for what you want', 'Respect other people', 'Don't indulge yourself'. There is too much self-assertion and too little self-restraint. And the police are as much affected by these trends as is the rest of society.

Take a typical incident – I have tried many such cases. A man is arrested in town late on a weekend evening for being drunk and disorderly, a breach of the peace or possessing cannabis. He does not go quietly and within minutes there is a howling mob, fuelled by drink, screaming hatred at the officers and attacking them with feet, fists and bottles.

Blood flows, and the whole messy business ends months later at a crown court where a jury has to sort it out. A few of the jurors may hate the police, so the result is uncertain. Defending barristers have the task of attacking the police, who accept that as part of their job. Excessive force or the extortion of admissions by force or threats may be alleged, some of which are true. For years I noticed that most jurors were reluctant to convict on police evidence alone, especially in London. How many bent coppers have been exposed in the last twenty years, including some very senior ones?

While police misbehaviour does occur, officers do not deserve all the scars. In 1990, 13,878 were assaulted; 13,568 of those had serious injuries and two died. When they are assaulted, alcohol in the attacker usually has a part to play. Britons now drink twice as much as they did in the mid-fifties, though less than in the eighteenth and nineteenth centuries. Men in the eighteen to twenty-four age group are the UK's heaviest drinkers, and drink-related car accidents are the number one killer of young people. Half of drownings of those under thirty involve alcohol, which is also a factor in 60 per cent of all murders, 75 per cent of stabbings, 50 per cent of domestic violence and 40 per cent of deaths by fire. More than a hundred thousand people a year are arrested for drinking and driving, and the same number again for being drunk and disorderly and the like. Ninety-five per cent of adults in the UK drink alcohol and £18 billion a year is spent on it – more than on new cars or on running hospitals or schools. The Government makes more than £7.3 billion a year – £230 per second – in taxes from alcohol. One way and another, alcohol plays a huge part in modern society; small wonder that the police are often on the receiving end.

I must have encountered thousands of police officers in court. Most are neither full-time angels nor full-time devils. Like the rest of us they are sometimes the one, sometimes the other, and generally somewhere in between. Daily they have opportunities for corruption or 'hardening up' evidence. Why should we expect them to be more honest than ourselves? Putting on a uniform – or a wig and gown – does not bring morality. But the abuse of power is more tempting and easier for police officers than for judges.

Why do people choose the police as a career, instead of, say, other public service jobs such as teaching, the Church or the probation service? Does it depend on how many GCSEs they have and what else is available? The opportunity for power over others must be a motive for some, though not the dominant one for all. So it must be for judges, who wield more real power than the police. We play God in people's lives and can make or break them, impoverish them, destroy their family life and social standing, and deprive them of their jobs and children. I have never heard of a UK judge being bribed, but that may be because the price would be too high. No one ever tried to bribe me.

A family company was being wound up and our accountant told me we had £700 for VAT which no one would ever discover: what should he do with it? I said it had to go to Customs and Excise. But did I say that out of honesty? Or because as a barrister I did not wish to lose face with the accountant? Or was I fearful of the consequences if someone did find out? Inherent morality – doing the right thing because it is right – is rare nowadays, and not to be expected from anyone. Most police officers appear to behave properly most of the time, but some abuse their position. Power tends to corrupt all who have it, unless there are correctives. Judges have the media and Court of Appeal looking over their shoulders. The police are often alone with suspects, and if they are investigated by other officers – well, things may get covered up.

One reason for the bad relations between the police and public is the way the police have for generations investigated offences. At that stage, even now, they have no independent authority to check or direct them. I prosecuted and defended countless times, and in many cases I was unhappy about what went on. Police malpractice does not happen as often as defendants allege, but it does still occur in my view, despite changes rightly introduced by the 1984 Police and Criminal Evidence Act (PACE). At the root of it all lie two factors: the loading of the criminal justice system in favour of suspects and defendants, and the need in most cases for police to obtain admissions – 70 per cent of prosecutions depend on that and only a few on patient Sherlock Holmes work.

A suspect has to be told he is not obliged to answer any questions put by the police. His silence cannot be held against him. Nor can his silence in court if he decides not to go into the witness-box. 'The burden of proof lies on the prosecution': jurors repeatedly hear that from the prosecution, the defence and the judge. 'If you have doubt at all, the defendant is entitled to be acquitted' – and they are, time after time, often in the teeth of evidence and despite a record for similar offences carefully hidden from the jury. You only have to watch the faces of the jury members when there is a conviction and the list of previous offences is read out: they look at each other as if to say 'If only we'd known, we wouldn't have had all that argument.' Convictions can sometimes be revealed during the evidence, as when the defence attacks the character of a prosecution witness (more on this matter later in the chapter), but usually the jurors' eyes are masked.

I defended a man for safe-blowing: he had traces of gelignite on his clothing and had been seen in the area around the time of the offence. The jury did not know that at his last appearance in court he had got five years for blowing the very same safe! What must the frustrated police officers have thought when the jury foreman pronounced him not guilty. 'Next time we'll verbal him' (invent admissions)?

The right to silence when questioned by the police is

judge-made law, and judges have got it muddled. The right to refuse to answer questions – coupled with freedom from ill-treatment or punishment because of such a refusal – is logical and right. But this has been mixed up with the supposed right to have the jury told that no adverse inferences should be drawn from a refusal to answer, or a failure to give an explanation. The latter 'right' was a consequence of the inability of an accused to give evidence before the 1898 Criminal Evidence Act. The judges or Parliament should then have made the appropriate changes; they should be made now. If there is evidence against a defendant that calls for an explanation, he ought to explain or have his silence held against him. Only the guilty need the protection of the existing rule.

As to the defendant's refusal to give evidence at his trial, I had to tell juries: 'Do not hold it against him. He is entitled to sit in the dock and tell the prosecution to prove it if it can.' This is nonsense. If an explanation is called for, he should give it or have his refusal thrown into the scales against him – it would not automatically lead to a guilty verdict, but it could be taken into account together with other points.

I understand the frustration of investigating officers who feel sure they have a guilty man in custody and are anxious to prove him guilty, even though that involves bending the rules in, as they see it, a good cause. Inventing evidence against those whom they do not believe to be guilty is rare, though I remember Detective Sergeant Challoner who nonchalantly planted a brick in a suspect's property. He was prosecuted and subsequently went to a mental hospital. In case after case, especially pre-PACE, I heard defendants deny they were ever cautioned – that is, told they were not obliged to answer questions. Sometimes they thought it was only an off-the-record chat. If a defending solicitor was present at an interview, he often felt it his duty to advise his client to say nothing. So the police tried to exclude solicitors and either told the court there had been no request for one

118

or exercised their discretion to refuse the request for 'unreasonable delay or hindrance to enquiries'.

There were two ways in which some officers broke the rules in putting 'admissions' before a court: extortion and invention. Extortion was usually by threat or inducement – both forbidden by the old Judges' Rules. It was rare to find a defendant alleging severe physical violence; that was too dangerous, in that marks could be seen and careers ruined. Also, most cases did not arouse police anger to that extent, though in Sheffield, as a 1963 inquiry found, it had been policy for many years – and approved by the chief constable – to use routine violence, including a rhinoceros whip. I had appeared in cases at Sheffield where defendants often alleged violence by the police, but it was brushed aside by prosecution and Bench as unworthy invention.

Intensive and persistent questioning by the police has always been legitimate, provided it falls short of oppression, though I saw many cases where, by implication, the jury found there had been oppression. If a suspect refused to cooperate by saying what the interrogators wished to hear, various devices were used. Some are suggested by the defence, even today.

First, there would be an attempt to convince the suspect it was in his interests, to tell all he knew. 'Your pal has admitted the burglary and he says it was all your idea. Are you going to let him get away with that? What's your version?' If the pal had said that, there was nothing wrong. If he had not, there was no breach of the rules, but it was getting near.

The next play went over the border: 'We can keep you locked up for weeks if you don't confess.' Or the same thing in effect: 'Give us a statement and you'll get bail.' Or: 'We'll put in a good word with the judge, tell him you've cooperated with us and tried to go straight.'

Other improper pressure includes threats that a wife, girlfriend, child or relative will be arrested and charged, or not bailed; prolonged and bullying questioning that breaks down resistance so that the suspect will sign anything; insufficient food; no bed or blanket; and a cold cell.

Invention of admissions, as alleged by a defendant, included putting words in a statement that he had not said and then getting him to sign it without reading it. More likely to be true was the assertion of 'verballing'. Pre-PACE it was common for the police to take no notes during an interview, even when it lasted for thirty minutes or more. They were allowed to wait until the interview ended and then write down the questions and answers from memory. If there was more than one officer present they could make a joint note, so their notebooks were word for word the same. Sometimes several hours passed before notes were made; that was permitted if they said it was the first opportunity they had had and events were still fresh in their memories. The reason they gave for not making notes during the interview was that it would interrupt the flow of question and answer. That was unconvincing, and sometimes a note was made at the time.

Serving and former officers have told me off the record that 'verballing' did happen – not that *they* ever did it, though! In any view, the system was wide open to abuse and errors. It was absurd to claim, as interrogators did, that they remembered every word exactly as it was spoken in an interview recorded in several pages of typescript. If two interviewers had had to write up their notes independently, there would have been wide discrepancies – as there have been when an interviewer has had a hidden tape-recorder. One of the worst features of the old system was that a defendant did not take notes during an interview or afterwards and only learned what was in the police notes weeks or months later, when the prosecution statements were served on him.

After years of increasing dissatisfaction with the system, in 1978 I sent detailed evidence to the Royal Commission on Criminal Procedure. I recommended, as others probably did, that where practicable interviews should be recorded on sound or videotape. The Commission's report led to PACE, which sets out in detail the rights of police and suspects, with a view to holding the balance fairly and avoiding the flaws in the old system. A very detailed custody record has to be kept for every arrested person, from his arrival at a police station and throughout his stay. The custody officer has to open the record, secure compliance with PACE and protect the suspect's rights. PACE lays down the procedure for road checks; stopping and searching people; entering and searching premises and seizing objects found there; making arrests; conducting searches; and fingerprinting suspects. An officer of superintendent rank or above can delay a suspect's consultation with his solicitor in specified circumstances.

Where an interview takes place in a police station it must be recorded at the time unless that is impracticable – for example, where the suspect refuses to talk if the conversation is recorded. The wish to keep an interview flowing is not a good reason for failing to make an on-the-spot record. Where an interview is held in a police station the record of it must be given to an interviewee if he is still there when the record is completed. The sound-tape recording of interviews is now virtually universal. Videotaping would be better still and may come eventually. A court may make any order necessary to secure the fairness of the proceedings, and exclude evidence if its prejudicial effect outweighs its probative value. A confession obtained by a trick, deceit or oppressive behaviour may be excluded. A confession is inadmissible unless it can be shown not to have been obtained by oppression and in consequence of anything said or done which is liable to make it unreliable.

Police malpractice can still happen despite PACE, but it is less likely. Officers can 'verbal' a suspect about what was said at his home or in a police car, though that was not often suggested in cases that I tried. The police could threaten a suspect before an interview, telling him what to say during it, but I cannot recall such a complaint being made by a defendant. PACE has created a big improvement. Disputes about what was said at an interview used to occur in about half the jury trials in my court. PACE reduced that to no more than about 10 per cent.

Could the appalling injustices of the Guildford Four, Birmingham Six and Maguire Seven cases happen today? There is no need to recite the facts of these infamous cases. We all know what happened, though we do not all agree why, who was to blame and what changes are needed. The top judges, led by Lords Lane and Donaldson who both played unfortunate parts in those cases, are as complacent as the Establishment always is. Ranks have been closed and mouths kept tightly shut. The old boys reassure each other that all is well. Has one apologetic word fallen from the lips of any Establishment figure, political or judicial? 'Never apologise. Never explain.' Top people certainly practise that: it could be their motto.

There was understandable horror and alarm when the bombs exploded in Guildford and Birmingham, killing and wounding innocent people. The public wanted justice – even vengeance. One likes to think the police only wanted justice, properly arrived at. But police officers are human underneath their uniforms, and despite their training they too felt angry. They were determined to cage those responsible, and knew from experience how hard a crime can be to prove. They had suspects in their power and they could beat confessions out of them. Provided the police did not break ranks (impossible for an officer to do if he wants to stay in the force and not be taunted or ignored until he is hounded out) no one would know. For all those years no one in authority did know – or rather no one admitted they did.

The Irish cases tell an awful tale of police brutality, suppression of evidence by them and the prosecution lawyers, inefficiency verging on incompetence by forensic scientists, the bias of Establishment-minded judges, and jurors' gullibility. They reveal the failure of an antique system to detect and right those scandalous wrongs for year after year while innocent people languished in jail, separated from their partners and children. The public saw indifference of top politicians and judges to wrongs when finally exposed – mainly by the efforts of journalists and, in the Birmingham Six case, of one man in particular, Chris Mullen MP, as he is now. Derided and ignored, he did not give up. His excellent book *Error of Judgement* influenced public opinion.

All judges – including me, were I still one – should learn from the way Mr Justice Nigel Bridge, now a Law Lord, handled the forty-five day Birmingham Six trial in 1975. Take the 'trial within a trial', which lasted eight days. As counsel and judge I did dozens of those, though not so many post-PACE. They arise when a defendant argues that evidence such as a confession by him should not go to the jury because it was obtained by violence, threats, inducements or other improper pressure. The police and defendants gave evidence to Mr Justice Bridge in the absence of the jury, and he had to decide whether to admit the confessions. I sympathise with him here. I usually accepted police evidence and rejected that of the accused. The police have so much to lose by misbehaving; and the more officers involved, the less likely for all to conspire. But a defendant has every reason to disown his confession and nothing to lose by trying.

On one side Nigel Bridge had fifteen officers, some high-ranking, from two separate forces. On the other side were – as many judges would see it – six scruffy, low-class Irishmen, five of whom had been on their way to an IRA funeral when arrested. No wonder he rejected their evidence and believed that of the police. As he said, the Lancashire and West Midlands police were complete strangers; the Birmingham officers would be taking a risk that the Lancashire ones might report them. He underestimated, as I have done, the ability of detectives to stand together in serious cases. 'Don't let the side down' is an attitude that Mr Justice Bridge must have known since his schooldays. Judges identify with the Establishment, as I did on the whole in the crown court. Police officers are part of the structure which preserves society from those who attempt to destroy it.

Nigel Bridge's belief in the guilt of the Six coloured his summing-up, which lasted three days. He said it was the gravest and most important case he had tried. He went further: 'I am of the opinion, not shared by all my brothers on the Bench, that if a judge has formed a clear view, it is much better to let the jury see that and say so, and not pretend to be a kind of Olympian detached observer.' I never went as far as that. Bridge did remind the jury that the decision was theirs and theirs alone. While accurate on the law and the evidence – 'impeccable', as the Court of Appeal say when upholding a conviction – the summing-up was, when taken as a whole, a cogent, final speech for the prosecution. It was unbiased neither in tone nor in content.

One of the main defence points was that the confessions signed by four of the Six did not tally with each other or with known facts. Yet the judge gave an interpretation to the prosecution's advantage. He said: 'Of course it is inescapable that these statements are not accurate in detail. But do they necessarily show that the statements are not genuine?' He went on to say that it was fairly common for criminals to seek relief from inner tensions by confessing. Those who confess often seek to minimise their role. 'They are often anxious to show that somebody else has really induced them against their better judgement to do what they had done, to shift the main responsibility on to someone else's shoulders. Read through, if you will, the statements of Power and Walker in particular to see if you cannot detect that psychological process at work.' The judge even suggested that the same explanation might apply to Callaghan's confession; that he had placed the bomb outside the pub when, in fact, it was placed inside. 'When he realised the enormity of what happened . . . would it not be a way of seeking to minimise the extent of his own responsibility, even while making a partial confession?' Was that fair, coming from one who was surely supposed to be impartial? There were passages in Mr Justice Bridge's summing-up which could have come from a crown counsel – which he often was when he was still at the Bar, though in civil rather than criminal cases.

If the defendants were telling the truth, the police had been involved in a conspiracy unprecedented in the annals of British history! It involved innumerable assaults and the fabrication of false evidence, he went on. It involved per-jured evidence on which the police must have spent many hours trying to ensure that their various lies would accord with each other. (The judge did not know about Detective Superintendent George Reade's 'schedule' which, when it surfaced years later, appeared to have that very object, though Reade did not explain what it was.) Bridge said: 'Consider the scale of the conspiracy in terms of those in-volved.' It would have ranged, he said from constables up to the chief superintendent in charge of the whole of the West Midlands CID, who had been promoted to assistant chief constable.

The Six were found guilty on all counts, and when sen-tencing them Mr Justice Bridge said: 'You stand convicted on each of the twenty-one counts, on the clearest and most overwhelming evidence I have ever heard, of the crime of murder.' If the death penalty had still applied, those six men would now be names remembered by a few in the UK, forgotten by the public and excoriated by the tabloid press.

What changes are needed in the judicial field to prevent or remedy injustice as in the Irish cases? First, we need fewer judges like Lords Lane (nice and able though he is), Donaldson and Bridge. All three should have the Irish cases engraved on their consciences, though I doubt they have. Such people are so confident they are always right. Lord

Havers, as prosecutor in the Guildford and Maguire cases, had questions to answer, but refused. Donaldson, as the judge in those cases, refused to attend the May Inquiry into the Maguire case in 1991.

The major public school/Oxbridge oligarchy, to which those and other peers belong, has to be broken. How? It will take time – at least twenty-five years. Working-class Bar students should receive more help to go to and remain at the Bar; eventually more of them will qualify for appointment as judges. Some aspirants cannot even afford to read for the Bar: local authorities commonly refuse grants. The £6000 a year payment during pupillage will be some help but will reduce the number of places available. The Bar Council and Inns of Court should provide funds for beginners. There could be a levy on those who have been in practice over, say, ten years.

Would working-class barristers be appointed to the Bench? A Lord Hailsham would be unlikely to give them priority over Etonians. Lord Mackay is much broader-minded, but he will not be there for ever. A board or committee including lay people should scrutinise applicants and appoint, promote and discipline judges.

A judge should be prevented by law from telling the jury his opinion as to a defendant's guilt. It is too easy for a clever judge to influence the jury's verdict. I have found that myself, though I do not claim to be clever. A judge who tries too hard for a conviction, as I did at times, can get a bloody nose from the jury. While on the High Court Bench the great Norman Birkett wrote in his diary: 'There is no satisfaction in work on the Bench at all comparable with the work one used to do at the Bar. There is no scope for fine speaking or for playing on the emotions. I still have the power of dominating juries, however: they do whatever I wish.'

Is a 'court of last resort' needed to counteract the consti-pated approach exemplified by Lord Lane in the second

126

Birmingham Six appeal? It has been suggested that such a reviewing tribunal should include lay people. The idea of such a tribunal is misconceived. It would not fit well with the existing hierarchy of courts.

The truth about Lord Lane in the Birmingham Six case is that he and his two fellow judges could not accept after all those years that the criminal justice system had got it wrong. He was proud of that system understandably, from his angle. And let us be fair. Lane has done his conscientious best as the 'Chief'. He is well respected by lawyers and popular even with me. However, he is a man with limited vision. He is too close to and too enamoured of the dinosaur-like apparatus over which he presides to take a critical viewpoint, which would be as alien to him as to almost all present or past judges, especially the senior ones.

It is too hard for an appellant to have a verdict overturned on appeal, even when there is cogent new evidence, as in the Birmingham Six case. No jury would have upheld those convictions as Lord Lane did, rejecting every bit of new evidence with the selective sleight of mind that every judge recognises and some, including me at times, have used when hearing and deciding appeals. Parliament could easily widen the scope of the Court of Appeal's powers or alter the way it uses them. Retrials should be obligatory where there is new evidence which might cause a reasonable jury to acquit. There are difficulties in retrying a case after years; witnesses may be dead, have poor memories or be senile. But appropriate legislation could deal with that; parts of the old transcript could be allowed in evidence, for example. In the case of war crimes, Parliament has decided that fifty years is not too long for justice to be done.

Finally, the key to reform in the judicial area is the appointment of a Lord Chief Justice not addicted to those 'three Cs' – complacency, conservatism and conformity. We need a radical, open-minded, go-ahead person – all the things that Lord Lane is not. The new man (there are no

eligible women within sight yet) will also require character-
istics that Geoffrey Lane does possess: a bright brain, a
sense of fairness, tolerance, humanity. Is such a person
available? Candidates have been referred to. But more of
this in Chapter 8.

Police officers, as well as judges, have too much unsuper-
vised power. They tend to abuse it in serious cases where
they feel sure of a defendant's guilt and where they are
anxious not to let technical rules in his favour cause an
unjust acquittal.

In some respects, however, the present system can ham-
per a defendant unfairly during police investigations, the
trial and afterwards. So we ought to tighten the rules against
a defendant while making the changes in his favour. We
have to get the balance right.

If a suspect or defendant exercises his right of silence
when answers are called for, that should be a factor for the
jury to consider. The Law Society's *Gazette* for May 1991
contained an article by Sir Frederick Lawton, the distinguished and sensible ex-Lord Justice of Appeal. He
advocated an end to the right of silence and went further. He
wrote that the prosecution should be able to tell the jury of a
defendant's previous convictions. These are usually suppressed unless, for example, the defendant attacks the
character of a prosecution witness, when the judge may
permit his character to be revealed. Sir Frederick stated that
continental jurists are astonished by our refuşal to reveal
convictions. In French courts an accused is questioned about
these early in the trial. 'There would be much less temptation for police officers to fabricate evidence if more use
could be made of previous convictions during a trial.'

Respectfully, I agree with Sir Frederick. The trial judge
should be able to authorise revelation of convictions that are
relevant to the charges. Old offences, say beyond fifteen
years, or those that are trivial or of a different type from the

current charges, should not be revealed. But take my client charged with safe-blowing described earlier in this chapter: his conviction for blowing the same safe was surely relevant.

Jurors should not be thought stupid, at least not all; the stronger ones who lead the rest are presumably the more intelligent. To suppose they will automatically assume guilt from a previous conviction is almost to discredit the jury system itself. In my experience, juries which know of a defendant's bad character may still acquit him. Under Sir Frederick's system they would be told how to regard convictions, as they are now when these are revealed.

Sir Frederick's article contained a further wise observation. 'Police standards of behaviour will never improve as long as officers think that those responsible for discipline look the other way when there are allegations of malpractice.'

Who investigates complaints against the police? The Police Complaints Authority (PCA) was set up under PACE. The old system was unsatisfactory. Police investigated police, and laymen did not come into the investigation or the adjudication. Dog is reluctant to eat dog, except in the judiciary, where – as will be seen later – some top dogs do like the taste of upstart little dogs like me! When I was at the Bar a colleague who had been involved in a case in which someone had complained about the police was visited by officers from another force who were looking into it. My friend was appalled by their attitude: they were only going through the motions.

The present PCA chairman is a circuit judge, Francis Petre. The Authority has two basic functions: first, to supervise investigations into the most serious complaints; and second, to review the reports of all investigations and decide whether the officers concerned should face disciplinary charges – if their chief officer has not already decided on that course. There is a staff of 54½ – the half being a part-time police adviser. All PCA members are appointed by the

Home Secretary. I do not like that; ministers have too much power and influence over such appointments, and there is an obvious temptation to pick 'safe' and reliable people who are unlikely to rock the boat or stand up to the Establishment. I prefer most nominations to be made direct by outside bodies such as the TUC, the CBI, the Law Society, the Bar Council and the Lord Chancellor.

Anyone may complain about a police officer. Some complaints are dealt with by 'informal resolution' – this means the complainant is satisfied with an explanation or apology. If he is not satisfied, or if the complaint is regarded as serious, a full investigation is conducted by a senior officer, who interviews the complainant and the officer(s) concerned.

The PCA supervises the serious cases and must do so if an officer is alleged to have killed or seriously injured someone. When the PCA decides to supervise an investigation, one of its members becomes responsible for the case. He approves the appointment of a senior officer to investigate and keeps in close touch with him, giving him directions throughout. The reports of all cases which are not withdrawn or resolved informally are looked at by the PCA, whether these are cases supervised or not. If the report indicates that a criminal offence may have been committed by a police officer, the matter is referred to the Crown Prosecution Service for a decision on whether or not to prosecute. The chief officer of the force concerned must then decide whether the officer may have offended against the police disciplinary code and send his recommendations to the PCA, who may direct that disciplinary charges be brought. At the end the PCA writes to complainants, telling them of the outcome.

In 1989 the PCA began the supervision of 879 cases, some of which were withdrawn. It reviewed and adjudicated 5308 cases, of which 664 resulted in some form of criminal or disciplinary proceeding against a police officer. At the end of a disciplinary hearing the complainant is told the finding, but not what disciplinary action has been taken: the PCA itself thinks this unsatisfactory.

There is much police dissatisfaction with the PCA. The Police Federation, their trade union, has been openly hostile, referring to a 'drip, drip by accusation' that is damaging morale. In 1989 the Federation passed a vote of no confidence in the PCA. A year later the Federation's chairman, Alan Eastwood, said: 'Nothing that the Authority has done in the past year suggests that we should change our minds.'

Senior officers do not criticise the system so openly, but have pointed out that a small number of highly publicised cases have been reported in such a way as to suggest that corruption is widespread, and have thus undermined public confidence. However, a recent *Which?* magazine survey found that 80 per cent of the public were satisfied with the police in general terms, though there were complaints about the fairness of investigations, discrimination and lack of accountability.

Barry Irving, director of the Police Foundation, an independent research body, believes it wrong for the PCA to argue, as it has done, that it should not be schooled in police management and culture. 'It seems impossible to have an efficient supervisory body without such expertise.' The PCA, he believes, was a negotiated settlement between public concern and the police service. 'The result has been less efficiency in the investigative process, more police investigating each other and more civil actions. Neither side is happy, and so maybe it is time for a renegotiation of the agreement.'

A complaint against the police is still investigated by other officers. That is wrong in principle. Understandably, camaraderie exists between officers, and it is not automatically removed merely because the investigators come from another force. There is a similar objection to senior officers deciding whether to discipline their juniors. Police morale is a proper concern of any chief constable, and he may feel that laying disciplinary charges will undermine that.

We need a new body, divorced from serving officers. It would work with the PCA. Call the new body, say, the Criminal Investigation Monitoring Authority (CIMA). The president of the Association of Chief Police Officers would be an ex-officio member of the governing body. CIMA would be centrally based and staffed at the top by lawyers, ex-senior police officers, ex-public servants and industrial managers. It would be an élite corps with wide powers to investigate. Its officers would be able to go without warning to any police area at any time, during or after police investigations into crime; they could demand production of documents and interview police officers, suspects, defendants or convicted prisoners.

In each area, CIMA would have approved volunteers such as magistrates or retired magistrates, who were authorised to visit any police station at any time without warning and speak to any person in custody, not about the alleged crime(s) but about how they were being treated while in custody. Such visits would not be frequent unless there was thought to be a local need, but could be made at any time. These volunteers would also be available on a rota system when a subject wished to have an independent person present at an interview but his solicitor could not be there.

Yet another body is also required. Call it the Department of Public Defenders (DPD). It would be headed by someone of the status and experience of a judge (I am not looking for the job myself, interesting though it would be!). The DPD would be available to any defending solicitor, mainly but not exclusively in legal aid cases. Its officers, principally solicitors and former public servants, would advise defending solicitors on policy and on specific points in answer to queries. Where necessary it would refer cases to CIMA. Representations would be made to the Home Office in such matters as the need for access to forensic science or other specialist services. At present a defending solicitor, even in an important case where he is advised by counsel, is left too much to his own devices. The prosecution have all the resources of the state behind them. My proposal would be a counter-balance. One of the DPD's functions would be to keep an eye on solicitors acting under legal aid. Inefficient ones would be investigated and either warned or struck off the legal aid list.

The above measures would hit police morale at first. This is an extra reason for building up their morale. Increased public confidence in the police would help. Those who distrust the police will decline to co-operate with them by reporting crimes, for instance. They may even obstruct the police when there is trouble on the streets. The disaffected may refuse to tell officers what they have seen, and be reluctant to sign statements or go to court.

In his report into the 1981 Bristol riots, Lord Scarman recommended the setting up of Police Community Forums to improve relations between police and public. There are now twenty-six such forums in my police area, West Yorkshire. The Police Authority has used them to gauge public opinion on matters like the use of 'baton rounds', more commonly known as plastic bullets. If my visit to the Huddersfield forum on 28 September 1989 revealed a typical attendance, I doubt whether they have had much influence.

The chairman of the West Yorkshire Police Authority presided; also present were three senior officers, a constable, a magistrate member of the Authority, two Authority employees, twenty-one members of the public plus a few more who declined to sign the attendance sheet (one wonders why). Represented were Neighbourhood Watch, the Pakistan Association, the Polish community, a Sikh temple, a tenants' association and Women's Aid. The forums have no executive powers and might be likened to discussion groups. However, they must do some good and I would not abandon them but rather try to make them more representative. It might help to televise some meetings.

At Huddersfield I spoke on sentencing policy and prison overcrowding, and my talk had an interesting sequel – though I did not learn of it until months later. I knew journalists were present, but was surprised that only one reference by me alerted their pens: drugs. I said prison numbers could be reduced in various ways, one being the legalisation of drugs, starting with cannabis. I also said that I disapproved of drugs and had never even tried cannabis.

Following press reports and an interview with me on a BBC radio programme, Lord Justice Tasker-Watkins VC, the assistant Lord Chief Justice, phoned Mr Justice Paul Kennedy as senior presiding judge of my circuit and said I must be taken off drugs cases. No one asked for my comments or told me about the black-listing! They might have pointed out the possible lack of public confidence in me as a judge trying drugs cases or asked if I felt embarrassed at trying them. But there was no word to me at all. That is how things have worked for centuries in the judiciary – whispered words between old pals. Ironically, the directive did not apply when I sat at Isleworth Crown Court in Middlesex which, being near Heathrow Airport, gets more drugs cases than other crown courts. I had to apply the law and could not change it, so I sentenced in accordance with the guideline cases decided by Lord Chief Justice Lane. Only by chance did I learn of the black-listing; I will explain in Chapter 6 how that came about – it formed part of a more important revelation.

Lord Scarman's forums are not the only bridge between police and public. Neighbourhood Watch schemes have this effect, and at the same time probably help to combat crime. A few years ago I rang the local police station and asked if there was a scheme covering my area of Halifax. The answer was no and the police could not impose one, but they would co-operate if residents took the initiative. So I set about it.

WAS I TOO EASY ON THE POLICE?

We formed a committee, called a public meeting and it now has more than one hundred members. I had to withdraw at an early stage – I could not be too closely involved with the police. Now the local constables know many people in our area; one occasionally calls to see me. He has given a human face to a helmet and uniform. We know whom to contact if something arises – not necessarily a crime; it could be a traffic hazard or nuisance. How far Neighbourhood Watch reduces crime is hard to prove. My PC friend believes it does, and a man whom I sentenced for burglary and later met when appearing on TV said it was a deterrent to him.

Reducing points of friction helps to improve relations with the police. Every time they have to search and arrest for cannabis, otherwise law-abiding people are alienated, including young people and ethnic minorities. This is an argument for decriminalising such drugs.

The law should be enforced in a commonsense way, so as to reduce friction. Stonehenge was built by our ancestors four thousand years ago. English Heritage, which I support, owns the stones and the National Trust, of which I am a member, owns the surrounding land. In a broader sense those megaliths surely belong to all of us, but are we allowed to go there? Not at any price. On 21 June 1990 the midsummer solstice 'passed off peacefully', said a press report – but only after eight hundred police officers had sealed off the mysterious monument, turning away hundreds and arresting twenty-five. What an appalling waste of police time! Why should we dissidents, hippies, gypsies, oddballs and druids not go and worship or camp nearby, provided we don't do damage? Too many officious people want to stop others enjoying themselves, and in doing so alienate the otherwise harmless.

Police morale is better than it was. Whereas four thousand officers left the force in 1977 for other jobs, in 1989 only fourteen hundred did so. This may be mainly due to the better pay the police now get. Between 1979 and 1990, basic pay in real terms went up by more than 41 per cent. During the same period there was an increase of nearly 59 per cent in total police expenditure. Despite that, the massive growth in crime and Treasury control of spending has left some disturbing signs. For example, in 1990 Derbyshire police suffered a 90 per cent cut in capital expenditure; crime statistics were still being recorded by hand instead of computer, and police cars were becoming increasingly outdated. Since then HM Inspector of Constabulary has refused to certify that the Derbyshire police are efficient, and they need the certificate to obtain the Home Office grant.

Modern aids should be more widely available. I have found video equipment useful in several court cases. In one, a youth alleged to have pushed a wall that fell at a fight during a football match could be seen doing so. In another, when a fight broke out in a pub three video cameras which took pictures every few seconds pinpointed who did what. Witnesses can lie or forget, but cameras cannot.

Video cameras were installed in Halifax town centre, where street fights are common after the pubs and clubs have closed. The town has twice as many licensed premises per head as Leeds or Bradford. The equipment was, in my opinion, mistakenly removed after complaints about 'Big Brother'. Street cameras do no more than the police already do – observe and detect crime. Innocent people have nothing to fear. At first there must have been opposition to the idea of plain-clothes detectives. As to unmarked police cars on motorways, which some forces use, if ordinary middle-of-the-road drivers resent their use then they can be counter-productive. Should there be automatic cameras by the road and at traffic lights to detect offending drivers? I see no objection in principle, and fewer drivers would defy the law. But to be effective such innovations must have public opinion on their side, and so they have to be introduced gradually and reasonably.

I favour the compulsory carrying by adults of an identity

card with a photograph and signature. Here again, there would be 'Big Brother' objections, but in the former West Germany they had such a law for years; the document could also double as a passport. In case after case before me, defendants have used stolen credit cards bearing other people's names. Millions of pounds a year are lost to credit card companies. Most of that fraud would be prevented if a purchaser had to produce an ID card which bore the same name as on the plastic and a photo of himself.

There are other ways in which the police could be assisted in preventing crime. Most cars are still too easy to break into and drive away. Manufacturers could build in alarms and other anti-theft devices cheaply. Offences in this area are so common that legislation should require this. Insurance companies should in the meantime give discounts for cars which are protected. And why does the Government not work with manufacturers to produce cheap mass-produced burglar alarms for houses? They would have to be simple for householders to operate and hard for house burglars to get round. We could all make it easier for the police to protect us.

I was too easy on the police at times, as other judges have been. But we are learning all the time.

6

Was I anti-women?

This is an absurd notion; anyone who knows me well will
confirm that. How then did I acquire such a reputation?
There were two reasons. First, I made some remarks in an
interview with *Woman* magazine; and second, I decided
some cases which – because it was me – received wide
publicity. I have been misunderstood in both areas. Putting
the record straight means delving into matters that are not
often looked at honestly or spoken of frankly.

I told the magazine interviewer of a real incident. I was
walking along a London street behind two young men when
a bra-less young woman came bobbling and bouncing
towards us. As they passed her, both men did an eyes-right
and there was a look of smug satisfaction on the young
woman's face. Was that her object, or was she bra-less for
sartorial comfort? Both, probably. I do not condemn bra-
less females; they add to life's enjoyment. Female attire is
based on sexual attractiveness. It is part of the sex game that
runs through all life. Without it there would be no life. With
it, life is continuously uplifting. Life without sex is as unthinkable as life without oxygen. There is no need, however,
to be continually obsessed with either commodity.

I have never said that a bra-less woman deserves to be
raped. But by her dress and manner she may in some situations give or appear to give signals that are open to
misinterpretation. If she seems to want sex but does not, a
man who tries to grab it from her cannot be excused but she
must share the blame.

*

Even today, sex cannot be openly and sensibly discussed. For centuries it was whispered about as though it was sinful; the Churches are to blame. There has been a healthy revolution in my lifetime, but it is not yet complete. My parents never said one word to me about sex; it might as well not have existed. At my all-boys prep school we were told, in a hesitant, roundabout way, not to have it with each other – but there was no word about girls. At home I hardly ever saw a photo of a naked woman, and when I did I devoured it. At sixteen I went out with a girl and my parents reacted as if I was up to some sort of unspeakable crime (which I was not).

In my youth well-known people never publicised their sexual activities, and certainly not their 'indiscretions'. Film stars who we now know were rabid as rabbits pretended to live like saints. Female stars were never photographed topless, and one actress snapped thus at a Hollywood party was so shamed by the publicity that she committed suicide. What appalling hypocrisy! Prominent people presumably played around as they do now, but it was curtained off.

Today some public figures boast of their affairs, and five-times-a-night Sir Ralph Halpern was eventually humbled because of his performance not in the sexual field but in the industrial one. Most people feel only envy when they read of sexual adventures. The notion that sex before marriage is morally wrong, which my parents believed and in the shadow of which I grew up, is no longer widely accepted. Some preach it, a few practise it, but for most people it is not only ignored but derided.

Centuries of Christianity have left birth-marks on millions alive today, but its teachings now go no more than skin-deep. Most people who go to church do so for social or family reasons; they do not so much believe as conform, zombie-like. More people have been murdered in the name of God or Allah, more books burnt and more opinions suppressed, than in the name of anything else. A plague on all your religious houses, I say – though I would not hurt the feelings of the sincere, however misguided I thought them. That is the key to morality as I see it: respect for others. And those ideas have to be applied to our feelings.

The very idea of marriage is now out of step with many people's thoughts. In church, which they visit rarely, or the register office which they also rarely visit – but most likely more than once – the couple may think at the time that their feelings towards each other will last. But they are wrong. 'Love' in the early stages of a relationship is an illusion, though a pleasant one. We wish upon ourselves a state of mind that soars deliciously. But it has no rational basis and, as the mature know, will not endure.

This early 'love' is based mainly, but not exclusively, on sex. Sex is selfish, but there is or should be an unselfish side to 'love'. The heady intensity of sex cannot last, because it is based on newness. It is like the smell and feel of a new car. Daily use dulls the joy of it. The newness fades and we hanker after another new car. Then problems arise – I used to see them daily in the divorce courts.

The time has come to divorce marriage from religion. This has happened in fact and should happen in law. We need a civil contract imposed in part by law and in part by the two parties concerned. One spouse should not be able to avoid all obligations merely by dominating the other. The essentials of a civil contract already exist in our muddled law: the division of property and liability for maintenance; the rights of the parties to the marriage to end it. It needs a complete re-think, though this is not the place to do that.

The complicating factor is children. A couple should please themselves if there are only themselves to please. If their life together has given life to other beings – one aim of marriage but not the only one – they should not part without considering the young symbols of what once was. Yet people do. As a judge I saw hundreds of divorcing couples with very young children, even babies, whose lives were being crippled by those who should have cared for them – and in varying degrees did.

Should parents who no longer 'love' each other, but love their children in a different, deeper sense, stay together in hostility, or is it better for the children that they part? There cannot be a rule applicable to all, though the Church teaches that there is. Each case has to be considered by the parents on its own merits – but as the parents are at odds this is not easy. If they do part, one spouse may want them to stay together, so bitterness spills over on to the children. They may not wish to see the deserting parent. 'He [or she] left us'; I often heard that pathetic cry. As to custody and access, and I did many such cases, court hearings only increase the acrimony and hostility.

Marital fragility has two main causes. Many young people seem to regard marriage as a recipe for constant sexual ecstasy, and when that goes they look for it elsewhere. Related to that is the second cause: most spouses are not monogamous. Only one in three marriages ends in divorce, but that is no test. Most spouses hanker for sexual variety, and an increasing number find it. The Church says, 'One man, one woman, for life', but that does not reflect human nature. As a generalisation that is bound to be false, but it does apply to the majority of people in Western society today. In Eastern society, men have always taken their own pleasures and denied it to their wives: female 'circumcision' mirrors that. Western woman is now being liberated after similar subjugation.

Should a husband or wife stay with a partner when the fire in their relationship has been reduced to embers and the flames are leaping elsewhere? The same rule applies: respect the other. And there should be no difference, whether the partners are married or not. Religions lay down rigid rules, but though it is convenient for society's governors to lay them down, such rigidity does not accord with people's ideas and feelings. They will break the rule or break with the religion.

Implicit in tabloid newspaper stories is the idea that there is something scandalous about a spouse who strays, even if it is a momentary diversion. The tabloid press pilloried Major Ronald Ferguson for visiting a massage parlour, and Frank Bough for drugs and sexual jinks. Significantly the broadsheets correctly ignored those stories, as I recall. Major Ferguson is not a public figure but merely the father of one. Frank Bough is a public figure in a sense, and the BBC dropped him. I suppose it was morally entitled to do so if it was responding to public opinion, upon which it depends. Also, Lord Reith's writ still runs in the BBC.

But I would have been happier if that organisation had taken the view that what Frank Bough did in his own time was his own affair. Only if a public figure behaves in his private life so as to contradict a public stance should the media spotlight him. Tory MP Cecil Parkinson as 'Mr Clean' could be said to have done just that. In any event, the full story behind his demotion from party chairman was of legitimate public interest and had to be told. The fact that a woman scorned chose to tell was irrelevant.

As to a non-public person's right to stray, that must depend on circumstances. Outsiders should not condemn hastily; they cannot know all the facts. Who would consign to chastity a man who is still sexually active when his wife no longer is? The Church, yes, but not most people. A man can surely respect his wife's interests without denying his sexual nature.

Conventional morality is based on a misconception. Whatever the Bible or Hollywood films may have assumed, a marriage that begins in hope will almost certainly dwindle into indifference and then peter out into hostility. The best recipe for endurance is mutual respect based on shared experience, children and grandchildren. Sex means a great deal, but should not mean everything.

My impression of present disharmony and unhappiness in relationships, whether between spouses or partners, is coloured by what I saw as a judge. Only a fraction of warring men and women can have come to court, but it seemed a large fraction. Usually a woman came to me for protection from a violent man. Almost invariably this was in civil proceedings, though occasionally I met such cases in the crown court too.

The general picture was of women patiently trying to keep the home together, tending the children, yearning for emotional and material security; and of men selfishly wanting more than domesticity. They expected women to be there on demand – for sex, food and shelter, mainly – but they themselves wanted to go out and have fun when and how they chose, womanising and drinking the housekeeping money, yet becoming angry, resentful and violent when chided.

A queue of women walked through my chambers when I sat in county court. Some hobbled on crutches. Others came bandaged or black-eyed. One man who told his pregnant partner he would 'kick it out of her', and tried to, was worse than most but not unique. All the women had misery in their eyes and fear in their minds, and looked to me for protection. If there was a dispute I usually found for them. The press was always excluded – except for applications to have a spouse sent to prison for disobeying an order or breaking an undertaking – so the public knew nothing of my sympathy or how I expressed it. I was condemned and unjustly labelled anti-women on the basis of a few notorious cases.

The different attitudes of many men and women towards relationships bring me back to the bra-less issue and Page Three. In no area is there such disagreement and misunderstanding between the sexes. Tactlessly, I said in public that I liked looking at pictures of naked women, and that added to the anti-women indictment. Yet any man who does not care to look at such images is senile, gay or a liar!

Women are different. Sensibly, they are rarely intrigued and hardly ever turned on by the mere picture of a man, clothed or not. Young women may be moved by the physical presence of a strong-looking man. More mature females go for subtler qualities, strength of character rather than of body; kindness and humour. A man's brain rather than his brawn excites them, though puniness must have some limits! Men, and we are so made not by choice but by nature, are easily aroused by what we see with our eyes and feel with our bodies.

And to talk of bodies leads us to breasts. Women do not understand why men are fascinated by these appendages, but they know what they themselves can achieve with them. One woman told me she hated Page Three as she had had a mastectomy. This is the key to female condemnation of nude photographs. Those girls have better, more exciting breasts than theirs, and so should be covered up or their depiction even banned by law. Their men may see them and compare. Women are reminded of their own inadequacies in the eyes of men as they daily catch sight of the pin-ups, and feel insecure.

Labour MP Clare Short may genuinely believe that top-less pictures 'demean' women, but she is wrong. They deify the female sex, in men's eyes. All this may make men look foolish in baffled females' eyes, but it happens to be true and I see no harm in it. As for suppressing Page Three by law, the notion is ludicrous and dangerous. I admire Ms Short for her honesty as a politician, but not for her lack of common sense as a person.

I have Ms Short's Indecent Displays (Newspapers and Work Places) Bill before me – she kindly sent it to me after a couple of occasions on which we met and clashed on TV. Section 1 reads: 'It shall be an offence to publish in news-papers pictures of naked or partially naked women in sexually provocative poses.' Section 2: 'It shall be an offence to display indecent material in any public place being a workplace.' Dear Clare – I have a measure of affection for her – you may not have thought it through. So many unanswered questions.

Why only newspapers and not magazines, books or paintings in art galleries? What is 'partially naked?' Surely we all go about in that condition; even Muslim women are permitted naked eyeballs. Is it all right if nipples are covered by stars? If a man has a sex-change and grows breasts through hormones he remains a male by law, so is he exempt from section 1? 'Sexually provocative poses' is not defined. Page Three girls are usually seen naked from the waist up and wearing a pleasant facial expression. Is that sexually provocative? All right, yes, but what's wrong with that? Attractive women provoke sexual thoughts of some kind in men, or they would not be attractive. Are they all to be condemned? Is sex itself being put in the dock by those no longer interested in it? Are the *Sun* pin-ups any more provocative than those who parade in the flesh with exaggerated cleavage and – ah, yes! bra-less, bobbling breasts? Be logical, Clare.

As for section 2, there is no definition of 'indecent matter'. It must mean something different from 'sexually provocative'. Why the difference? What does 'indecent' mean? Giving rise to sexual thoughts? Or are we back to the ancient and nonsensical legal notion of 'tending to deprave and corrupt'. I know of no evidence, nor did the eminent philosopher Professor Sir Bernard Williams (once called the brainiest man in Britain) and his distinguished committee. No one was ever depraved or corrupted – whatever that means, and it must impute something harmful – by anything looked at in a photograph, book or film. Excited, yes, in some cases – but so we are by a thousand impressions, including the way women dress. Excited but not harmed. The men who read 'pornographic' material and then assault women have not been changed in character; they have fed a

145

tendency they already had. Whatever their actions, are the rest of us to be coddled and blinkered by law because of them? What is meant by 'any public place being a work-place'? A public place means one to which people have a right of access, and so workplaces are not public except where, for example, men are digging up a street and unlikely to have a calendar pinned up!

In turning back the clock, how far would Clare Short go? Topless bathing would certainly have to cease. In Spain, soon after the end of the Second World War, women bathers had by law to wear a costume with a skirt. Even Ms Short would presumably bridle at the Victorian fear of nakedness leading to frills on piano legs – but who knows? I think we should be told.

Clare Short and her parliamentary antics would be merely laughable if she were not an educated woman, a former top civil servant and now a legislator paid out of taxes. But she and the large number of female followers she claims have a simple remedy that would need no new statute and create no new crime. The *Sun* sells about 3.6 million copies daily and is read by about ten million. A fair proportion of readers are women. If they refused to buy the newspaper and put press-ure on their men not to buy it or bring it home, Rupert Murdoch – not insensitive to falling sales – would drop Page Three as if it were alight. That is the democratic way. As a left-wing socialist, does Clare Short believe that the state should tell us how to live our lives and what we may look at? Censorship is at the heart of every dictatorship, left or right.

Whether my principle is right or wrong, I apply it consist-ently to prostitution and drugs as well as to Page Three. What a tart and her client choose to do to each other is no concern of the state provided they do not harm others – those who live in the area and see their homes devalued and their wives and daughters pestered. We need licensed, inspected brothels away from residential areas. They would reduce disease, cut out pimps and make stealing from clients difficult.

Clare Short, Mary Whitehouse and the Churches would form an ill-sorted alliance crying 'The state would be approving and encouraging prostitution.' The state would no more be doing that than I am. Prostitution is degrading to both parties, but it has always been there and always will be. There are men who want quick, anonymous sex without emotional strings, and women who are ready to provide it for payment. The state should accept that situation and channel the trade less harmfully while trying to dissuade women, especially the young, from it.

The state should start to withdraw from the drugs field. If an adult wishes to take a harmful substance into his own body, whether it be nicotine, alcohol, cannabis or heroin, that should be his own decision. I abhor drugs and my decision has been not to take any. Present official policies are making things worse, as Prohibition in the USA did with alcohol from 1919 to 1933. The illegality of drugs drives up prices, the huge profits then attract gangster importers and pushers, and force addicts to steal in order to buy drugs. Large groups, including young people and Afro-Caribbeans, become anti-police through raids, searches, arrests and prosecutions. Riots can be sparked off. Since the drug trade is conducted underground, many addicts fear going to the authorities for help. Most doctors are unsympathetic. Yet this is an area for clinics and hospitals rather than police stations, courts and prisons. Under legalisation, the law and order budget would decrease more than health costs would increase.

We have got things hysterically out of proportion and are led, as in so much that is bad, by the USA. In the UK, one hundred thousand people a year die as a result of smoking and ten thousand from alcohol. For heroin and cocaine the figures are between fifty and two hundred a year, and some of these die through the effects of dirty needles and impure drugs which are by-products of illegality. No one ever died of cannabis.

I do not expect politicians, 'Shortists' or not, quickly to see the logic of any of this or to act on it if they do. Fear of party bosses or voters closes their minds, blinkers their eyes and gags their mouths.

I turn now to those cases which I decided that involved female defendants or victims. Notice two things about these cases. They represented a minuscule proportion of all those I tried in the twenty-eight years I was on the Bench. The press was not interested in most of the others, so the public knew nothing of them. Second, the four cases received the publicity they did mainly because I was involved. There is not as much press mileage in condemning an unknown judge. Shortly after the Renshaw case, in which I imprisoned a woman for refusing to give evidence, a woman in the south of England was similarly treated. It received three lines at the foot of a column. If it had been my decision imagine the headlines!

A great deal more lies behind those notorious cases than the public yet knows. I was misunderstood by the public, and in part dealt with unjustly by Lord Chief Justice Lane. My pen is now free to tell all.

Lord Lane did not come into the first case. On 25 January 1989 I sentenced W. who was in his forties to a probation order for two years, with a condition of residence at the probation hostel where his specified needs were already being attended to. He had pleaded guilty to indecently assaulting a six-year-old girl while baby-sitting. He got into bed with her and simulated sexual intercourse on one occasion. The defendant had had a dreadful life: when he was young he had lost his parents and six of his seven siblings when their home collapsed. He never got on to his feet. His wife had died and he had various ailments when, a pathetic figure, he came before me. I said he would be picked on if he went to prison. The law did not permit me to pass a suspended prison sentence and order him to remain at the probation hostel. The case attracted publicity and I was criticised by the tabloids. But there were interesting sequels.

On 14 February 1989 I was at Leeds prison to open the new prison officers' club. A man who had been a dock officer when I passed sentence told me that W. had been so 'shattered' beforehand that it took them forty-five minutes to get him up into the dock. If he had been sent to prison he 'would have been finished within a week', he said. On 11 October 1989 I went to an open day held by Huddersfield Probation Service and was shown a painting by W., done at the hostel, where I was told he was making excellent progress.

Earlier, in about March 1989, I was told by a court clerk that I had been black-listed (my word) for 'sex cases'. No one had officially said anything about this, asked me for any explanation or told me what I had done to deserve this 'sentence'. I was disturbed that some court staff must know about my black-listing, knew that I did not know, and might therefore be put in an embarrassing position. However, I decided to take no action at that time.

In August 1989, four pleas of guilty were allocated to me at Leeds Crown Court, and I read them. One was an indecent assault case. Then they were whisked away, and when I asked why I was told there were counsel difficulties (listing officers have to transfer cases from one court to another to assist barristers). My fears were now increased, so at my request the circuit administrator – the top civil servant on the circuit – came to see me. Wynne James is a nice Welshman and I do not blame him for the invidious position he had been placed in. He assured me I had not been black-listed, and that he would know about it if I had been.

I then decided to go to the top: to Mr Justice Paul Kennedy, at that date the circuit's senior presiding judge. I have known Paul Kennedy since he joined our circuit. He is a very able man, and when he took silk I recommended him as a leader in several cases. He is cast in the typical top public school/Oxbridge mould, and his marriage to a daughter of Lord Devlin's cannot have hindered his ambition to become a High Court judge and higher. Smooth, tactful, discreet, he would never open his mouth to his own disadvantage, as by criticising anyone influential, whether a solicitor or a judge. He would make a good papal adviser, and he reminds me sometimes of Cardinal Richelieu; he is charming on the surface, but his dark eyes are always peering through the mask of his expressionless face, eager for the main chance. A very good judge, Paul Kennedy will go beyond his present High Court office. If he were older (he is ten years my junior) he could be a contender for Master of the Rolls, when Lord Donaldson finally relinquishes that prestigious seat.

On 25 October 1989, at Carr Manor, the High Court judges' lodgings in Leeds, Kennedy told me that I had indeed been black-listed and that he had done it because of the publicity arising out of the W. case. He did not say my decision had been wrong. I said he should have told me at the time, and he replied that perhaps in my case that would have been advisable, but not in some other cases such as recorders! So black-listing was not confined to me, but was always secret. Richelieu would have approved.

Next day I wrote to Paul Kennedy, stating that I had forgotten to raise with him Wynne James's denial that I had been black-listed. Kennedy's reply was odd, to say the least. He said Wynne James did not know of the black-listing when it took place, in August or September, as he was on holiday. My presiding judge – usually so meticulous – must have forgotten that the W. case was held in January, and the black-listing cannot have been done seven or eight months later!

I then put the facts before Lord Chancellor Mackay, asking:

1. Should I have been black-listed at all? What were the reasons?
2. When was I black-listed?
3. In what circumstances should a judge be black-listed?
4. Should a judge be asked for his comments before he is black-listed, and told of any decision to black-list before the court staff are told?
5. At what level has the black-listing procedure been laid down? Or is it growing unplanned? Should you issue guidelines?
6. Has someone tried to deceive me? If so, who and why?

Lord Mackay did his best to do right, but he was naturally anxious not to let down a High Court judge or a circuit administrator while at the same time not misleading me, a mere circuit judge. His letter informed me that Mr Justice Kennedy gave instructions on 26 January 1989 that, while the case, file and transcripts were being obtained in relation to the W. case, no further cases involving allegations of sexual abuse should be listed before me. In August 1989 Kennedy heard that a case involving an allegation of sexual abuse was to be listed before me, and so he gave instructions that the case should be taken out of my list.

Lord Mackay went on to say that there are circumstances in which presiding judges may decide that, for a time at least, a judge should not handle a particular class of work. Reasons might include a decision by a judge or the way he has expressed that decision, which might affect public confidence in the administration of justice. A judge should normally be told of any decision that he should not try cases normally within his jurisdiction. A later letter from the Lord Chancellor's office stated that Wynne James 'did not recall' the January 1989 instructions, given through his office, when he spoke to me in August of the same year.

There are obvious contradictions and unanswered questions in all this, but it would be pointless to go further into them. There was nothing iniquitous in any of it. In so far as I was misled, it arose out of a system of 'whispered words between old pals' that has gone on for centuries. It is much better to be open and frank. A judge should be asked for an explanation and told he is being black-listed. Maybe I did some good in raising the issue. I doubt if Kennedy acted in that way afterwards, and presiding judges who read this may learn from it: the Lord Chancellor did not circulate his decision in this matter, so far as I know.

After the W. case I was interviewed once on TV about it. I considered there could be no objection to explaining what listeners could have heard for themselves if they had been in court.

As the Lord Chief Justice overruled me in the next two cases, let us take a quick look at him. Geoffrey Lane was head boy at Shrewsbury, and at Cambridge he gained firsts in classics and law. After five distinguished years in the wartime RAF (he was awarded the AFC) he was called to the Bar in 1946 at the age of twenty-eight. He soon had a large practice on the Midland circuit, being deservedly popular with everyone – he is a genuinely nice man. His ability as a judge can be gauged by his progress: to the High Court in 1966, the Court of Appeal in 1974, the House of Lords in 1979; he became Lord Chief Justice the following year. I appeared before him while I was at the Bar, and saw him when he visited the Leeds QC mess on judges' night. I join in the general acclamation.

In court, Lord Lane is usually a model judge: erudite, quick, patient, yet firm when necessary. Out of court, in the administrative field – to be as frank as I hope he would wish me to be – he has been less of a success. The Lord Chief Justice is the boss of the criminal courts. He presides over the Court of Appeal (criminal division), where he gives a lead on the level of sentences for particular types of crime. His is a demanding job, with many administrative functions.

He meets judges of the Queen's Bench Division of the High Court, who try the most serious criminal cases and sit with him on appeals. He advises the Lord Chancellor on the appointment and promotion of judges. He is in touch with the Home Secretary from time to time on such matters as prison overcrowding, sentencing policy and parole.

One of the keys to understanding Lord Lane is his antagonism to the media. He always refuses to give interviews, and he expects the same of other judges. Reporters of any kind are the 'enemy', to be frowned on and avoided. Investigative journalists stray into the judicial field at their peril. A reporter on BBC TV's *Rough Justice* had his career dented even though his work had led to an innocent man being cleared by the Court of Appeal. I put Lord Lane's distrust of the media down to his background and training. Barristers do not speak to the press, and have to shun publicity since it can amount to advertising. Lord Lane's reticence, and my lack of it, have been the main cause of conflict between us. I believe judges should on occasions use the media to explain themselves to the public, who are their ultimate employers and paymasters.

A good all-round Lord Chief Justice should be more active than Lord Lane has been. He should go round the country giving a lead to circuit judges who man the outposts and are struggling against the barbarians. He should work out and spell out penal policy – not only in the few areas such as drugs where he has issued guidelines on sentences, but in a comprehensive way. I shall try to do that later in this book. But write a book? A judge? Lord Lane must find the idea as repugnant as appearing on that confounded box.

As for remedying defects in the penal system, Lord Lane is not that kind, or any kind, of radical. While on the Bench I wrote to him about court delays, drugs in prison, the welter of bail applications to circuit judges, sentencing and parole. He always replied to the same effect: 'There is nothing I can do!' His complacency is not deliberate: it springs from his education and training. He must have muttered several times, 'Pickles has to be stopped. He talks too much. He is letting down the judiciary.' I believe such an attitude was reflected in several cases of mine which he heard in the Court of Appeal.

On 9 March 1989, at Leeds Crown Court, I was due to try a man for assaulting his ex-girlfriend, causing her bodily harm. There was nothing particularly unusual about the case, even when I was told that the twenty-four-year-old complainant, Michelle Renshaw, had now refused to give evidence for the prosecution. Although there was a strong case on paper, the defendant was never tried: he had to be found not guilty. In the end I sentenced Renshaw to seven days' imprisonment for contempt of court. (My sentencing remarks are in Appendix 3.)

I have not been able to reveal until now that it was Mr Justice Michael Davies who suggested that I gaol Renshaw for seven days. The reason for my going to see him was that I had to consult a High Court judge in a case like that, if one was in the same building, and ask if he wished to deal with it. Sir Michael Davies (he is now retired) – a pleasant man and not 'public school' – said he would let me deal with Renshaw. He asked how long I proposed to give her, and I said twenty-one days. 'No, make it seven,' he said, and I did. The responsibility was mine, of course. I had not gone fully into all the points with him.

When Renshaw applied for bail, Michael Davies, having been involved as I have indicated, let Mr Justice Jupp deal with the application. He refused bail, thereby condemning Renshaw to serve her sentence prior to her appeal. I assume he did that because Mr Justice Davies had told him what had happened.

The media showed intense interest in the Renshaw case. I decided that, as in the W. case, I could explain what had occurred. I appeared on TV several times, including a *Heart of the Matter* programme with Joan Bakewell, in which the issues were discussed sensibly. I also wrote articles in the press, including one for the *Guardian* (reprinted in Appendix 4). All this must have infuriated the Lord Chief Justice.

The Court of Appeal, presided over by Lord Lane, set aside Renshaw's conviction, even though her counsel had conceded before me that she was guilty of contempt of court. Lord Lane said I had asserted myself too much. There was truth in that, though such contempt proceedings are unique; they are initiated by the judge. The prosecution plays no part, so the judge has to play a bigger part than usual. The media, and therefore also the public, misunderstood the appeal decision. Lord Lane did not say I was wrong to send Renshaw to prison. On the contrary, he said imprisonment was the appropriate penalty in such a case. It was not what I had done that was wrong, but the way that I had done it. One cannot expect the media or the general public to follow such a refinement.

After the Renshaw case, a young Bradford solicitor issued a writ for libel against me on behalf of Renshaw's boyfriend, on the basis that I had inferred in the media that he was guilty. I had in fact been careful not to infer that. The writ was never even served. The solicitor announced that, as he could not obtain legal aid, he was not proceeding. One might have expected a solicitor – however young and in whichever city he practised – to know that libel is by statute excluded from legal aid. But the lawyer had achieved publicity for himself, including a press photograph taken outside Bradford County Court. As his client was unemployed, who paid the £60 for the writ? One can only speculate.

There followed an odd decision by Lord Lane in another case that I had tried while the publicity in the Renshaw case was going on. On 21 September 1989 he quashed the conviction of the appellant, Kenneth David Earnshaw, although I had handled the case properly. It was a case of a man kidnapping a woman, and Lord Lane said the jury might have been influenced against the man by statements I had made in the media: he made his disapproval of my actions apparent. Indeed it was the basis of the decision.

The Tracey Scott case came up at the end of 1989. Scott, a twenty-year-old single mother, pleaded guilty to theft of more than £4000 worth of goods from the supermarket where she was a check-out operator. She had simply waved through her friends, including one who wheeled out a bicycle. A video camera had shown the extent of the offending. Determined to get this one right, I pondered hard over Christmas. I was anxious to apply Lord Lane's guidelines while not parting woman and baby. Before I passed sentence a place was found for both of them.

In substituting a probation order, Lord Lane said, 'The judge seems to have been concerned more with the public impact of what he was doing and saying than with the justice of it.' Was the cat out of the appellate bag? I am biased, but this is what Cliff Moiser, the respected clerk to the Plymouth magistrates, wrote in *Justice of the Peace* magazine on 7 April 1990:

> Judge Pickles, always good for a bit of publicity, has recently been criticised again for his decision to sentence a young lady to six months' imprisonment. She was employed as a check-out assistant at a supermarket, and allowed many of her friends to pass through the check-out with goods that were not paid for. A loss to the store of somewhere in the region of £4000, but actually unquantifiable, was involved. The fraud had obviously gone on for several months, was difficult to detect, was a breach of trust, and was otherwise quite naughty. In the appeal, the Court of Appeal indicated that probation was the obvious answer, no question about it, and the judge at first instance was criticised for indicating that a female with a baby could not thereby escape a custodial sentence. But the very same judge (Lord Lane) in R. v Barrick, 1985 Criminal Law Review 602, said that in a case where the offender was in a

position of trust and used that privileged and trusted position to defraud his employers of sizeable sums of money, certain principles applied. That person, as in Judge Pickles' case, would be a person of hitherto impeccable character, practically certain that he would never offend again, and he would never be able to secure similar employment. What was to happen? A term of immediate imprisonment was inevitable, save in very exceptional circumstances or where the amount of money was small. The court should pass a sufficiently substantial term of imprisonment to mark publicly the gravity of the offence, and where the amounts involved could not be described as small but were less that £10,000, the imprisonment could range from quite short up to 18 months. Suspension of imprisonment was not appropriate and courts should take into account the quality and degree of trust reposed in the offender, including his rank; the period over which the fraud had been perpetrated; how the loot had been spent; the effects on the victim; and the impact of the offences on the public and public confidence; the effects on fellow employees, and then mitigation, illness, long delay, help by the offender to the police or excessive responsibility. If Judge Pickles was said to have strayed by caring more about a pregnant woman than the difficult task of sentencing in hand, *then the Court of Appeal would appear to be more concerned with putting down Judge Pickles, than bearing in mind its own guidelines in R. v. Barrick* [J.P.'s emphasis]. The offender being twenty years old further complicated the matter, of course, but what of the guidelines, never mentioned?

The fourth case was similar to the first, in that it concerned a man who had indecently assaulted women. Lord Lane had no part in this one. It did not attract a great deal of publicity, but the little it did get added to my ill-deserved reputation.

On 7 May 1991, twenty-two-year-old H. pleaded guilty to

assaulting two women on separate occasions. He had previously been put on probation for two similar offences. The pattern was the same each time: he approached women in the street and put his hand on their knickers over their private parts. The women were very frightened, but not harmed in any other way. The *Sun* described him as a 'sex fiend'. It failed to report that the defendant had never had a girlfriend; this was his way of approaching women. The newspaper did record my remarks: 'If I send you to prison you would be picked on. You would not have been taught how to behave towards women.' Apparently I had been 'slammed by women's groups'. A rape counsellor said that the offender should have been gaoled.

I considered the best way to protect women from that man was to teach him how to relate to them, and the probation service had a programme for that. Prison would have crushed him at public expense, but he would have come out no better, and probably worse, in his attitudes.

Sentencing is difficult and intricate. A judge should do what he thinks right, despite clamour in sections of the media or the public – more of this in Chapter 8.

When the evidence is examined carefully, the charge that I was anti-women is not made out.

7

Did I become 'media-infected'?

Just before my 'diary' article was published in the *Guardian* on 4 March 1989 (see Appendix 2), I happened to sit next to Mr Justice Michael Davies at lunch and told him about it. Later he wrote to me that he had read my *Guardian* article, and telling me he thought I had talked a lot of sense in my book. However, he went on to say that I seemed to have become so 'media-infected' that, like them, I had acquired a closed mind and would let nothing change what he called the 'fixed stereotype conception'. He quoted one example of what he said I claimed never happened. Efficiency in the courts, he wrote, had over a fifteen-month period produced a number of improvements. The list of non-jury cases waiting to be tried had been reduced from 7500 to 4000, while the waiting time after applying to the court for a hearing date had been cut from twelve months or more to three months. Additionally, the list of cases where a jury was to be involved had been reduced from 230 to 130, again over a matter of months. He finished by stating that the media were not interested in this kind of information, which might spoil their preconceptions.

I replied, defending my bringing matters to the attention of the public. I also sent a copy of a letter that Mr Justice Davies had himself written to me, on 17 July 1985, about a letter I had written to the *Guardian* on the iniquity of parole. In it he wrote that his clerk had just shown him my letter in the *Guardian*, a paper that he did not himself read. Mr Justice Davies said he wished to congratulate me on stating so clearly what he felt sure were the feelings of most of the general public and very many judges.

Unfortunately we did not in fact meet again until 1989. Did either of Mr Justice Davies's letters hit the nail on the head, or did they both?

On 26 May 1991 the *Sunday Telegraph* published an article by Megan Tresidder, based on an interview I had given her. I had at first refused, but I am glad I changed my mind. She sounded sensible on the phone and the *Sunday Telegraph* is a responsible newspaper – its sister daily played an important part in the history of my relations with the media. Ms Tresidder's article was fair and perceptive. She wrote:

> Pickles does have a lot to contribute to debates on legal reform. He has drawn attention to court delays and has suggested evening courts to try to reduce the backlogs. He strikes a chord in the public when he questions the need for judges to wear such awesome costumes and pendulous wigs. It is reasonable of him to attack the Oxbridge bias of the judiciary.
>
> His heart is in the right place but his mouth is all over the shop. He is a courteous and caring man but seems to get overtaken at times with a demon desire to go too far. During lunch for example he repeats his apology – already made on TV – for calling Hailsham (in fact, Lane) a dinosaur. 'It was rude and whether it was my opinion or not I shouldn't have said it.' But then within minutes he comes up with another new insult for him – 'an old Etonian windbag' [that *was* Hailsham].
>
> He is inconsistent partly, I think, because he wants to entertain. At one point, after talking quite seriously about the deterrent effect of prison sentences for football fans, he says: 'What you need is a stiff sentence at the beginning of the season and a booster halfway through.' Pickles

comes across as someone genuinely interested in reform.
He might have achieved much more if he had curbed his
tongue!

I wonder about that last bit, but I accept Ms Tresidder's
shrewd analysis after meeting me for seventy-five minutes
and doing her homework thoroughly.

How did I become involved with the media? Where did
the infection come from? Would I have been better if I had
inoculated myself against it, or been cured? On balance,
has it been good, bad or indifferent?

I sat on the Bench, part and full-time, for twenty-two
years before I became known outside Yorkshire – and it
happened by chance. Ironically, if Lord Chancellor Hailsham had treated me in a considerate, restrained way, I
would still be 'obscure', as he called me, though not I hope
as 'absurd' as I am anonymously referred to on pp. 430–1 of
his book *A Sparrow's Flight*.

For centuries our judges were rarely seen or heard outside
court. There were, and are, official processions in London
and some provincial cities to mark the opening of the legal
year, when the public gaze at the judges, recorders and
barristers – full-bottom wigs, silk stockings and buckled
shoes for judges and recorders. It looks a bit like something
from *Dr Who*. These men, and the occasional woman, are
from the past, stuck in a time-warp, as they solemnly and
silently process, carefully keeping in step and line. In cities
like York the procession ends at the cathedral and then goes
off for sherry with the High Sheriff. There is no harm in any
of this. Some love it and think it symbolises Britain – as it
does.

On ceremonial occasions, the judges do not speak to the
public. Until recently they were officially inhibited from
speaking outside court at all. In December 1955 the BBC's
Director-General, Sir Alaric Jacob, wrote to Lord Chancellor Kilmuir asking if serving judges could give a series of

radio 'lectures' on the Third Programme about great judges of the past. Who today remembers Kilmuir, formerly Sir David Maxwell-Fyfe QC, a thick-set and thicker-brained politician? Only a few, for his reply to the BBC rejecting its request, which laid down what became known as the 'Kilmuir Rules'. Boiled down, the letter said that a judge's reputation for wisdom and impartiality would vanish if he spoke outside court, as he would be criticised. (But criticism is good for all, surely?) Kilmuir also condemned judicial participation in 'entertainment', without defining it. My dictionary says 'to occupy agreeably'. A discussion on, say, sentencing that involved a judge would entertain many viewers or listeners, but be no worse for that. Lord Kilmuir did not think it through.

By 1979, judicial minds were starting to change. On 25 June that year Lord Scarman addressed Justice, a group which does good work pinpointing unjust convictions. He spoke about the desirability of judges being able to take part in public discussions. I wrote to Lord Scarman and he replied:

> I do believe very strongly in judges exposing themselves and their views to the challenge of public discussion, provided always they know the limits within which they may comment. I am sure that successive Lord Chancellors have allowed their fear of what might happen to the inexperienced or indiscreet judge to govern the directions, more or less unofficial and off-the-record, which they give to all of us. I made my breakthrough when I was chairman of the Law Commission, and I have never returned to the cloister.

Lord Chancellor Hailsham was not prepared to relax the 'Kilmuir Rules'. On 25 January 1980 he wrote to all judges: 'The independence of the judges depends on their immunity from direct criticism, and this cannot be preserved unless the judges refrain from expressing opinions off the bench and to the public at large, on matters of current interest . . . '

So now the gag on judges was necessary to preserve judicial independence. Kilmuir had not said that, and I cannot see how public criticism could undermine independence. In practice the 'Kilmuir Rules' were used to gag circuit judges. Only senior, 'reliable' judges appeared, new or dissenting notions being suppressed. For example, *The Times* of 19 June 1985 printed a letter from Judge Tibber, a circuit judge, about the right of a defendant to challenge three jurors without giving reasons (a right since abolished). One of the presiding judges on that judge's circuit was Mr Justice French, who – doubtless prompted by the Lord Chancellor's office – asked the circuit judge to undertake 'to refrain from these or other views in public in future'. I have the correspondence which a quite young and junior official of the Lord Chancellor's office had with the judge. To his credit, the latter stood his ground and refused to give the undertaking. No action could be taken against him: it was bluff.

Most judges are easily kept in line. They are used to it; they have been accepting it since prep school. And most of them want something from the Lord Chancellor: promotion, a title, membership of a royal commission or an invitation to a royal garden party. It happens that none of these interests me at all. I was able to stand up to Hailsham, who turned out to be better at making threats than at implementing them. However, I should not be rude about Hailsham even though on 27 May 1986, at the annual Bar conference, he called me a 'fool' and a 'nut case'. He did not name me, and even denied he was referring to me, but there was no doubt that he was.

Let us take a calm look at Quintin McGarel Hogg, now Viscount (or is it Baron?) Hailsham of St Marylebone. His father was twice Lord Chancellor, earning a reputation similar in some respects to the present Lord Hailsham's. Quintin Hogg had an outstandingly successful academic career at

Eton and Oxford. Whatever flaws he has, modesty is not one of them. On page 15 of his book, *The Door Wherein I Went*, he wrote:

> I have acquired, and have retained, an almost unlimited capacity to absorb information, great power of concentration, and meticulous habits of scholarship, marred only by the occasional carelessness caused by the speed at which I work. I was academically exceptionally gifted, and being intensely ambitious and competitive by nature, made full use of this gift.

Lord Hailsham has undoubtedly done the state some service. It is all set out in the thirty-eight lines of his entry in *Who's Who*. We write our own entries, length and content being some indication not only of achievement but also of modesty (I have three lines). Hogg was elected MP for Oxford in 1938 at a famous by-election in which he defended Neville Chamberlain's policy of appeasing Hitler. He served in the army in the Second World War, being wounded in action, but became Under-Secretary for Air before the war ended. He was First Lord of the Admiralty under Anthony Eden during the 1956 Suez Crisis, but though he was kept in the dark by the PM about the real aims of that disgraceful affair he did not resign, as some ministers did.

Hailsham rose to be Tory Party chairman under Harold Macmillan, and was photographed emerging from the sea like a monster – it was only a diving mask – and faithfully ringing the bell for the faithful at the party conference. Those pictures may have robbed him of No. 10; not enough *gravitas* (and he such a renowned classicist) for the men from the shires. So reluctantly Hailsham had to settle for the Woolsack, which has less power than the top job but more pomp – and how he relished both!

Before I pass to my clashes with him, I concede that not all he did as Lord Chancellor was bad; an able-brained, hard-working man, he must have good things to his credit. But he was there to preserve; he was instinctively for tradition and against change. It was natural for him to defend and justify the legal system, and in particular the interests of the Bar at which he had practised fitfully and cholerically. When interviewed by John Mortimer (see page 12, *Character Parts* by John Mortimer) he admitted he used to lose his temper in court. I saw him do it in 1948 when he was still at the junior Bar: he was gratuitously rude to a witness and was rebuked by Lord Chief Justice Goddard. Yet here was the man who later appointed and promoted all magistrates and judges.

When Lord Hailsham finally left office in 1987 after twelve years, not a great deal had been achieved and much remained to be done. He set his face against a Ministry of Justice: what heresy, to abolish or emasculate the office whose holder has custody of the Great Seal; the office he and his father held and towards which his son, Douglas Hogg QC, is now edging through the ministerial undergrowth. And while a third Hogg on the Woolsack would impress the untutored by dynastic endurance, it might depress the rest of us. Dynasties – look at the Hapsburgs – tend to produce bigger heads but smaller minds with each generation.

Criminal and civil cases gathered dust through delay in Hailsham's time, though new courts were built and more judges appointed. He was hostile to law centres which – publicly funded and staffed by salaried lawyers – help poor litigants who would otherwise be unrepresented. For the first time since legal aid was introduced for civil cases forty years ago, Hailsham cut it back. He incurred the wrath of the legal profession for this, though he protected them in other ways, fiercely upholding demarcation and restrictive practices. When former Prime Minister Margaret Thatcher wanted to let building societies do conveyancing, Hailsham protected solicitors' interests. Yet the Young Solicitors'

Group, representing 44,000 practitioners, accused him of 'blocking reform of the legal profession in order to protect his fellow barristers'. He clung to the adversarial view of divorce, where one party has to be guilty. He refused to take on responsibility for conciliation in matrimonial matters and failed to introduce family courts to replace the patchwork of procedures spread between the High Court, county courts and magistrates' courts.

In all that Hailsham has said and written during his long, distinguished life, I can detect no hint of self-criticism. He is right about everything and will listen to no one who disagrees, dismissing all criticism with a wheezy chuckle. Hailsham is a patrician, contemptuous of the plebs. Such people are dangerous, however well-intentioned they think they are. Humility, tolerance, the acceptance that one may be wrong: these qualities are found in the truly great, and intellectual excellence is no substitute.

Hailsham clashed inevitably with me and those like me – ordinary folk who jog along with their faults and flaws and know they have them, but are not prepared to be ridden over by those like him. I first came to the serious attention of Lord Chancellor Hailsham when I made a speech at the Inner Manchester magistrates' annual dinner on 14 October 1981. During my then five years as a circuit judge I had become increasingly frustrated by weak government policy on sentencing and parole. The public was not being protected. I had taken this up with fellow judges on my circuit, the permanent secretary to the Lord Chancellor, Sir Wilfred Bourne, and Hailsham himself. He did not even acknowledge my letter to him of 25 March 1981. So in my speech I criticised the Home Secretary, William Whitelaw, for 'waving the big stick' at courts by threatening to curtail our powers if we did not reduce prison sentences. Lord Chief Justice Lane wrote to me in restrained, reasonable terms, telling me I had embarrassed him in his discussions with Whitelaw, and asking me to please keep quiet in public.

I did keep quiet for more than three drifting years under Lord Lane, until frustration built up again and I wrote an article entitled 'A Place for Punishment' which the *Daily Telegraph* published on 22 March 1985. This produced letters from Sir Derek Oulton, the permanent secretary, and Hailsham himself, threatening to dismiss me if I offended again.

I managed to keep my nerve, well down the judicial ladder though I was, with no allies and no one with whom I could discuss it. I decided it was bluff: this was Hailsham's method, bullying judges in private. Significantly, his letters contained no word about the points I had made in my article. Did he care about sentencing policy? Or was he concerned because I was embarrassing the Cabinet, of which he was a member? I was stepping out of line, and judges simply did not do that. At the hint of such heresy the Lord Chancellor's office had for centuries only to touch its big stick and recalcitrants fell back into line. Hailsham was doing what came naturally. Lord Mackay would have agreed with me that there was a problem and discussed it, pointing out the official angle. Hailsham never even sent for me and I have never met him, save transiently at Oxford about forty-five years ago. He has always refused to debate matters with me on TV. What has he to be afraid of?

On 7 August 1985 the *Daily Telegraph* printed an article by me called 'Justice Delayed is Justice Denied'. Lord Chief Justice Lane then sent for me, and I met him for the first and only time on 18 September that year. He was polite and restrained, but said I should not have written the articles. I thought it wise to volunteer an undertaking not to write further articles before I retired: it was given on the basis that he would take up the points I had raised with him. Sadly, his response was minimal when I raised with him court delays and other matters I have already referred to. He had shut me up, but not kept his side of the arrangement.

My 'coming out' fully into the public arena happened by

chance. On 23 January 1986 Hugo Young lamented in the *Guardian* Hailsham's efforts to stop judges taking part in a radio programme. On 27 January there was a letter from Hailsham in reply. This was something I knew about and the public did not, so having withdrawn my undertaking to Lord Lane, I wrote the article which changed my life. The *Guardian* published 'Kilmuir Rules – OK?' on 14 February 1986 (see Appendix 1). It brought forth not one word of reply from Hailsham to the *Guardian* or to me.

An unexpected result of my stand was that, as soon as Lord Mackay became Lord Chancellor in November 1987, he abandoned the 'Kilmuir Rules'. Times had changed. He would not lay down rigid or detailed rules. 'Judges should be given more discretion when there were approaches from the media,' he said. 'It should be left to them to decide what to do about interviews by the press or broadcasting media, as long as they do not prejudice their judicial rule.'

All that effort, those threats by Hailsham and his men, the insistence that judicial independence rested on the 'Kilmuir Rules', were swept away in a few cool sentences by the gentle Scot. And the heavens did not fall.

In his memoirs, Hailsham refers to me:

> I was strongly advised by two of the most respected members of the judiciary and by my own office that a particular judge had been guilty of misbehaviour within the meaning of the Act and should be removed . . . the judge in question had among other misdemeanours made a number of what, rightly or wrongly, I thought to have been quite unjustified and scurrilous criticisms of myself.

He goes on to state that my only real claim to fame was the number of times my behaviour had been criticised and my judgements reversed by the Court of Appeal. He also accuses me of breaking my word to Lord Lane. He then defends and seeks to justify the 'Kilmuir Rules'.

But in his book Hailsham fails even to refer to the issues which arose between himself and me, or between Lord Lane and me. There is not a word about the contents of my *Daily Telegraph* or *Guardian* articles. Although he tries to justify the 'Kilmuir Rules' he does not add that Lord Mackay abandoned them. So much for Hailsham's intellectual gifts and the way he uses them.

Having left the dark forest of judicial reticence and stumbled into the open by chance, as I have described, I found I liked my new freedom. I had things to say and there was a need to say them. But there have to be principles in this area, and I see them as follows. They could be called the Pickles Rules if I had any sort of authority, but I do not. Nor do I claim always to have adhered to my own rules.

1. Those who appear or may appear before a judge should be able to feel confident that he can and will try to make fair, impartial and accurate decisions – that is, in accordance with the law and evidence.

2. A judge should not as a general rule comment in public about a case he has decided, so as to identify the case. The reasons for this are: detraction from judicial dignity, and the possibility of defamation proceedings (a judge has no immunity when outside his court).

3. A judge who is approached by the media should only co-operate if he can do so in a dignified manner on a subject he knows about from experience and/or study, and on which he therefore feels he can add to public discussion.

4. While playing a public role, in or out of court, a judge should not object to criticism, from whatever source or in whatever terms. He should feel free to reply, provided he does so in moderate, reasoned language.

5. While in the public sphere, a judge should be, and be seen to be, free from pressure by the Government. It is wrong for a minister, including the Lord Chancellor, to try

to silence a judge in order merely to prevent embarrassment to himself and his political colleagues.

In the years since my *Guardian* article I have had many approaches by the media. At first I was hesitant. This was new territory. The man who had the statutory power to remove me – unhampered, it seemed, by any procedure – might try to do it. Once over the parapet it was dangerous, and I had to tread warily. I turned down many offers but eventually accepted many – too many, some say. I never went to the media; they always came to me. I turned down an early offer by the *Sun* to write about Page Three girls, but have since written for it, as I have for the *Guardian*. I have been recorded at both extremes, then, and for various organs in between, including the *Daily Mail*, the *Mail on Sunday*, the *Listener*, *Punch* and the lamented *Sunday Correspondent*. Every journal has its own style, and it is demanding but can be rewarding in both senses to try to fill the bill.

I have done radio and TV programmes, including three appearances on *Wogan*. It would be hypocritical of me to say that I have always been reluctant to comply, or that I have found appearances nerve racking. It is satisfying to analyse a subject that I know about and that the public is interested in. I seem to have the journalistic instinct combined with histrionics – the wish to entertain, as Ms Tresidder found. The deeper the involvement, the better I find it. Radio and TV interviews can be boring and superficial; but not so the *Byline* programme on drugs that I did for BBC TV in June 1991. I learned a lot from that. I was in it from the start, saw the research, filming and editing, and wrote and presented the commentary.

Meeting and working with media people has left various impressions. The first is that most of them are my sort of people, as many lawyers – and judges especially – are not. The media do not care who your father was and where you went to school, only that you deliver what they want: relevant information presented agreeably.

I have worked with and spoken freely with many journalists. I have said indiscreet things about myself – a tendency I have – but no men and only three women have let me down. I speak the truth as I see it: it is my Achilles heel, and may be the death of me. Some of the journalists have been impressive: Alan Rusbridger of the *Guardian* comes to mind, as does Martyn Harris of the *Daily Telegraph*. The former told me he was surprised how frankly I had spoken about myself. Harris wrote of me on 17 March 1989: 'My interview with him was one of the very few I have conducted where I found myself censoring quotes for the protection of the interviewee. He demands that journalists paint him "warts and all", and they turn his warts into beauty spots.'

Nearer home Sheron Boyle, a journalist then on my local newspaper, the *Evening Courier* in Halifax, ranks along with Ms Tresidder as a writer of integrity.

In the interview she did with me, published on 10 December 1990, she wrote:

He claims to be a man with a mission. A rebel with a cause. Judge James Pickles is a professional anomaly – a figure of authority, yet one who revolts against it. Rarely a moment goes by without the maverick Halifax judge peering out over half-moon glasses from the pages of the press and TV screens . . . the words 'colourful' and 'controversial' are almost a part of his title.

Certain other women journalists merely sell their victims to the reading public. They do it for the money. They flatter a man they deal with, but have no affection or concern for him. And the men, myself included, are to blame for having anything to do with such women, whose reputations they should have enquired about beforehand.

Ms A. – I shall not bother to name these individuals – was

recommended by a publisher. In 1987 she came to stay the night with us after interviewing me with a tape recorder. Next morning I drove her to Leeds in my open-top car. The interview was over, as I thought, but I was dismayed to read in the *Sunday Express*: 'I could just hear Judge James Pickles as he roared down the motorway to Leeds in his open-top Jag XK150 (in fact, an XK120 replica): "I've got a self-destruct streak in me. I love driving fast."' I was annoyed about this at the time and wrote to Ms A. about it. She replied that it was all on the tape – plainly incorrect. However when I met her later I did not hold it against her, blaming my own lack of caution.

I failed to learn my lesson. Naïvely I thought *The Times* would be different. Ms E. came to see me at Leeds Crown Court in 1989. She is quite well known and has been on Radio Four. At the time I liked her; she gave me lunch while she took notes. I spoke to her further in my room at court, and then she left. Twenty minutes later E. returned, saying she was sitting in the train when she realised she had left her notebook in my room. We walked to the station together, and as I held my umbrella over us, she put her arm in mine. I light-heartedly told her that she should not do that as I was susceptible to such an approach. We chatted amicably, and when we arrived at the station I kissed her on the cheek and we parted.

The Times is still read by most judges and lawyers. E.'s article included these words:

A fine and dapper figure, Judge Pickles escorted me to Leeds City station at the end of our interview, enlivening the rainy talk with descriptions of his romantic fancies and asides about women in the media whose presence had excited him. Once on the platform he threw caution to the wind and pressed several kisses to my face. Judge Pickles has intelligence and personality, but it is hard to believe that his mind is always clear.

DID I BECOME 'MEDIA-INFECTED'?

At lunch that day, one of my judicial colleagues asked: 'What did you do to that woman from *The Times*, Jimmy?' What Lord Lane said has not been recorded – and could not be repeated in polite company, I suspect. That journalist set me up. I walked naïvely into her trap. She cannot have thought the interview was still going on in the street.

I am not the first man who, having vowed to learn his lesson, failed. I have no excuse for being seduced telephonically. What is more, the name of the paper J. works at should have warned me. *Today* is a journal of dubious parentage and history: I have since discovered that it was going downhill at the time. When she came to see me I should have done my homework, read the ailing organ and found out about her. I did try to avoid the trap E. had set, by telling J. about it. But far from protecting me, that merely played into the sticky hands of J. Her article was headed: 'I am susceptible to female charm. Please don't manipulate me.'

The piece itself made out that I was obsessed by sex and cars, which is an exaggeration. It ended by suggesting that I had indecently assaulted J. by touching her thigh as she got into her car! Admittedly she was physically attractive and therefore the suggestion was not unthinkable – but it was unlikely in theory and untrue in fact. And it came from the pen of someone whom I had invited to my house and offered lunch to.

I immediately cancelled several interviews I had arranged with women journalists. I had had enough of their breed. But L. writes long articles in the *Independent on Sunday*, which I confess I find interesting: I am addicted to the ritual disembowelling of the distinguished. How she captures her victims is hard to understand – but then some people are blinded by vanity and the urge to get noticed at whatever cost. L. wrote a diary for her paper in which she used material from J.'s *Today* piece and stated of me: 'He retires in July and not a moment too soon.' L. has never met me, and is never likely to, though she later had the nerve to ask me for an interview.

There are lessons in all this which I pass on to other naïve aspirants. Be wary of women journalists especially from the tabloids. I have had criticism from the press over the Renshaw and Scott cases. I did not object to that: I hardly welcomed it, but it did not affect or worry me. It was water off a judge's gown. The morning paper lies in the gutter by the evening, ignored by all except street cleaners. A week is a long time in politics, but with the press it is less than a day.

Not long after calling me a 'plonker' over the Renshaw case, the *Sun* rang and asked me to write an article. 'Just a minute,' I said, 'it's not long since you called me a "plonker".' The journalist agreed. 'So that's showbusiness, is it?' I asked. And in a way it is. They had a newspaper to sell, and I had views to express. So we did a deal, and I got 'damages' out of it that way.

What has been the public's response to my efforts to protect them in court and enlighten them in the media? Most who write to me have been overwhelmingly and consolingly favourable. I have a solid following out there, but I do receive the occasional hostile letter. I cannot say I dislike being a celebrity. To be taken notice of is on the whole better than to be ignored as being of no importance.

If I did become 'infected' by the media, the dose was mild and not unpleasant to me or anyone else.

8

How close did I come to being sacked?

There is an odd difference between the way that High Court and circuit judges are dismissed, for which Lord Hailsham is responsible. Since the 1700 Act of Settlement, and now by the Supreme Court Act 1981, a High Court judge may only be removed on an address to the Queen by both Houses of Parliament. However, under the 1971 Courts Act: 'The Lord Chancellor may, if he thinks fit, remove a circuit judge from office on the ground of incapacity or misbehaviour'. There is no definition of either ground, and no procedure has been laid down.

The reference in Lord Hailsham's memoirs, quoted in Chapter 7 of this book, indicates that he considered removing me without ceremony. In the same way he refused to renew Manus Nunan's recordership: he acted on reports that Nunan never saw and for two years did not offer Nunan any opportunity to be heard.

If Hailsham is correct in stating that two senior judges and his own office advised that I should be removed, we ought to be told more, though Hailsham is unlikely to enlighten us. Who were the judges and what precisely was their advice? Did they say I could be removed without any hearing or being permitted to defend myself? And who were the top civil servants in the office – Derek Oulton, the then permanent secretary, and Tom Legg, the present one? What qualifications had they to give such advice, save practising at the Bar for short periods and then opting for civil service security? In fairness, both men have excellent credentials and I have never quarrelled with Legg.

Hailsham goes on to state in his memoirs: 'The principle that justice should be seen to be done meant I could not act as victim, prosecutor, judge and jury in the same proceedings.' So his own statutory provision was unworkable, although he had eminent advice that it should be worked! How quaint and quixotic. The truth is that Hailsham dared not move to dismiss me, though he would have liked to. He knew that public and parliamentary opinion would have made his own position on the Woolsack untenable.

In 1987 Hailsham left office for the final time, to the final relief of many who had to work with or under him: few have actually said that, though I have. Lord Havers' tenure of the Woolsack was so brief that if you blinked you missed it: his four months' service earned him a £40,000-a-year pension.

Lord Chancellor Mackay, the present incumbent, is a different being. I concede that when he threatened to dismiss me I took him seriously. To have been threatened by one Lord Chancellor may be regarded as misfortune . . . and everyone who knows Lord Mackay would side with him, for he is a good and honourable man. Hailsham had not even dared send for me and confront me. When I briefly met him in 1946 he was young, pompous and arrogant; now he is old but otherwise unchanged. Lord Mackay did send for me and there are lessons in what happened. The details have not been revealed until now.

After the Renshaw appeal, Lord Mackay wrote to me:

From what I have seen, it appears that in the present case, at a time when you knew or should have known that an appeal was pending, you publicly defended your decision and commented on the case in a way which would have been regarded as improper if it had been done by any of the professional people involved . . . This caused me considerable concern at the time, but I felt it would not be proper to take any action until the hearing of the appeal had been completed. Now the appeal has been decided, I must consider what action I should take and, before I make any decisions, I would be glad to know whether you wish to offer any explanation in comment.

My reply ran as follows:

I have been in the law for forty-one years. I have tried criminal cases for twenty-six years; for half of that period, full-time.

I enclose a copy of the paperback edition of my book, *Straight from the Bench*. The hardback edition was published in April 1987, and the paperback in August 1988. I make no particular claims for the book, as to profundity or otherwise. I wrote it because I felt I had various things I should say to the public, arising out of my experience at the Bar and on the bench. The book speaks for itself (I do not expect you to read it all). No one has told me I was wrong to write it. I send it to you so you may, I hope, accept that I have taken my work seriously and written about it responsibly. In a sentence I have for some time felt that the judiciary has been too much of a self-perpetuating oligarchy drawn from a narrow social group, and operating too remotely from the public. If we are to have the confidence of the public as a whole, we must from time to time leave our ivory tower and let laymen look round it. We are accountable to the public for what we do on its behalf and at its expense. I know, from the many letters I have had from lay people, that the book and the approach it represents have been appreciated.

Not surprisingly, Lord Hailsham did not agree with my approach as set out above. He tried to silence me, applying the 'Kilmuir Rules' and even threatening to dismiss me, for writing the article that is reprinted in the book on pp. 184–6. If I may say so, you appear to have accepted my arguments when you abandoned the 'Kilmuir Rules'.

As I wrote in 'Postscript 1988' to the book (see pp. 177–83) I welcomed your appointment as Lord Chancellor. I have a genuinely high regard and respect for you. I have given general support to your efforts to reform the legal system. I have no wish to become involved, privately or publicly, in controversy with you.

I accept that as a general rule it is wrong for a judge to comment in public out of court about his decision in court. With all respect, the reason for this is not that the Court of Appeal might in some way be prejudiced: I do not see how that could happen, whatever may be the position where jurors are involved. Better reasons are that such comments may detract from judicial dignity, and – not being privileged – attract proceedings for defamation.

In all my experience the Renshaw case was unique. No decision of mine has attracted such publicity and criticism of myself in the media. I did not approach the media, but they approached me. I accepted some approaches, but not all. I considered I had been misunderstood as to what I had done and why. Rightly or wrongly, I decided that the situation raised an exception to the general rule against judicial comment. I tried to explain, to those who had not been in court, what they would have heard had they been there. Nothing I said or wrote was in any way directed at the Court of Appeal. Several people wrote that they now understood the case better. There was public discussion of important legal principles, which cannot have harmed anyone and must have done some good. For example, in the BBC TV programme *Heart of the Matter*, presented by Joan Bakewell, participants included John Stalker, Helen Kennedy QC and myself. The issues were aired in an educative, dignified, balanced manner.

It is my duty to defer to your ruling. I give you my undertaking that in the relatively short period prior to my retirement, I will not comment publicly on any judicial decision of mine, in a manner which identifies the case concerned.

Lord Mackay accepted that, and wished me well for the remainder of my judicial career. That was in October 1989. At the end of that year came the Tracey Scott case. I was in Lanzarote when I read of the Court of Appeal decision, and about to return after a healing week by and in the warm sea. I was staggered, not only by the decision but by Lord Lane's words: 'The judge seems to us to have been concerned more with the public impact of what he was doing and saying, rather than with the justice of it.' In the plane going home I saw in the *Guardian* of 17 January 1990 the headline to a leading article: 'Pickles Preserved'.

When I arrived home the press had been seeking me in force. Two reporters had flown to the Canaries, but gone to Tenerife. I knew I was about to endure the 'rat pack' tactics which the press had used over the Renshaw case: house besieged, court building exits manned, a horde of photographers following me in the street, running ahead and snapping.

On the morning following my return, after several reporters had spoken to me through the letter box, I made a decision which with hindsight was unwise. I would hold a press conference at lunchtime that day in Wakefield, where I was sitting at the crown court. I had no intention to talk about the merits of the Scott case, but I wished to disperse the 'rat pack' and correct a mis-statement.

I had said in court that if young women thought that by becoming pregnant they could be sure to escape imprisonment, since the lapse of time between offence and trial was so long, some of them might be tempted to become pregnant deliberately. I was reported as saying that I was sending Scott to prison in order to deter accused women from becoming pregnant.

Obviously I could not invite the press into the crown court building where I was sitting. So I rang the licensee of the

179

adjoining aptly named Inns of Court pub, where I sometimes had lunch. The conference was well attended by
reporters, photographers and even a TV crew. I corrected
the misunderstanding and what I said was duly reported. I
also called the Lord Chief Justice 'an ancient dinosaur living
in the wrong age'. I should not have said that, but this book
indicates why I felt the frustration that now boiled over so
inappropriately.

For all his good qualities, Lord Lane was blocking progress in the criminal justice field. It is not enough for him to
be a good judge in court, as he is – despite his dreadful gaffe
in the Birmingham Six appeal which led to my supporting
those who called on him to resign. Someone had to apologise and accept that the system had gone terribly wrong.
Lane's resignation would have done that to some extent.

In court Lane is for the most part a big man. In his work –
or inactivity – outside court he has proved to be a little man.
He is incapable of understanding or grappling with the need
for reforms, even of the court delays for which there are
obvious remedies. He is likely to retire within a year or two.
I wish I could see a successor with the necessary qualities.

There are two front runners for the job of Lord Chief
Justice. Both happen to be Jewish – a tribute to that most
talented of all races – and Oxbridge. Lord Justice Harry
Woolf is very clever; I have only met him once, briefly, but
have heard nothing to his disadvantage. He appears to be
unstuffy and prepared to stand up in court to the Establishment. The main reason why he may not head the criminal
courts is that he might be even better fitted for the civil side
as Master of the Rolls when Lord Donaldson finally leaves
that post.

I happen to know the other candidate, Lord Justice Peter
Taylor, very well. I was against him at the Bar, and he also
led me. I saw him in action as leader of the north-eastern
circuit and then as its presiding judge. There is no more
ambitious man. He is an excellent judge in court, especially

in criminal cases. He is not in the same intellectual class as Woolf, but the Lord Chief Justice does not need to be outstandingly clever.

As I would expect, Peter Taylor is preparing the ground carefully. He is a man for detail and I admire that. I have seen reports in the media about his being evacuated during the war and living frugally. They can only have come from him, and Lord Mackay – of humble origin himself – must be impressed. Taylor is even on record as saying that we may have to abandon wigs and scarlet-and-ermine. He would never have said that in Hailsham's time.

Smooth, polite, restrained and proper in court, Peter Taylor can be irascible, intemperate and overbearing out of court. Worse, he does not know how best to deal with people. He is a bit of a bruiser with a strain of arrogance.

In about 1978 I went as a guest of the circuit to a judges' night, presided over by Peter Taylor QC as leader of the circuit. Also present were two or three High Court judges. In his speech, Taylor said: 'Judge Pickles writes melodramas. We could do with more of the mellow and less of the drama.' It was not intended as a joke, and no one laughed. Peter lacks the light touch, except at the piano where he is an excellent performer. The remark had some basis, in that one or two barristers had complained about the way I had treated them in court. There was substance in their complaints, and I did my best to restrain my tendency to be impatient and speak sharply. But what a way to raise it with me!

If Taylor had had insight and knew how to deal with people, he would have taken it up with me personally or in writing, asking me to tone down a bit and remember how I had reacted to judges when I was at the Bar. He should have realised his remark was likely to antagonise me. After dinner, several barristers were chatting to me and someone said I looked like Ernest Hemingway (I had grown a beard). I observed that he had shot himself with an elephant gun.

Taylor – trying the light touch, I think – said I'd have plenty of people to do that to me. I responded: 'You would. You'd shoot me in the back.' And he walked off and out of my life for a couple of years.

On 18 September 1980, S. appeared before me at Sheffield Crown Court. His solicitors had been unable to obtain his instructions, and so his case had been listed to clarify the position. Counsel A., representing the solicitors, was present – he was in Taylor's chambers – and I decided to have the case mentioned again on the following day. The transcript reveals my question to A:

> Judge Pickles: 'Are you in a position to act or not?'
>
> A: 'The position is this. I have spoken with my chambers and, unfortunately there was no one present at the time who could give me information about this. I must say therefore that I know of no other commitments that I have at the moment and no impediment.'
>
> Judge (to defendant): 'What I am going to do, Mr S., is ask Mr A. to take over legal aid without a solicitor for the time being and to see you, preferably today, if he can. Can you?'
>
> A: 'Your honour, yes.'
>
> Judge (to defendant): 'He will have to get the documents and he will see you today and possibly tomorrow as well, and if he finds that he needs a solicitor we will arrange that, you see, but he can start off on his own.'

When I arrived home that day there was a message from Peter Taylor asking me to ring him. I did not do so immediately, and when he rang he angrily demanded if I had got his message. He went on to accuse me of compelling a member of his chambers to take on a case which he did not want to, and refusing to assign a solicitor under legal aid. Taylor had spoken to Mr Justice 'Roddie' Smith, a presiding judge of the circuit, who had authorised the assignment of another counsel to the case, with solicitors. I said I would obtain a transcript at my own expense, and I did. It vindicated me; on that occasion I had acted with complete propriety. I sent it to Taylor, with a copy of a letter I had written to Lord Chancellor Hailsham about the incident. Peter Taylor then panicked. Unknown to me, he was about to be appointed a High Court judge, and was afraid Hailsham might change his mind – which he was capable of – and there was nothing to prevent him: the decision was his alone.

I then received a message from Taylor asking me to ring him – I did not – and a letter from Mr Justice Smith trying to smooth me down. Taylor's appointment did go ahead, and Derek Oulton, of the Lord Chancellor's office, rang to say that Hailsham had been very concerned, but as Taylor was now a High Court judge that ended the matter. What was the reason for Mr A.'s strange behaviour in misleading Taylor about me? He must have told his clerk that he had agreed to do the case the next day, and when his clerk asked why (having accepted other work for him) A. said I had compelled him. A small incident and of little consequence now, but in its way revealing.

In July 1985 I circulated a paper to judges on my circuit about court delays, and it came before a judges' meeting presided over by Mr Justice Taylor, then a presiding judge of the circuit. He seemed mainly concerned about my reference in the document to complacency, which he did not like. He, and it is right to say most of the circuit judges there, gave my document a cool reception.

If he had imagination and drive, Taylor would surely have taken up the subject and introduced reforms, but his mind was not geared to it. The gross injustice involved in defendants waiting for many months, sometimes in gaol; the difficulties for witnesses in remembering, for jurors in deciding and for judges in sentencing – these factors did not urge him to action, any more than they have done in Lord Lane's case. The two men are indeed in the same mould.

In February 1986, a few days before my *Guardian* 'Kilmuir Rules' article appeared, Mr Justice Taylor phoned me at home. Was it true I was going into the press again? Yes. He told me he had read the correspondence between Hailsham and me, and the Lord Chancellor could not be expected to back down. Peter Taylor, at the instigation of the Lord Chancellor's office, was repeating the threat to dismiss me. I told him that if Hailsham did try to sack me, the public fuss might be bigger than that over the Westland affair. 'Oh, who's threatening now?' said my presiding judge.

If Taylor does become Lord Chief Justice, he will earn and deserve a similar reputation to Lord Lane's: very good in court, but not so good at out-of-court administration. It is academic to me now, but whoever does get the job I wish him well (there is no woman in sight) and I hope this book may be of some assistance in a mammoth task.

Lord Mackay fired his first salvo on the Tracey Scott case just twenty-two days into 1990. In that and later letters he took a tough line, alien to the man when I met him. I wondered who wrote the letters – his civil servants? They may have been urging him to take a strong stance, saying I had got away with it previously and all control over circuit judges would go if the same happened again.

The letter said I had broken the undertaking I had given after the Renshaw case not to comment in public about my cases. Lord Mackay asked for an explanation; he was considering whether to remove me from the Bench for misbehaviour. I replied, saying the matter could hardly be dealt with satisfactorily by correspondence, and offered to go and see him. He refused: my response was 'wholly inadequate and suggests you are not taking the matter as seriously as I do'. He sent me a 'statement of facts', culled from press cuttings, and asked me to verify its accuracies.

I never complied. As the Lord Chancellor's office was

taking an adversarial approach, threatening to remove me from the Bench for misbehaviour, it was for them to prove their case and I was not prepared to assist by making admissions. Also I decided to 'play it long', dragging out the 'procedure'. I knew that as time went by the original sting – especially of the pub press conference – would be felt less, and it would be difficult to dismiss me for something that had happened months previously, since when I had continued in office.

Two further counts were then added to the indictment. On 4 April 1990 I spoke at the annual dinner of the Fylde Medico-Legal Society. In view of what follows, it should be noted that I was offered a fee; but I asked that it should be given to a medical charity – it went to a local hospice. Although it was a private function, the wife of one of the officials was a journalist and asked if she could report my speech. Naïvely, I said I had no objection, but did not trim my speech accordingly.

What I said was part serious but mainly 'knockabout': such audiences want entertainment rather than instruction. A cuttings service sent the report of my speech to the Lord Chancellor, and it included this reference by me to Lord Lane: 'He is a nice man really though I know I called him something I shouldn't have done. He is a good judge in court, but he hasn't stood up to the government as much as he should have done.'

The third count in the indictment arose out of a report in *Today* newspaper that I had a 'top showbiz agent' who would hire me out for £800 an evening. Since I became notorious I have had a large postbag. Every week I receive requests to speak, together with pleas to right injustices or even to help students write essays. I reply personally to all letters that call for it. I have to reject most requests to speak, especially where distant travel would be involved. But I have spoken to university students, rotary clubs, magistrates, solicitors and charities. There is no question of asking for a fee on such occasions, though sometimes I receive hospitality or expenses. On a few occasions while I was a judge I spoke at dinners which were commercial in nature and I received fees, though never as much as £800. This helps to subsidise other charitable functions and postage.

When I appeared on *Wogan* for the first time in 1987 I asked the amiable Terry to introduce me to his agent, Jo Gurnett, and she agreed to act for me. I was getting approaches from the media, and it has been convenient to have them filtered and arrangements made by someone experienced in that field. It never occurred to me that there was anything iniquitous in any of this. Those who listen to me, in whatever medium, seem to appreciate my efforts.

On 27 April 1990, after previous delaying letters, I asked what procedure had been laid down for the operation of section 17 (4) of the 1971 Courts Act which permits the Lord Chancellor to remove a circuit judge. Lord Mackay replied that none had been laid down, but there were three stages. The first was to establish the facts. The second was to determine whether the conduct described in the statement of facts constituted misbehaviour. 'I am advised that the conduct described really does, in law, constitute misbehaviour. In order to reach a conclusion on this issue I am willing to consider any argument you may wish to put before me as to the advice I have been given.' The third stage: if misbehaviour was established should I be removed?

On 14 May that year I addressed the Conservative Backbench Legal Committee at the House of Commons. It was a dull Monday and many MPs were still in their constituencies, but about six gave me a courteous reception. One of them, a barrister called Budgeon, questioned me rather acidly – but I was told this was his usual style. By the time I dined at the House afterwards the chairman, Ivan Lawrence QC, told me that he had already put one of my points on sentencing to the Home Secretary and another Cabinet minister. I told Lawrence about Lord Mackay's letters, adding that he had refused to see me and that I might have to 'go public' in order to pre-empt a move to treat me in the cavalier way in which Manus Nunan was treated. Lawrence offered to take up the matter with Mackay and let me know the results within a week or so. Strangely I never heard another word from him until we met after my retirement. Lawrence should surely have let me know something.

I was on my own, confronted by one of the most powerful men in the land. He was a good, fair man but also courageous. He would not bluff as Hailsham had. If I drove him to it, he was capable of removing me. He would, however, be reluctant to do it. Very intelligent, he must have known that the procedure is open to criticism as unfair, and there could be a backlash in Parliament and the media. My object was to come out of it unscathed. That required me to be firm yet reasonable; to put up a strong defence but yet be open to discussion. After Ivan Lawrence offered support and then tip-toed silently into the darkness, I discussed it with no one at all. That is how it has always been: I have made my own decisions at times of crisis. I have been a loner since prep school days, marked out from the crowd, standing up for myself.

On 26 May 1990 I wrote to the Lord Chancellor:

I am always ready to have my conduct as a judge scrutinised, provided that this is done:
    (a) In accordance with the principles of natural justice
    (b) In public
    (c) So as to investigate the whole of my career on the Bench from October 1963.
    I shall probably retire in a little over a year and I am not happy to have my position, reputation and pension put at risk by a 'procedure' which I regard as inadequate. The hostile tone of your letters disturbs me, though I do not seek to impugn your motives or your integrity.
    If you feel you have to pursue section 17 (4), I shall be

unable to defend myself properly without calling in aid members of both houses of Parliament and the public through the media. I hope that this does not become necessary as it may aggravate existing problems.

Lord Mackay replied that he was not acting out of any sense of personal hostility. If I wished to submit evidence or representation from MPs or the public, I could do so.

I decided to take a firm stance and broaden my defence, and on 14 June 1990 I wrote:

1. Section 17 (4) gives you power to remove a judge for 'misbehaviour', which has not been defined. It does not provide you with any other disciplinary power.

2. No judge should be exempt from scrutiny and discipline by an appropriate authority. I do not claim to be so exempt. If I have erred – as I may have – I deserve to be dealt with appropriately. But by whom? In what conditions? Subject to what sanctions? In public or in private? Subject to natural justice or at the whim of the appropriate authority?

3. Some, probably almost all, Western countries have a Judicial Commission or the like, to supervise and if necessary discipline members of the judiciary.

4. Lords Kilmuir and Hailsham, when dealing with the 'Kilmuir Rules', accepted that the Lord Chancellor has no disciplinary control over judges. Instead, covering part of the ground, the Rules provided a voluntary code which enabled the Lord Chancellor or usually his civil servants to decide which judges should appear in the media (in practice, the senior pro-Establishment ones). Apparently accepting my arguments, deployed in my controversy with Lord Hailsham – especially in my *Guardian* article of 14 February 1986 – you abandoned the Rules. Judges are now free to decide whether to accept media invitations, provided their judicial work is not prejudiced.

5. It would have been easy for Lord Hailsham or you to introduce disciplinary power by statute. The decision not to do so must have been deliberate. Presumably there were these reasons:

(a) Discipline by the Lord Chancellor might appear to be interference by the Executive with the Judiciary: and

(b) Discipline by a judicial commission would limit your power. The commission, not you, would decide which judges should be removed or disciplined otherwise. And inevitably there would be a call for the commission, or a similar body, also to appoint and promote holders of judicial office. That would further limit your power and that of your top civil servants. History has few if any instances of politicians or civil servants voluntarily surrendering power. The tendency is for them to seek to increase it. You have yourself stated that you intend to retain in your sole hands the final decision as to appointments.

6. There is therefore a gap, deliberately left open by you and your predecessors. You have power to remove a circuit judge, but no power to do less than that to him. You have influence. Most judges want something from you: promotion, honour or title, membership of a royal commission. They gladly eat out of your powerful hands. Difficulty has arisen in my case because:

(a) I have no ambition whatever for anything you could give me; and

(b) After twenty-two years on the bench, part-time and full-time, during which I was unknown outside Yorkshire, the Kilmuir article in the *Guardian* brought me into the public eye, and I have felt it right to respond to some media invitations. Some people have resented this.

7. What sort of disciplinary code is it that provides for dismissal but nothing less than that? What criminal code in any civilised country would provide the death penalty and nothing less? Thus you have been constrained to interpret 'misbehaviour' to cover a few (ill-chosen) remarks by me

out of court. I am being threatened with loss of position, pension, reputation, ruin; yet I have, over forty years in the law, twenty-six of them on the bench, a long record of service to the public. I have addressed magistrates, gone round penal institutions, given evidence to royal commissions, put forward ideas on why crime has increased, sentencing, parole. It is all in my book, a copy of which I sent you on 17 August 1989. I have committed no crime, done nothing mean or sordid. Yet all that counts for nothing. I have dared to be different, to step out of line. Conformity is all. So you think you can crush me in a private 'hearing' and it will soon all be forgotten. If you think that, Lord Chancellor, then with all respect, you may discover you are wrong. I do not lack either supporters or the ability to defend myself.

8. How does a contested section 17 (4) operate in practice? The only instance I know of is Recorder Manus Nunan. (I appreciate that the removal of a judge is not exactly the same as the non-renewal of a recordership). You are familiar with Nunan's case (I have the correspondence between him and you). You declined, albeit in gentle terms, to re-open the case. Nunan sat in the Crown Court as Deputy Judge from 1975–1978, when he obtained a recordership which was renewed in 1981 and was due to be renewed again at the end of 1984. He had never been told of any complaints or warned about his performance. There had been no successful appeal against him. On 7 December 1984, Tom Legg (as he then was) wrote saying, 'The Lord Chancellor has decided not to renew your recordership when your current term runs out on 31 December 1984.' . . . No one would tell Nunan – or me, when I enquired – what he had done wrong. After agitation in Parliament and the Press, Lord Hailsham saw Nunan at the House of Lords on 26 September 1986. The full transcript is attached hereto. The 'hearing' was a shambles. There was no procedure. Lord Hailsham was prosecutor

and judge. He conducted a rambling discussion. He acted on reports which Nunan never saw. Not a single instance of misbehaviour or inadequacy was ever quoted. It was never explained why, if he was incompetent, he had been appointed in 1978 and renewed in 1981. Lord Hailsham, who appointed all judges and sat at the very heart of British justice, showed that he had an insufficient notion of how to act judicially (he never sat at first instance). After the 'hearing', Lord Hailsham refused to read a document I sent him (see Oulton's letter to me of 13 January 1987). He read documents from anti-Nunan people, but would not read one from a judge known to be pro-Nunan. Lord Hailsham's 'decision' letter in the Nunan case reveals that he was afraid of an application for judicial review. I know Nunan well. He is a nice, inoffensive man. He served this country well for many years, abroad and here. Whatever the real merits, he was not treated in accordance with the rules of natural justice. He was crushed and humiliated. His case remains a disgrace to English justice.

9. You appear to be contemplating a private Nunan-type 'hearing'. I hope it will not surprise you when I say, 'Certainly not. In no circumstances.'

10. What remedies have I, if you do intend a 'Nunan-hearing'? Application to the High Court for prohibition before such a hearing, or for certiorari afterwards. If I have to, I will go to the High Court doing the case myself. (What will the media make of that?)

11. Alternatively, I could go to the media, preempting your decision under section 17(4) and hoping that pressure from the public and Parliament will be brought to bear upon you. I doubt if you realise what a storm would break. I have no wish to do it – the Judiciary as a whole would be harmed. But if you drive me to it, I will not fail.

12. I will cooperate in a section 17 (4) hearing provided it is held:

(a) In public

(b) In accordance with the rules of natural justice

(c) So as to take into account my whole record in the law.

13. On 9 March 1990 I wrote to you suggesting an informal discussion with you. You rejected that, being intent on section 17 (4). I still feel that such a meeting will be in your interest, mine and that of the public. You have never met me, but you will not find me unreasonable.

14. Please let me have your observations. In particular, I would naturally like to know which path you propose to take, so that I can prepare myself.

The Lord Chancellor then asked me to go and see him on 20 July 1990. The Head of Judicial Appointments Group – I do not suppose they have a group for dismissing judges – wrote stating that the 'hearing' would be in a committee room in the House of Lords at noon. 'The Lord Chancellor would like you to put your case in the way you wish with the minimum of preliminaries and interruption.' A proposed press notice was enclosed.

I had no intention to submit myself to 'trial of a judge'. Lord Mackay would sit there and ask me what I wished to say showing every courtesy. But there would be no one to present the 'case' against me – only the Lord Chancellor himself. The onus would be on me. So I wrote declining to attend a hearing 'which would not accord with the rules of natural justice'. In reply I was given 20 October 1990 as the new date for my 'trial'. I replied, setting out my side once again, in this ritual dance in which I was anxious that the music should not stop with me left standing in silence and awkwardly before Lord Mackay, but looking foolish before the nation's eager press.

My letter went:

I have tried more than once to discuss all outstanding matters informally with Lord Mackay, but he has declined.

His insistence on the section 17 (4) process has put us at arm's length. I am therefore not prepared fully to disclose my hand. It also indicates to me that Lord Mackay does not approach these matters with an open mind.

I am unable to agree the Statement of Facts or the Press report about fees. As to the report of the private dinner at the Fylde Medico-Legal Society, I have not been told what is complained of.

Parliament cannot have intended to suspend the rules of natural justice in the application of section 17 (4). If it had so intended, it would have said so expressly. Lord Hailsham, who was responsible for drafting the section, takes the view that it is unworkable. Thus, on p. 430 of his book, *A Sparrow's Flight*: ' . . . the principle that justice should be seen to be done meant I could not act as victim, prosecutor, judge and jury in the same proceedings.' He goes on to refer to the desirability of superimposing on the statutory duties of the Lord Chancellor the Scottish, Canadian or Australian methods of securing a fair trial of a judge compatible with judicial independence.

I agree with Lord Hailsham that a situation in which the prosecutor is also the judge flouts natural justice. It would put the onus of proof on me. I am not to be treated as Manus Nunan. Further, if I were to attend a hearing of the type proposed, it would create a precedent which is undesirable and contrary to the interests of other holders of judicial office.

I deny that any of the matters alleged can amount to misbehaviour – whatever else may be said about them. Paragraph 80 of the Notes for Circuit Judges has to be read with paragraph 78 which states that the Lord Chancellor 'does wish to emphasise, however, that it is not his function to give directions to a member of the judiciary and that the decision as to what course the judge must take must be his own.' The same must apply to a speech at a private dinner. As to my press conference, I had no intention to break my undertaking, and I was at pains not to discuss the Tracey Scott case. There were special factors leading to my decision to hold the conference, including the need to correct mis-statements in the media about the reasons for my decision in that case, and a particularly wounding and unjustified remark of Lord Lane about me. (I have never criticised Lord Lane as a judge – save for that remark. I have real reservations however about his fulfilment of his wider duties as Lord Chief Justice.)

I consider it unfortunate at least that Lord Mackay did not invite representations from me before accepting advice from some unspecified person(s) that the matters complained of can amount to misbehaviour.

A further letter arrived, dated 26 September 1990. My heart always quickened a beat or two when I saw his black-crested envelopes lying inside the back door. But this letter was different: it gave me a tactical opening, a key to the end game – if that is not mixing metaphors. Lord Mackay, despite all his power, must have wondered how best to tackle this situation which I assume was a new one for him. He wrote: 'I am willing to see you formally in public or informally in private, as you wish'. After nine months' skirmishing he was offering me what I had requested in the first place.

I replied: 'I have always been prepared to discuss outstanding matters with you informally'. I felt that in such a situation I could win, that is, induce Lord Mackay to drop his menacing stance – or had it really been that of his top civil service advisers? I could negotiate a settlement in which neither of us climbed down. I realised I was likely to be rebuked, but that did not matter.

On 2 November 1990 I entered the panelled room in the House of Lords in which I had been sworn-in as a judge by Lord Elwyn-Jones fourteen years before. Nothing seemed different except the man in charge. Lord Mackay is a most

194

formidable person, because he is so pleasant, friendly, unaffected, reasonable – and intelligent. He does not have the public school manner of the Hailshams, Haverses, Donaldsons and Kilmuirs which arouses hostility in ordinary people like me. 'They' are different from 'us' – they were educated to be superior and they talk down to others. Lord Mackay is one of us. He rose from a railwayman's cottage by brilliance and effort to teach maths at St Andrews University, go to Cambridge and then become the Scottish Lord Advocate before settling on the Woolsack, to the surprise of most and the consternation of the English Bar and Bench – except for a few, including me.

I expected to find, as Manus Nunan did, two civil servants and a shorthand writer, but there was only Lord Mackay. He did not even sit at his desk. We settled into armchairs and talked. There followed the two most fascinating hours in my life. We conversed as if we were equals – and James Mackay is in fact a few months younger than me.

In his friendly, unaffected way, the Lord Chancellor went through the various complaints. He did not do so in a hostile manner and could not have been more reasonable. I did not do justice to myself at the 'dinosaur' press conference, he said, and I had to agree. We went through the other complaints, and at the end he called in an assistant secretary and dictated a résumé of our discussion in the fluent way one expects of a top mathematician. It is set out in Appendix 6.

The upshot was that I am now a fervent admirer of our Lord Chancellor. There is little I would not do for that man, and for the rest of my time on the Bench I was careful to adhere to the rules. What a contrast in style and outcome with Lord Hailsham. He handled me entirely differently, and we know with what result. Mackay and Hailsham are both very able men, but one has the common touch and the other does not.

On 28 November 1990 Lord Mackay wrote me a letter which he released to the media. In it he rebuked me for the press conference. I suspected that the civil service had penned the document, but it did not matter. I was free to serve out the few months before my retirement.

What conclusions do I draw? First, single-handedly I managed to get the judiciary freed from the Kilmuir gag with which Hailsham and his predecessors had silenced it for generations. Second, we need a judicial commission which not only appoints and promotes judges but also disciplines them when necessary. It is absurd that the Lord Chancellor has no effective control except the power to remove circuit (not High Court) judges for 'misbehaviour', with that term undefined and the procedure non-existent. Lord Mackay is a fair and reasonable man but he will not be there for ever.

With hindsight I did not come all that close to being sacked, but how could I be so sure at the time? So although I lost no sleep, my heart did miss the odd beat.

9

Did I send too many to prison?

Prisons are 'penal dustbins', as one ex-prison governor called them. They cry out for reform. Yet they are society's main weapon in its war against crime. Whether to send a defendant inside and for how long was one of the most difficult parts of my work on the Bench.

Prisons were originally intended for holding offenders before sentence, which usually consisted of death, transportation, branding or a fine. They were owned by dukes, landowners, the Church and local authorities, and run by gaolers who made profits from them. Conditions were scandalous. The Home Office inspected prisons from 1835, and took them over in 1877, when a prison commission was set up. They were built on the cell system, the Victorian notion being that solitude, silence, hard humiliating tasks and the Bible would instil penitence. The notion was mistaken. Prisons do not make people better, and they make them bitter. The unpleasantness of it may, however, make them behave better for fear of returning. Although prisons have become unpopular with left-wingers, social workers and others who make simplistic statements such as 'Prisons do no good', I know of no country which manages without them.

Today, England and Wales have about 130 prison establishments, which vary widely. I have gone round at least one of every type, except a women's prison. The 'local' prisons, as at Wormwood Scrubs in London, Winson Green in Birmingham and Armley in Leeds, are overcrowded Victorian buildings, where slopping-out, lack of work and confinement to cells for long hours bring unnecessary humiliation and waste. In contrast, a semi-open prison such as Ranby, between Worksop and Retford in Nottinghamshire, which I have visited, is not overcrowded. There is no slopping-out and life seems relaxed and civilised. That was an army camp originally; recently built prisons such as Swaleside and Garth have even more modern facilities.

After sentence there is a regional system for allocating prisoners, according to various factors. The first is length of sentence. If it is a month, say, they stay in local prisons which also hold people on remand. Prisoners are put into categories according to the risk to the public should they escape. Category A is for a prisoner whose escape would be highly dangerous to the public or police or state security. Category B is for a prisoner for whom the very highest condition of security is not necessary, but for whom escape must be made very difficult. Into category C goes a person who cannot be trusted in open conditions but who does not have the ability or resources to make a determined escape attempt. The category D person can be reasonably trusted to serve his sentence in open conditions.

Categories A and B go into the 'dispersal' system – seven or eight prisons such as the Isle of Wight's Parkhurst and Wakefield in West Yorkshire, which take inmates serving medium or long sentences. Where a prisoner and his family live is taken into account, as are the particular needs of the prisoner. In practice, however, the main determinants at present are available space and security. There are about one hundred prisoners who are moved to different establishments every twenty-eight days. They are mentally ill but beyond the help of the prison system, since prison hospitals will not take anyone whose mental illness makes them violent.

Since about 1955 crime has risen year by year. Until Home Secretary William Whitelaw started a building programme in 1980, the politicians' attitude to the inevitable overcrowding was that it was for the courts to solve the problem by avoiding or reducing prison sentences. And we complied, though with some reluctance and insufficiently to end overcrowding. Parole was introduced in 1968: at privately held meetings the executive – Home Office officials who receive recommendations from the Parole Board – decide whether to cut sentences passed by the judiciary in public. As Home Secretary, Leon Brittan extended parole generally while curtailing it in some serious cases.

To tell a criminal he would go to prison for three years when everyone knew he would almost certainly be freed after a year was farcical. As a result of the Carlisle Report, prisoners will in future serve at least six months or half their sentence whichever is longer. I would like to see parole abolished apart from a few exceptional cases. Prisoners dislike it. They can only apply once a year and are not given reasons for refusal or told whether there is any point in applying again. Some refuse to apply at all.

The prison population has varied in recent years:

1984-5	43,600
1985-6	46,600
1987	49,000
1988	50,500
1989	48,600
1990	45,600

Spending on prison building has more than doubled in real terms since 1980. Under the current programme, twelve new establishments have opened, providing 5,997 places. A further nine are under construction, providing nearly 5,117 more places.

The Home Office works from hand to mouth, from day to day, and lurches from crisis to crisis with little enquiry into what prisons are intended to do and little concern for the needs of individual prisoners. Security is the key – keeping them in until it is time to let them out. We need a more constructive approach. I would like to see Britain lead the world with a modern policy on penal reform. At present we are light years from that, with little prospect of getting nearer.

What features do prisons have? First, they are expensive for the community. The weekly cost of keeping an inmate at a dispersal prison in 1990–1 was £616; for an open adult prison it was £293; the overall average was £386.

The impact of gaol on a criminal obviously varies with the individual. The effect on multi-millionaire businessman Gerald Ronson must have been devastating, even though after two nights he went, with unusual speed, to an open prison where he had his own room and access to a telephone. At the other end of the scale, an old lag soon settles into a familiar regime which holds no special terrors: he knows how to play the system. But for all there is humiliation. They are ordered around and herded about by powerful prison officers and are at the mercy of brutal inmates from whom they cannot be protected all the time. This even applies to those on rule 43 – segregated at their own request from non-rule 43 prisoners, usually because they are in for sex offences and so liable to be attacked by other prisoners who call them 'nonces'.

All prisoners are cut off, wholly or partly, from the things they cherish. Their job, if any, is probably lost. Family life is interrupted and threatened, normal sex forbidden. They cannot go out to the pub, though alcohol and drugs are available in prison at a price. And above all, prison life is boring.

There can be problems on one's release, as even Gerald Ronson will have found. Any hopes of an honour or title will have crumbled. He may be shunned in the 'best' society circles, even though the Queen Mother shook hands with him at an opera performance. His good character has gone, and even in the cut-throat world of commerce that means something. Who would now employ Ernest Saunders in a responsible position? If he had retained his liberty, the offences would not have carried such a stigma. Once he has been inside, the prison tag never entirely leaves a man.

Those distasteful features of gaol have consequences. Although some do not fear it, almost all wish to avoid it and will accept any alternative. The one question most defendants want to ask at court is, 'Will I go to prison?' If a man can be assured he will not, he relaxes and breathes easily again. He does not mind a fine; payments are tailored to the pocket, are usually by instalments, and if he is on state benefits they will be little more than nominal. Community service is irksome for the lazy and wilful – which most prisoners are – but preferable to prison.

Probation by itself means little: an occasional thirty minutes with a probation officer. I preferred probation orders to have conditions, such as being required to attend for up to sixty days a day centre where structured work is done in such areas as awareness of self and others, rights and advice, offence avoidance, literacy and numeracy, parenting, values, beliefs and attitudes, use of leisure, health and safety, housing and accommodation, job search, living alone, personal communication, sex and sexuality, and cooking for survival.

An absolute discharge means there is no punishment at all. A conditional discharge means that if for the prescribed period – usually one or two years – no additional crime is committed, the offender hears no more about it; but if there is a further offence within the period he can be recalled and sentenced afresh. A conditional discharge is no hardship in the mind of the defendant when he receives it. Likewise suspended sentences, which I do not like. To say to an offender, 'You should go to prison for six months, but you're not going to. I shall suspend it for two years,' is an absurdity. If he deserves to go immediately, he should. Some say that by passing such a 'sentence' the court somehow expresses the community's disapproval for the crime. But the public is not so naïve. People are interested in what actually happens to the defendant.

The suspended sentence is a Home Office device for reducing prison overcrowding, but one of its results is to reduce respect for the courts. Another is that, on balance, overcrowding may not be reduced: when a sentence is suspended there is a tendency to make it longer than it would otherwise be, yet it may have to be served later when added to a new sentence for another offence. I had one man before me who was subject to three suspended sentences, all passed by magistrates on different occasions and running at the same time. He must have thought – until I sentenced him – that the courts really had gone soft.

No one will ever prove how much crime has been caused by Home Office weakness, but I believe it has had an effect. The criminal fraternity may be fools in many respects, but they catch on to such matters; they know all about parole, remission and suspended sentences. For my part I learned to act on the assumption that a fair proportion of actual and potential offenders are affected in the way they treat others by the likely sentence if they are caught. Many are gamblers and, if they think they will escape detection, the likely sentence is no deterrent. But would anyone say that thought and conduct in the City had been unaffected by the sentences in the Guinness case? Would anyone seriously contend that, if prisons were abolished for house burglary, the figures would not leap? Imprisonment is the main weapon that judges have when dealing with serious crime. We know penal institutions are not run properly, but we have no control over that. Loss of freedom is the big gun in our attempt to punish the wicked, deter the wavering and contain the incorrigible. And there is no other way to compel a recalcitrant to obey court orders.

Some say that prisoners, especially young ones, learn about crime while inside. There is something in this, but it has been exaggerated. Most detainees come from a community where they mix with wrong-doers. And when doing community service or attending a day centre they rub shoulders with such people. It is true that in prison they have more time for idle chatter. But if a defendant said to me, 'Don't send me where I'll learn new criminal ways,' I would reply, 'Then I'll send you there for longer, to delay putting your new knowledge into practice.' However, I admit the need to treat prison as a last resort, and agree that constructive non-custodial methods should be tried first.

There has been controversy about remands in custody. Such people, especially when under twenty-one, should not be held in prisons at all but in separate remand centres. Critics go further and point to the injustice of locking up the unconvicted. They say that in court a large proportion either get off or do not get a prison sentence. I heard many bail applications after magistrates had refused them, and I rejected about 90 per cent. In most cases they were already alleged on prima-facie evidence to have offended on bail at least once in the present proceedings; to have granted them bail again would have been like issuing a licence to commit crime. They usually have lengthy records, which sometimes include absconding while on bail. So if it is considered that an applicant is likely to commit further offences, abscond or interfere with witnesses, bail has to be refused. As for the argument that some do not receive a prison sentence, that may be because they have already been in custody for several months awaiting trial; if they had been allowed bail, they would eventually have gone to prison.

Whatever else is done with prison regimes, priority must be given to improving conditions. A circuit judge, Stephen Tumim, is HM Chief Inspector of Prisons – an imaginative appointment. His 1989 report to the Home Secretary reveals that he has a deputy, a staff officer, two teams of inspectors (each including two prison governors and a principal officer), a specialist inspector of buildings, a specialist in medical matters, a research consultant, a secretariat of seven and a driver. Full inspections usually last from Monday to Thursday, but are not unannounced. In 1989, twenty-one gaols received full inspections; twenty-two had visits, seventeen of them being 'short'. The report contained some illuminating details. In Birmingham the bath-house used by convicted men was seriously damaged and infected by cockroaches and rats. The spartan and basic slopping-out conditions at Wandsworth Prison were accepted by inmates and staff as standard. Inmates saw them as part of the package for being in a 'hard' prison. Many staff took the view that such conditions kept inmates in their place.

By the year 2000 the Home Office intend to provide incell sanitation or twenty-four hour access to sanitation for all except eight thousand prisoners. A surprising number of establishments were found to suffer from leaking roofs, even in newer buildings. The older prisons, not all dating back to the last century, had extensive areas of brickwork in need of repointing. Very few of the managers of the prisons visited by Tumim had a clear view of the developments to buildings or land which would be needed in the future. He considers each inmate should have his own cell with a bed, table, locker and chair, but to spend twenty-four hours a day alone in his cell would be inhuman. In Birmingham Prison nearly six hundred inmates, convicted and unconvicted, were housed three to a cell. There was not enough space for each to have a chair, locker and table. Meals were eaten sitting on beds. Dormitories, housing an even larger number of prisoners, provide no privacy, peace or quiet and can give rise to bullying, theft and physical abuse; but they usually have toilets and sinks to which there is twenty-four hour access.

The inspectorate has recommended that inmates at Ford Open Prison, where the Guinness Three – Saunders, Ronson and Anthony Parnes – went, should each have their own TV set. For the last few years all French gaols have been cabled for colour TV, which can be hired, and this has transformed the prisons. Inmates are ready to work in order to pay to hire sets; television calms minds which would otherwise be bored or planning mischief. In one French prison, the use of tranquillisers dropped by 70 per cent after this innovation; violence, suicide and self-inflicted injuries also decreased.

The availability of work for English prison inmates varied remarkably, according to the 1989 report. At Wandsworth Prison, only 560 of the 1550 prisoners were usefully employed. But at Strangeways Prison in Manchester, work was available for all but 300 of the 1600 inmates. The reasons for Wandsworth's poor position were given as shortage of discipline staff to supervise workshops and the diversion of officer instructors to discipline duties. This led to workshops becoming unprofitable and so being closed.

Low Newton, a remand centre for men under twenty-one, found work for virtually everyone. At Pucklechurch, a women's remand centre, employment opportunities were few and limited to kitchen and general cleaning duties. Even training prisons had problems. Ranby (short- and medium-term training and lifers) and Wayland (medium- and long-term and lifers) had excellent workshop facilities, but staffing difficulties, shortage of work and 'poor inmate motivation' (in other words, very bad wages) resulted in low production. Despite their best efforts, many prisoners receive as pay considerably less than the pocket money given to those in local authority residential accommodation. Kitchen staff are the highest paid at about £5 per week, but they earn this by very long hours and no day off. New pay scales are being considered. The prison service is almost self-sufficient in vegetables, dairy produce and meat. An inmate who learns to drive a tractor can be certificated and so qualify for similar work on building sites.

Association – inmates mixing with each other – when it takes place, normally runs from after tea to between 8 p.m. and 9 p.m. Depending on staff availability, some inmates may be offered association in the afternoon and sometimes during the whole weekend. What is available on association varies enormously, but in general inmates can watch TV, play small board games, snooker or pool, visit each other's cells and have their hair cut.

Now let's take a look at prison life from a different angle – a prisoner's. I have been corresponding with one whom I never sentenced, but who wrote to me after reading *Straight from the Bench*. Mark Leech is a remarkable man: well above average intelligence, articulate and with insight. I am much indebted for what follows and have modified my views in the light of his, which he kindly sent me in detail. Now I am trying to help him in his efforts to prepare himself for a better life on his release from prison than he has had so far. He has had articles published in the *Guardian*, and written a radio play as well as his autobiography; I have given him advice in these areas based on my (limited) experience. Mark agreed with Donald West, who wrote in *Delinquency: Its Roots, Careers and Prospects*, that it is not difficult to predict which ten-year-old boys are going to get in trouble with the law. In a study of the backgrounds of four hundred males aged between eight and twenty-four, West identified the following key factors contributing to criminality:

1. A low family income.
2. Membership of a large family in which parents were identified by social workers as being bad at raising children.
3. Parents who were themselves criminals or possessed a criminal record.
4. Low intelligence through non-attendance at school or poor educational opportunities.

When Mark tested this by questioning one hundred fellow inmates at Blundeston Prison, Lowestoft, he found that:

1. 83 came from large families on low income or state benefits.
2. 76 were from large families where at least one parent had a criminal record – 23 had both parents with records.
3. 79 had no formal educational qualities at all.
4. 84 completed their education in an institution such as approved school or Borstal.
5. 52 could not read properly and 21 not at all.
6. 93 of them came from inner cities such as London, Birmingham, Manchester or Liverpool.

Mark is now thirty-four and has spent twenty years in institutions. He is the youngest child of Roman Catholic parents. His brothers and sisters, who are between ten and twenty-one years older than him, have done well in life. His mother was forty-six when he was born, unwanted, and he was often palmed on to his siblings to be looked after – which they resented. He used to hear his parents arguing during the night. Mark was regularly beaten by his mother, brothers and sisters. He says he committed his first crime at the age of six when he threw into the fire the wooden spoon with which he had often been beaten. Two years later he found his mother dead on the floor; he shed no tears for her. The family then broke up and his father took to drink.

Mark was put into local authority care at ten and sent to a boarding school where a house-master sexually abused him on four nights a week for three years. He kept absconding and on one occasion took a bicycle, for which he was sent to an approved school. He did not trust adults and had become anti-authority. Next came Borstal, where he says he learned everything from how to steal cars to chequebook fraud. He has had six prison sentences. He went to Dartmoor in 1981 and twice since then: he spent more than four years there, finding the regime oppressive and brutal. In 1982 there was an extensive police inquiry into assaults by prison officers at that prison. Mark went back there in February 1984 from

Long Lartin, where he had taken part in a twelve-day roof-top protest. At Dartmoor he was put in the punishment block. Within a week he was involved in a mini-riot caused, he says, by a prison officer assaulting a prisoner. Two staff and three inmates were injured.

In October 1986, after five years in which Mark had 'given them hell and had been brutalised beyond belief', he was suddenly released from his punishment cell into the outside world. Within a few days, using false documents, he obtained a job as an area manager for a security company. Five weeks later he was appointed head of security for a large company. He had risen from a prison wage of £2.50 a week to £22,000 a year. Then he burned down the firm's computer room and while on the run he made a hoax call to a mountain rescue team in Scotland. All this led to a six-year sentence which he had almost completed when I met him for the first time in June 1991. Two days later he absconded from prison and was on the run for several weeks before giving himself up. His parole had to be postponed.

The turning-point in Mark's life came when he was sent to Grendon Underwood Prison in May 1989. During the previous two years in prison he had decided to reform; he had not had a single disciplinary report, whereas during his last sentence in the same period he had had eighty. Grendon is situated in pleasant countryside eleven miles west of Aylesbury in Buckinghamshire. Opened in 1962, it marked a major change in penal thinking. All the inmates are volunteers, and they can return to their sending prison whenever they wish. Normal treatment lasts between eighteen and twenty-four months, but a fair number do not stay the course for so long and either choose to leave or are voted out by the inmates for breaking the rules against drugs, sex, violence, drinking or gambling.

A prisoner who applies to go to Grendon is subjected to a searching period of scrutiny. If selected for it, he spends two months in the assessment unit where potential 'Therapeutons' have to undergo educational, intelligence and psychological tests. They are also required to present their life story to the inmates of the assessment unit at one of their weekly meetings. Mark says of it: 'Presentation can be a harrowing experience, for not only can it result in discussion of experiences long since locked away and painful to recount (for example, sexual abuse as a child) but it is frequently the first of many face-to-face sessions with reality that people have to experience in Grendon as part and parcel of their daily life in therapy.'

The staff meet at the end of the two-month assessment. They consider the results of the tests and the candidate's commitment to change as demonstrated by him. A vote is taken as to whether he should be accepted for therapy. If he is rejected he returns to his prison of origin. If he is accepted he is allocated to one of the four therapeutic wings known as 'communities'. Each is split into five groups of eight for therapy, and this forms the backbone of the Grendon regime. The group meets three times a week for an hour, and the community as a whole meets twice a week. Each community has its own policies and ways of doing things.

On B Wing, where Mark was, a new arrival is allocated a group and a sponsor – an experienced member who guides him through the first two weeks of therapy. A reception board is held within twenty-four hours, consisting of the chairman (an inmate) and a member of each group. Soon after that the new arrival goes to a staff group meeting, consisting of all the uniformed discipline staff, probation officers, psychiatrists and psychologists who are attached to the wing. He has to sign a 'treatment contract' which binds him to the major policies of the wing.

Every Grendon inmate is directly answerable to his group and to the whole community for his behaviour and attitude. If he intimidates others or does not show consideration for others' feelings, he can be 'grouped' by any member of the community. He then has to discuss the incident at the next group meeting or answer to the wing where, if his commitment is in question, he may be voted out of Grendon.

Group meetings, at which there is no smoking, eating or drinking, can be heated. Mark says that coming face-to-face with your faults and problems in a brutally frank way can be a painful experience.

Group therapy is a very hard way by which to realise the effects you have on others, and I learned from my time there that there can be no more ruthless examination of behaviour than that carried out by one's peers. On a number of occasions I have stormed out of group meetings (known at Grendon as 'throwing the dolly out of the pram') only to realise that I went there to change, and no one promised me it would be a bed of roses. The forthright manner of group therapy helped to build a strong bond between members of a group and the relationship can be quite caring.

In addition to the main therapeutic wings, Grendon has an acute psychiatric unit for severely disturbed and potentially violent prisoners who are waiting for a place in a special hospital. Mark worked there as a cleaner. He wrote of one morning cleaning a large floor and talking to a cheerful twenty-three-year-old West Indian serving life for the rape and murder of an old woman. That man had spent the whole of the previous day in a strip-cell after having an argument with another patient.

Like all patients in that unit, he is volatile and has to be treated with care. The unit's staff are on first-name basis with everyone, as are all the Grendon staff. I have come to admire the way in which they do their work in an atmosphere which is both stressful and demanding. The vast majority of the psychiatric unit staff are externally qualified in general or psychiatric nursing, and often both. Sadly that cannot be said of the hospital officers in other penal establishments.

Mark described for me a typical day's routine at Grendon:

7.45 a.m.: Cell door unlocked. Breakfast.
8.30 a.m. to 11.20 a.m.: Work.
11.40 a.m.: Lunch.
1 p.m.: Exercise. Mark used to jog around the yard and lost three stone in weight.
2.45 p.m.: A community meeting (not daily) to discuss whether X should have home leave, for example. Inmates vote and it is later considered by the staff group.
4.30 p.m.: Tea.
5 p.m.: Inmates vote which TV programmes to watch.
8.45 p.m.: Mark collects a flask of hot water and returns to his cell, where he keeps a budgerigar named Eddie the Eagle. He reads and listens to the radio.
11 p.m.: Lights out.

There are only three hundred places there for a prison population approaching fifty thousand. None of the new prisons being built are on Grendon lines.

Having experienced every type of incarceration, Mark Leech believes our prison system has to be moved from its basis of 'Wake up. Unlock. Slop out. Bang up' to a situation where prisoners have to think for themselves, question their own behaviour and work towards change. Referring to the present system, he says:

From the very moment that the prisoner arrives at the prison, he is thrust into a sharply polarised regime where, simply in order to survive on a day-today basis, he is forced to circumvent the rules. He learns to respect authority by being placed in a cell for twenty-three hours a day with two others he probably does not know but is forced to live with. His toilet facilities consist of a plastic bucket, and he is forced to watch as others use it then throw the contents out of the window. He is placed on reports for breaching of rules he has probably never seen and is told do not exist. He is placed in solitary confinement after a hearing which the High Court has revealed falls far below standards of fairness. He may be hundreds of miles from his family and friends, and sees a probation officer once in a blue moon.

Typical prison days, according to Mark, are like this:

> *Local prisons:* Locked in a cell for twenty-three hours with one or two others. A video may be shown at weekends and two at Christmas.
> *Training and dispersal prisons:*
> *8 a.m.:* Cells unlocked. Breakfast.
> *9 a.m.:* Work.
> *11.15 a.m.:* Lunch.
> *Noon:* Cells locked.
> *1. 15 p.m.–4.15 p.m.:* Work. Return to wing, collect tea.
> *5 p.m.:* Cells locked.
> *6 p.m.–8 p.m.:* Association, gymnasium, evening classes.

Mark states that conditions in local prisons are better imagined than described.

> Slopping out filth and human waste is never a pleasant task, as any nurse will tell you. But you have five hundred men in an old Victorian prison (A Wing at Strangeways, for example) and they are all attempting to do the same. And they have just four sluices for all of them, and not more than fifteen minutes to complete the task. Add to that the fact that this takes place within five minutes of getting out of bed, and you can almost begin to understand what it is like and imagine the ammonia-like stench which permeates the whole wing – and then everyone goes for breakfast.

I agree with the following points made by Mark:

Telephones: Category B prison inmates have no access at present, as the Prison Officers' Association feel it would undermine security. Yet in Scottish prisons, except for Peterhead, there are pay phones in each wing.

Censorship of letters: The reading by staff of prisoners' letters is a waste of time; prisoners cannot express their feelings to their loved ones.

Visits: These should be more frequent and for longer than the current thirty minutes allowed. Conjugal visits should be introduced, whereby a man can have sex with his wife or girlfriend. (My comment: to deprive a man of heterosexual activity for long periods not only encourages homosexuality but builds up frustration.)

'Democracy': Except at Grendon, inmates are not involved in running their prison. If they ran their wings through committees, many disputes could be resolved.

Clothing: Women are allowed to wear their own clothes, but men are not. There is no logical distinction.

Probation officers: Every prison has its resident probation team seconded from the local service. In theory they are there to help in the reform process and to pass on their expertise to staff and inmates. But probation is under-resourced. Officers in prison do little more than make phone calls and write reports. They could hold group discussions on offending behaviour with specialist groups for lifers, alcoholics and drug addicts. But very few such groups are held. 'Welfare' should be carried out by prison staff. It would help to forge relationships between the two sides that are currently so far apart. This would free probation officers for group work and other reform-based activities. More than three years into his current sentence, Mark's parole reports were being compiled for the third and final time, yet how often had he met the man who is to be his probation officer if he does get parole? Once, for thirty minutes, two years ago.

Surely it is time to consider not only who should go to

prison and for how long, but what should happen to prisoners while they are inside. I believe Mark Leech's experience and views point to the way ahead. Meanwhile, judges have no control over those whom they have sentenced. They know about prison overcrowding, and Home Office pressure to reduce it by shorter or non-custodial sentences. They have wider considerations, however, and I now turn to them.

What should judges do about crime? It is tempting to suggest we should all resign and give way to more educated, enlightened and representative people. We have seen how ill-equipped we are. Judges come from a narrow, white, middle-class segment, and are dominated by men who have been to certain public schools and Oxbridge.

There is no more insular and self-satisfied group of people than English judges, and the higher they climb, the worse they are. On the Bench I tried to regard myself as accountable, not to the Lord Chancellor, Lord Chief Justice or the system but to the public as a whole, or its right-thinking members.

Most judges go on doing things with a zombie-like insouciance. They behave as they always have. Any novelty is heresy. Innovations are wrong, by definition, because 'British justice is the best in the world'. Those who say and believe that do not hear the guffaws that this remark draws forth around the world, especially in Ireland and even in large sections of our own island. Judges continue to pass customary sentences without knowing why, or caring to ask. When I had correspondence with Lord Lane in 1981 concerning my 'Whitelaw speech', I sent him copies of addresses I had given to magistrates. They contained fairly elementary propositions about crime and how to deal with it, but Lord Lane was evidently impressed because he wrote: 'I am most grateful to you for your long and interesting letter and the enclosures, which I have read and intend to read again more

214

carefully when I have a bit of time to spare. It is only fair to say that I agree with almost everything you said.'

Lord Lane has never had to think out penal policy. He has run the system in the way it has always been run – pragmatically. He is there to keep the monster of a machine running along the existing track, not to divert it or even overhaul it. And he is one of the nicer, blander, more amenable judges. Let me try in my humble, halting way, to do what Lord Lane and other senior judges should be doing, by going back to first principles.

The essence of criminal law is to protect A from harm by B that A (being a sane adult) has not consented to. 'Victimless' crimes have to be looked at carefully. The law should not try to protect A from harm he chooses to inflict on himself. Unfortunately, owing to past hang-ups still lingering on, our present law does that. Examples are drugs, pornography and prostitution. Fresh thinking is needed in those areas. I do not claim originality, but here are my thoughts.

Making drugs illegal drives up the prices. It becomes profitable to import and push drugs. Users have to commit crime to pay pushers. That causes four out of ten property crimes in the USA. If drugs were decriminalised, the prison population would fall. There would be nothing in it for pushers. We would know who the addicts were and treat them as patients, instead of chasing them into back alleys where they use dirty needles and impure drugs. If a person became dangerous to others through addiction, that would be an offence. That is the point at which the law should intervene. An addict could be sent to an institution for treatment.

I would start by decriminalising cannabis, as Holland and eight American states have. Since 1976 it has been available in five hundred coffee shops in Holland. Yet is that country full of stoned people? There has been no increase in its use there since the early 1970s. Only 2 per cent of ten to eighteen-year-olds smoke it; only 6 per cent of them have tried it. If the experiment with cannabis succeeded, I would go on to decriminalise other drugs. Preferably this would be done by international agreement, or Britain might become a mecca for drug users. We also have treaty obligations concerning drugs.

I am a libertarian. The state should not dictate to us on matters of taste or morals. Adults should be free to choose how to use or abuse their bodies, provided they do not harm an unwilling adult or a child. This also applies to so-called pornography and prostitution.

As for children, they are essentially the responsibility of their parents or guardians. A child has to be protected until he is old enough to make his own decisions. But beware of the argument that 'this magazine or photo must be banned because children might get hold of it'. That is an argument which can be used to ban anything.

'Enlightened firmness' expressed my attitude when sitting in the crown court. If a defendant left court laughing, feeling he had got away with it, then I had failed. But judging is like batting at cricket. A good batsman treats every ball differently, according to its merits. A judge who is tough or soft on principle is a bad judge. All the facts and factors have to be fed into the mental computer, and then almost automatically the appropriate sentence – as it seemed to me at the time – emerged. I had in front of me the prosecution witnesses' statements in the case, including what the defendant said when questioned by the police. There was a list of any previous convictions and sentences: it was vital to know what non-custodial sentences he had had in the past. Almost always there was a social inquiry report by a probation officer, detailing the defendant's early life, difficulties, jobs, relationships and response to probation, with a recommendation as to sentence.

On a guilty plea the defendant hardly ever gives evidence, so he cannot be assessed by the judge as he is if he pleads not guilty and gives evidence. Yet I had to peer into his mind. Through his counsel he insisted he was sorry, had decided to reform and would never offend again. How many times had he said that before? He may even have believed it as he stood there, his heart beating fast, facing the man who held the future in his hands. The past may hold the key to his future. If a defendant has thrown away chances in the past, he is likely to do the same again – though we must remember Mark Leech and those who eventually do reform. If a man has not had a chance for some time, now may be the time to try a non-custodial sentence – especially one such as attendance at a structured day centre as a condition of probation, which will show him how to improve himself. I often took a risk with a man in that situation, especially if the present offences were not that serious.

We all change our minds: we have one attitude or aspiration today and another tomorrow. That is particularly true for the offenders who have never had to sit down and sort out their thoughts or redirect their lives. They have not been brought up or educated properly. They have lived their lives from one disordered day to the next, their steps not being guided, their futures not planned. They have been swept along with their peers, indulging themselves today with no thought of tomorrow. So we try to give them a helping hand, but there are limits to that. The time comes when they have to be treated as sane adults who can make choices and must accept the consequences.

There is an assumption in defending counsel's speeches in mitigation that basically every defendant aims to live an honest life, and his present predicament represents a temporary aberration: underneath he wishes to be as honest and industrious as the rest of society. This is fallacious. Some offenders have no wish to go straight and despise those who do. They are not necessarily professional criminals, equipped for and planning activities like an organised business. Most defendants are aimless drifters who, from

217

time to time, are tempted by circumstances and by other people to take part in crime and are too weak to say no. There is some hope for them. Statistics show that most crime is committed by young men. They may grow out of it, fearful of losing home, job, partner and children by being sent away again. So prison and the fear of going back plays a vital part in their reform.

Punishment should fit the criminal as well as the crime. The Criminal Justice Bill, introduced by Home Secretary David Waddington in November 1990, was originally to have set down that a judge should generally disregard a defendant's previous convictions when sentencing. Happily, after judges and magistrates had strongly protested, this was watered down. Courts will be able to take into account the 'circumstances' of past offences. Relevant factors can include whether previous crime involved violence or the threat of violence. Mr Waddington said the bill was a 'balanced package' designed to satisfy the public's demand for exemplary penalties for criminals such as rapists, murderers and drug traffickers, and the need for more property offenders to be saved from hardening and costly jail sentences.

But the distinction he made between offences involving violence and those involving property was a false one. Was the Home Secretary saying house-burglars should not go to gaol? If so, he was profoundly and dangerously wrong. Such offences, which are increasing, represent a gross intrusion which causes enormous fear, damage and loss, whether there is someone at home or not. Bogus officials who trick their way into old persons' homes and steal their savings may not use violence, but they have to go to prison.

The Court of Appeal has in recent years tended to fall for the notion that a man is not to have his past offences held against him. As an example, extended sentences – which are longer than the normal maximum or the normal 'tariff' – have virtually fallen into disuse. Under the 1973 Criminal Courts Act, where an offender is convicted of an offence punishable with imprisonment for two years or more, and where because of his previous convictions the judge considers he is likely to commit further offences and the public need to be protected from him for a substantial time, an extended sentence may be passed. I favour this approach, but on the few occasions on which I adopted it the extended sentence appears to have been set aside by the Appeal Court. A defendant's war on society should be looked at as a whole. If he is a menace to others when at liberty, he should be put away for a long period where he cannot do harm. Lord Chief Justice Goddard would not have let extended sentences wither away, as the last few LCJs have.

Whatever else is said about prison, while an offender is inside we outside are safe from him. At present we almost encourage him in his criminal ways. The risk of detection is slight. If an arrested man keeps his mouth shut, he may never be prosecuted. If he does go to court, the system is loaded in his favour. There is always a chance, with a jury. Then there is the Court of Appeal, to say nothing of the Parole Board.

So when should an offender lose his liberty? I think in the following cases:

1. To punish for wickedness. By wickedness I mean a deliberate decision by a clear mind to do a criminal act, knowing that it will substantially harm another. A decision is not deliberate if made spontaneously. A goes to B in a pub and without a word strikes him, perhaps mistaking him for someone else against whom he has a grievance. B does not expect it, but happens to be holding a glass in his hand as he instinctively strikes back at A. He may be acquitted for self-defence. If not, prison may be inappropriate. But if B deliberately smashed his glass on a table and then went for A, that would be wicked and merit imprisonment. Kicking someone who is lying on the ground is always wicked. Suppose a mind is unclear through drink? We often say

219

drink is no excuse, but it can be a mitigating factor. Not if a defendant drank to give himself courage to commit the offence, or before going to a football match where he knew there might be trouble. But in the above example, B standing there affected by drink had no means of knowing that A would attack him, and so his less than clear mind is in his favour on sentence.

2. To deter – usually others, but possibly this defendant also. Some clever criminologists – who have a few things to teach us – say there is no evidence that long sentences are a deterrent. I believe some people are deterred from some crimes because of sentences they have had or have heard about. This cannot normally be proved, but I have a piece of 'anecdotal' evidence (how the criminologists will scoff at me for that!). In 1969 at Leeds quarter sessions I sentenced the 'King of the Cop' to a total of thirty months' imprisonment for assaulting two police officers at Leeds United's football ground. The case had wide publicity: it was the first time I had featured prominently in the national media. Later the police gave me figures for arrests at United's home games, and there was a startling drop after my sentence. I happened to meet the 'King of the Cop' on a radio programme in 1986. He said he had learnt his lesson. The short sentences he had received previously had done no good. Since my sentence he has continued to attend matches, but he has been very careful not to get involved in violence.

Recently I was upheld by the Court of Appeal in a case where the appellant had sold T-shirts which he knew were illegal copies of copyright shirts. He made his situation worse by selling a consignment after the enforcement officer had been to his premises. I sentenced him to six months in gaol. The news of it must have passed round that particular community of traders within hours. Does anyone deny there would be a deterrent effect upon them or some of them? Conversely, a non-custodial sentence such as a fine would have come as a relief or even encouragement. Dishonest traders would have thought, 'If we do get caught we can always buy our way out of it.'

3. As punishment for defiance of a court order. Some people will not do as they have been ordered if they are merely talked at for disobedience. If they get away with it, others follow suit and, ultimately, law enforcement breaks down. That is why at present a defendant who fails to pay a fine, although he has the means, goes to prison. A person who is ordered to come to court to testify can be gaoled if he refuses. Failure to do community service properly must lead to imprisonment, or that excellent scheme would have no teeth and few would attend. I put driving while disqualified in the same category, though magistrates before whom most such cases come do not appear to. Most courts accept that refusal to carry out a condition in a probation order about attending a day centre, or the commission of a further offence during the order, usually merits loss of liberty.

4. Where a dangerous criminal has shown it is not safe to leave him at large. He may not have a long record. Ian Brady, the Moors Murderer, is too dangerous ever to be released; Peter Sutcliffe, the Yorkshire Ripper, is in the same category.

Partial loss of liberty is developing as a concept without anyone spelling it out. It makes sense: prison is expensive and disrupts an inmate's life severely. So can there be loss of liberty which will be cheaper and less disruptive yet achieve the same aims? Can partial loss of liberty punish, deter and contain? To some extent, yes. Where it can, it should be used instead of imprisonment, or as an adjunct to it: a prison sentence need not be as long as it might be if it is to be followed by partial loss of liberty. Partial loss takes, or could take these forms: extended community service, curfew, electronic tag and tracking. Let's look at them in more detail.

At present community service is done a few hours at a time, to fit in with the offender's other commitments.

Houses are painted, gardens dug or rubbish cleared. Although the scheme is run by the probation service, there is no supervision except of the work itself. It must be irksome, but can hardly be called punishment.

But if an offender had to work for a period of several months, five days a week between 9 a.m. and 5 p.m. in factory-type conditions, this might be regarded as a suitable alternative to gaol. There would have to be no scope for slacking. There would be no pay; the offender would be unable to do any other work and would receive state benefits on an unemployed basis. His life would not be totally disrupted, and the scheme would be much cheaper than prison. An all-day Saturday and all-day Sunday order would be appropriate in cases where a man had a job he ought not to lose. This could be a suitable punishment for driving with excess alcohol on a second or third occasion, or for a soccer hooligan not of the worst type. The Home Office is supposed to have plans for an extended scheme on these lines, which I suggested in my previous book, but I have not yet seen it in operation.

I also suggested curfews and the Home Office plans to introduce this idea as part of a sentence. As I pointed out, we sometimes make a curfew a condition of bail – the defendant must not leave home between, say, 7 p.m. and 7 a.m. – but not as part of a sentence or a condition of parole. The problem is that a curfew is not policed. No one calls at the house to ensure the defendant is there, and the defendant knows this. Only if a police officer happens to see a person who he knows is breaching his curfew or is arrested for a further offence do the breaches come to light. The curfew could be extended into 'house arrest'. If it were possible to contain a man in his house and only let him leave within specified hours, with specified people and to go to specified places, that would be some guarantee against criminal activity. Regular checks would have to be made, however, by a special corps similar to traffic wardens: an ideal job for an ex-police officer, though he would not need to be young or highly trained.

The idea of the electronic tag came from America, and is a means of ensuring that an offender adheres to a curfew. A 'manacle' is placed on the defendant's ankle. It sends out continuous signals which are passed by a short-range transmitter in his home to a communications centre monitored by private security guards. There is a 'Big Brother' aspect to this, though a defendant is much less restricted and watched than in gaol. If he leaves home or tries to remove the anklet, an alarm sounds. A £500,000 pilot scheme in London, Nottingham and Tyneside was unsuccessful. A report from the Association of Chief Probation Officers said that suspects in two of the projects preferred to remain in custody. They realised that time remanded in prison would be taken into account if they later received a prison sentence, whereas time spent at home tagged would not.

The Home Office planned to have 150 defendants awaiting trial tagged, but magistrates found only fifty who were suitable. Of those, eleven committed further offences before their trial and seventeen breached their curfew. In only seven cases was the tagging a success; and a man was alleged to have been involved in a killing while wearing an anklet. Two Scotsmen in London obeyed the curfew until they were interviewed on TV about it; then they blew their appearance money on a West End pub crawl and were arrested a few days later. It seems that in parts of America where tags have succeeded they were mostly fitted to minor offenders, such as those convicted of motoring offences and living in comfortable, middle-class homes. The Home Office scheme was applied to those who would normally have been remanded in prison, including poor young men whose chaotic lives did not fit in with house arrest. Curfews of twenty hours a day or more meant that a significant number of unemployed people confined to the house lost benefit because they were unavailable for work. So far so bad, but I would not rule out tagging altogether.

Tracking is an old name for what is now called the Leeds Intensive Supervision Programme (LISP). As with electronic tags, the original name had too much of a 'Big Brother' association, I believe. Tracking was started in 1985 as one of two pilot schemes. LISP is a very useful alternative to custody, and involves a partial loss of liberty to the offender. I used it more than once. LISP is for people of twenty-one or over facing more than six months in gaol. The offender is assessed after expressing remorse, a wish to change and willingness to work on his offending behaviour. Intensive supervision lasts for a maximum of sixty days within the first six months of a probation order. The programme is individually tailored for each offender. Although contact is for a minimum of one hour per day – but often much longer – at the outset offenders are expected to account for their behaviour, and to plan and have their activities approved every day in advance, in order to avoid situations in which they might re-offend.

During the assessment, usually a period of twenty-eight days, an offender is seen six times a week by a programme worker. He is expected to keep appointments with the latter, stick to a programme agreed daily with the programme worker, and not to deviate from it without the knowledge and agreement of the programme worker. A 'contract' of aims is commenced, and the offender is expected to attend any meetings the liaison officer or probation officer convenes, work permitting. At the end of the assessment period a report is produced for the court.

From January to October 1990, LISP orders were made in 45 per cent of the cases where it had been recommended. If the court takes that course, initially contacts with the programme are high, and the offender may be expected to give a daily programme on four or more days a week. There are regular reviews with the offender, programme worker, probation officer and liaison officer. Throughout Intensive

Supervision, requirements are strictly adhered to. Any failure to comply may be dealt with by a verbal and written warning or a return to court depending on the seriousness. Non-cooperation results in the court being asked to sentence again for the original offence and discharge the probation order.

Analysis of LISP orders between January and October 1990 shows that 91 per cent of offenders were male; 41 per cent were aged between twenty-one and twenty-five; 23 per cent had been convicted for violence; the same percentage for house burglary; 21 per cent for non-house burglary; and the same percentage for theft. All had previous convictions.

I received 'ending reports' on offenders who had done 'adult tracking' – when it was still called that – and here is one: 'John Smith' was twenty-one and had been convicted of two offences of taking a vehicle without consent, two of theft, and receiving stolen goods. Smith's 'identified issues' were:

Alcohol: He had kept to his agreement by not going to night clubs and being home at midnight. He did not drink often because his budget did not stretch far, but he still had a problem. He drank far too much when he did go out, and this was the reason for his last breach.

Friends: He still kept in touch with his past associates, maintaining that they did not lead him astray. He said that some of his past friends had been to see him and asked him to carry out burglaries, but he had declined.

Use of time/employment: He spent most of his time at a day centre. He had been to the Job Centre with his tracker many times, with no success; he had had three job interviews, all unsuccessful. He refused to go on training schemes, saying they were a waste of time. The tracker explained that at the end he would be better qualified and his prospects of employment far greater, but he would not listen to reason on the subject.

Accommodation: Smith had settled in well, and his home

was always clean and tidy – this was one thing he saw he had achieved.

Budgeting: He had cooperated on trying to live within his means by giving the tracker all his money on Giro days, so she could give him so much back daily. This was the only way he could make his money last until the next payment day. His probation officer had been doing this for some time, and when Smith began tracking he asked the tracker to carry it on. However, this had not helped Smith to learn to budget for himself.

Attitude: He was still determined to commit no more burglaries; he said it was not worth the risk, that in the long run crime did not pay. Though his attitude towards work was somewhat laid back, this was his top priority in life.

Thinking ahead: This had been Smith's downfall; he found it very difficult from the start, not knowing from one day to the next what he would be doing or how he would be spending his time. Again he saw the need for work, saying: 'If only I had a job.' His poor response led to his being sent back to crown court for resentencing.

Tracker's summary: 'Most of these issues need looking at again, the main one being alcohol. Though this case has been challenging and at times stale, I must say I have enjoyed working with Mr Smith and pleased to say he has got through his sixty-day condition without re-offending.'

Many people point to the *variations in sentencing* that occur in the English courts. It is impossible to eradicate this situation. No two cases are alike when you examine all the facts – which the press does not and cannot do. No two judges are alike.

Variations between English courts are nothing compared with those between different countries. The International Bar Association, which represents three million lawyers, published comparisons in September 1990. Judges and legal experts had been given hypothetical cases and asked to estimate the heaviest sentence their countries' courts would impose.

The rape of a sixteen-year-old girl at a bus stop, beaten and threatened with a knife by a twenty-seven-year-old man with a history of minor sex offences, would attract a sentence of eighteen months in Ireland, three years in Denmark, and five years in Holland and Norway. England weighed in at twenty years, while Canada, Hong Kong, Kenya, Nigeria and the United Arab Emirates would give him life.

A severe assault involving a stabbing at a party would result in a suspended sentence in Ireland, twelve months' jail in India and Norway, two years in Holland, three in Hong Kong, four in Canada, five in England, Germany and Greece, six in Spain, seven in Nigeria, ten in Texas and life in Kenya.

A twenty-four-year-old man with a record for theft who sold £26 worth of cannabis could expect a fine in Denmark, twelve months' jail in Texas, four years in Spain, ten in the United Arab Emirates, twenty-one in Nigeria and life in Hong Kong. The sentence in England is given as one year, but I consider that to be unrepresentative; I would have imposed a fine.

Sentences for a £25,000 tax fraud ranged from 'repayment' in Ireland to a large fine in New Zealand, eighteen months imprisonment in Canada, three years in Scotland, Kenya and India, ten years in Germany and ninety-nine in Texas. The sentence for England is put at three years, but I consider one year to be more likely.

A nineteen-year-old armed robber who stole £800,000 with four others in a bank raid could expect two years in Norway, five in Canada and Ireland, six in Spain, ten in Germany and Scotland, fourteen in England, twenty in Greece, ninety-nine in Texas and death in Kenya and Nigeria.

The Scandinavian courts are the most lenient sentencers, the African countries and Texas the most severe. The above figures are, however, 'gross' and there must be wide variations as to the availability of remission or parole. In practice, ninety-nine years in a Texas gaol probably works out at considerably less than that.

To indicate my approach to imposing loss of liberty while on the Bench, here are details of some cases which I decided in the crown court in 1989.

A MAN WHO ATTACKED WOMEN A, aged thirty, pleaded not guilty to two counts – one of assault occasioning actual bodily harm on a fourteen-year-old girl, and the other of common assault on a girl who was then thirteen. He invited the first girl to go for a walk with him, then tried to kiss her and held her by the arm while attempting to do so, causing bruises to the arm – which were not serious. When the other girl came upon the scene the accused spat at her. The second girl became upset while giving evidence, and in the end the prosecution decided to let those matters lie on file on the basis that A would be bound over, which he was. He promised to keep the peace for the next twelve months, on pain of paying up to £100 if he did not.

The accused then had to be dealt with by me for an offence to which he pleaded guilty – an assault causing actual bodily harm on a nineteen-year-old woman on the day following the other matters. He had seen her in the street, and because she had not met him when she had agreed to do so, he said, he had punched her once on the right cheek, causing some redness and swelling.

He told the probation officer compiling his social inquiry report that he had had a confused childhood. He had had a reasonable relationship with his mother but a poor one with his stepfather, which deteriorated as he got older, and he felt he was the family scapegoat. Social workers became involved with the family while the accused was at junior school, because of behavioural problems. At eleven he was transferred to a special school. His behaviour still caused concern and he was moved to an assessment centre. On leaving school he was unemployed until the age of seventeen when he went to Borstal, obtaining there a certificate for painting and decorating. Then he obtained work as a cleaner, and since then had had various manual jobs. From November 1988 he had been undertaking temporary work for an agency, earning an average of £90 a week. He was a single man. His mother worked as a home help and had expressed concern about her son's behaviour.

A's difficulties were in forming relationships with women. Until four years previously he had been involved in the Rastafarian religion for about nine years, although he was white; he was said to have become 'stigmatised' by local people, and his leisure time was spent playing either the guitar or keyboards. He did not attend when asked to go to the community service unit for assessment, because of 'transport difficulties'. It was suggested that we should obtain a psychiatric report. I decided, however, that the best thing in his case was to give him a sentence of eight months suspended for two years, with a two-year supervision order. His previous convictions had ended in 1979.

I told A that he had to be very careful, because there are too many attacks on women these days and he ought not to approach them in a hostile way. It was the sort of case where a suspended sentence could make him restrain himself when dealing with women. I also ordered him to pay £100 prosecution costs.

A DRUG ADDICT D, twenty-four, pleaded guilty to four offences which all took place on the same night. One involved breaking into a car in a street, causing damage valued at £432, and stealing two pair of sunglasses and a radio from it; the items were later recovered. He tried to steal from another vehicle and when he was arrested, having been seen by somebody who lived in the area, amounts of heroin and cannabis were found on him, both for his own use.

D had been dealt with in various lenient ways in the past. In 1984 and 1985 he had been fined for theft; in 1987 for possessing drugs, when a probation order was made with a condition that he should attend a drug centre for treatment. He was given community service once in 1988 for attempted burglary and again that year for actual burglary, and for the offences for which he had been put on probation he was given a total of four months' imprisonment. On 21 March 1989 he was put on two years' probation for stealing goods worth £1000 from a house.

The accused had been taken into care at birth and fostered at the age of four, but during the last ten years his attitude and behaviour had increasingly become matters for concern. He had developed a drug problem over the past six years, escalating through the use of amphetamines to heroin. There was a significant link between his drug addiction and criminal behaviour, which he seemed unable to do anything about. He had previously spent some time at one of the drug rehabilitation centres run by the charity Phoenix House, but had left there after he was put on probation. Since then he had been prescribed a reducing course of methadone which he had completed, but he did not look to the future with much optimism, realising that the majority of drug users relapse.

Over the previous four months he had been employed as a builder's labourer, his first job for several years. He saw it as a good influence in terms of his drug abuse, as it helped to keep his mind occupied. He earned £95 a week net and lived with his girlfriend. He had no debts and owed no fines.

The social inquiry report's conclusion was that over the last four years D had continued to offend periodically, the majority of offences being directly related to his drug problem. He was once again very much at risk of receiving an immediate gaol sentence, but there did appear to be other options. For the first time in many years he was working reliably and his income and expenditure were such that he could pay a fine. He had done community service in the past, but with full-time work he now felt a further order of that nature would place too great a pressure on him and it would probably be breached. The probation order had made little or no impact on D, and the probation officer suggested it be discharged.

I could not allow D his freedom, one of the reasons being that he had been on probation at the time he had committed these offences. It was a sad case of a man who was addicted to drugs and had to steal in order to supply them. If I had done something which let him remain free, it would only have reinforced his criminal activities. In my view, the effective way of deterring him was to send him to prison for nine months. When considering whether to gaol a person it is vital to know how he has responded in the past to non-custodial approaches, and this man had responded badly.

A FORTUNATE ROBBER I had to sentence twenty-year-old E for robbery and drink-driving on the same night. He was of previous good character. Soon after midnight he went to a petrol station kiosk and asked if there was a petrol can for sale, having parked his car in a nearby street. He produced, in a partially wrapped plastic bag, a ratchet and pointed it at the attendant, who thought it was a gun. The accused said: 'Give us your fucking money or I'll blow your head off.' The terrified attendant handed over £28. Two men saw what had happened and told two police officers. E's car crashed when being chased by a police car; the money was recovered. He was found to have nearly double the permitted amount of alcohol in his body.

At first I thought I would have to send him to a young offenders' institution since he was under twenty-one. His background showed that his parents' separation had caused him much confusion of loyalties during adolescence. He went with his father, who was a labourer, but after two years moved to live with his mother, who eventually remarried. E had a sound relationship with his stepfather. He left comprehensive school at sixteen, having obtained eight CSEs. After that he worked on a pig farm for a year but was then dismissed, apparently because his personality had been damaged by his parents' separation.

At the time of the offence he had just had two cheques returned by the bank and thought he did not have enough in his account to cover them. In fact it was the bank's mistake and it should not have returned the cheques.

It was pointed out in a psychiatric report that E did not show any mood disorder or any other evidence of serious mental illness; his intelligence was at least average. The offences perplexed him and he expressed considerable concern. As a result of his parents' split during his adolescence, his father had become a distant and possibly idealised figure. His two months in custody had already affected him and he displayed considerable remorse. In his normal life he showed self-discipline, and further prison training was unlikely to have a beneficial effect on him. If the court was disposed to deal with the case by means of a non-custodial sentence he would not be further exposed to figures who might influence him towards crime in the future.

E's employer, Mr R, gave evidence for him. He had employed E for three years. Before his arrest he had been his head pig-man for nine months. They knew he had had a rough family life as a youngster and that he got upset because of family circumstances. He was very keen on his work; he could not be faulted for time-keeping. His interest in his job amazed Mr R. His work was nearly equivalent to that of a vet and he virtually lived with the animals. He had never shown any signs of going off the rails and was the most kind-hearted young man Mr R had come across; he had five full-time staff and wanted E back. E had been saving while working for Mr R – first £20 a week, then £30 and then £40. Just before the robbery he had moved into a flat with his sister and a friend, and that had entailed a fair amount of expense. It was in respect of that that the two cheques had bounced. In all of the very special circumstances referred to, I decided to release E immediately. The two months he had served were sufficient. He was banned from driving for twelve months.

I read in the newspapers that the police were concerned about the leniency of my sentence. But six weeks later Mr R wrote to me:

> The real purpose of my writing, with full approval from E, is to thank you most sincerely for listening, throwing the book away and giving your personal judgement. You will be delighted to know that your trust has been upheld. E came home with me and went straight to our pig unit to see how it had fared. He is living a good, honest life. He has repaid me, at the rate of £10 a week, the money I loaned him to clear his debts, and is saving at the same rate towards another vehicle when he regains his licence. He is at present cycling nine miles each way to work daily. He sends his many thanks and good wishes for the future also from myself.

THEFT FROM EMPLOYERS T, twenty-seven, was convicted by a jury of stealing £2764 from the committee and members of a working men's club. He had been a member of the club and, as the only willing candidate, had been appointed secretary by the committee. He was paid £500 a year and held the post from February to September 1987. T attended an evening book-keeping course organised by the Club and Institute Union (to which working men's clubs are affiliated) and had taken an accountant's advice about keeping books. When T left the job a note was found addressed to the auditors, stating that he had not paid in the sum of £2764 takings from the bar, pool table and cigarette machines – but had kept the money back so as to have the club redecorated. Later he claimed the full amount to cover expenses occasioned by loss of earnings and the near-breakdown of his marriage.

When he was interviewed by police he gave a similar account. However, when he gave evidence before the jury he said he had spent £800 to pay off his mortgage arrears. He had paid £200 into the club as money he owed on a loan, while the rest he had put into a locker and left it there for several weeks, locked in the office. When he went back in September he found that the lock had been broken into and £1700 stolen.

I had to explain to the jury that dishonesty was an essential ingredient of the offence. T said he always intended to pay the money back, hopefully before its loss was discovered, and the jury must first consider whether the accused acted dishonestly by the standards of ordinary and decent people. If they found that he had done so, they had to consider whether he must have realised that what he was doing was by those standards dishonest. After being out considering their verdict for about two and a half hours, the jury pronounced him guilty.

T had no previous convictions except one when he was a juvenile for several burglaries, for which he received three months in a detention centre. At first I thought it essential that he should go to prison. He had to be punished and he and others like him had to be deterred. He had enriched himself at the expense of those who had entrusted him with the money, and I intended to gaol him for twelve months. When I came to hear from T's counsel, he said that the £2764 was now available in the form of a cheque. He had borrowed the cash from a money-lending institution, no doubt at a high rate of interest, on the security of a second mortgage on his home, and both he and his wife were working. If he went to prison he would be unable to repay the loan. He would lose his house, and I thought in all the circumstances, since he had been foolish rather than wicked and the club needed to be compensated, that I could pass a suspended sentence. As the cheque was drawn on the accused's account and various of his cheques had previously bounced, I adjourned the matter until a cheque was obtained from his solicitors. The twelve months' imprisonment was then suspended for two years.

A CLEVER THIEF O, twenty-five, pleaded guilty with another to stealing from cars. He was with another man in his vehicle when on a number of occasions he was seen observing people leave banks and go to a car. He followed that car and, if the person concerned parked nearby, he and his colleague stole from the car. On one occasion a pub landlord was seen to leave a bag of change. He went to his pub and the accused and his colleague then stole £175 and caused £60 damage to the car. Another time, a bank clerk saw O's van acting suspiciously and wrote down the number; the van was then seen going up and down as if looking for vehicles to break into. The next day the van was observed outside a bank, obviously watching it and looking for potential victims. A fish and chip shop owner went to the bank, parked, came out with £60 in change and put it into the car. The car was followed, the windscreen smashed and the £60 taken; damage of the same order was caused to the windscreen.

O had previous convictions for theft in 1979 and 1982; then at this same court, on 16 February 1989 (after the present offence), for thirteen offences of handling stolen goods he was sentenced to fifteen months' imprisonment and had since been released. He was engaged to be married and had worked in the car industry since leaving school. Before his arrest he had been working as a self-employed car salesman, but he now had a job as a panel beater and sprayer. His prison conduct was described as average, and it was said that he appeared to be adopting a low profile and trying to keep away from trouble.

The social inquiry report said that his time in prison was a sufficient deterrent and he was fully cooperating with the conditions of his parole licence. The probation officer suggested a conditional discharge because the offence did not involve violence. He had technically spent four months remanded in custody for these offences (I am not sure about that; I think he was still undergoing his fifteen months' sentence) and he was subject to the stringent conditions of a parole licence.

I decided that something more than that was needed for what was really a wicked and considered series of offences involved in the conspiracy. I ordered O to do 200 hours' community service and to pay £400 prosecution costs.

CASH IN THE ATIC P pleaded guilty to handling stolen goods. A travel company's offices were broken into and cash, travellers' cheques and currency totalling £20,000 were stolen. The same weekend the burglar apparently phoned P and arranged to leave the proceeds with him. He never came back for the goods, but according to P he had said P could have the £2385 of foreign currency, which was mainly in travellers' cheques. The accused said he had cashed only £300 worth.

P had had several previous appearances before courts – three for violence, one for burglary in 1981, and one for receiving in March 1988, when he had been fined. He had never been given a custodial sentence. He had married in 1981 and lived with his wife and child, but they had separated in the mid-eighties and divorce was pending. After first moving back with his parents he was now living with his girlfriend. He had had various jobs, but had been virtually unemployed between 1986 and 1988. For the previous few months he had been working with a roofing firm. It was permanent work and he earned £150 net a week. P had had a stress illness about three years earlier and had to take tranquillisers. Much of his spare time was spent doing DIY jobs in the house. He did weight training and went out two or three times a week, drinking up to six pints of beer. He had an offer of a job.

The social inquiry report suggested community service. I felt, despite the delay that had taken place since the offence, that it was too serious for a non-custodial approach. If there were no receivers there would be fewer burglaries. He was sentenced to nine months' imprisonment.

DID I SEND TOO MANY TO PRISON?

*

I probably did send some to prison whom I ought not to have, and some escaped who should have gone. But I did my best to get it right.

Afterword

There it is. I have said all I have to say after all my years in the law. I have tried to pass on what I have lived through and learnt. This book is my final statement – well, as final as I can make it!

The law is a fine profession. I have met some noble people, and some not so noble. I have tried to tell it as I saw it. Now it's all water under the bridge, and there are new ways to negotiate, new people to meet, new lessons to be learnt. Maybe one day I'll tell about that. For now, it is enough to look to the future – my new life, and to contribute to and learn from that.

Postscript

The hardback edition of this book, which was published in April 1992, was well received by the public. Some of them came up to me in public places and said how much they agreed with me. Press reviews were on the whole favourable, with one exception. The *Yorkshire Post* for 25 April 1992 had a review by Gilbert Gray QC that surprised me by its vitriol. We both grew up on the north-eastern circuit and were good friends; years ago we were on visiting terms. We never fell out. I conclude that Gray was the self-appointed spokesman of the legal establishment when he wrote:

'This is a book by Jimmy Pickles about Jimmy Pickles, but unfortunately he never explains why he fell in love with himself. It is a lonely book by a lonely man looking at his reflection in a forest well and wishing it were a TV set. Modesty in no way disfigures this book. What does disfigure it are the vituperative attacks on his elders and betters, page after page of the spiteful, the rancid and the inaccurate.'

The reader will decide to which of us those epithets apply. But I understand the feelings of judges and would-be judges: they resent my telling the public how the legal system fails to serve them.

Various welcome things have happened since this book appeared. Lord Chief Justice Lane retired. He is the man I called 'a dinosaur'. I shouldn't have, but it was true. He was a nice dinosaur; you couldn't have met a more pleasant one, but he stood stolidly in the path of reform, refusing to admit that anything was wrong or that there was any improvement he could make. Other welcome retirements included Lord Donaldson, the Master of the Rolls, and Law Lord Ackner. Both typified the public schools/Oxbridge dinosaurs who dominate the judiciary.

As I predicted in this book and my previous one, *Straight from the Bench*, the new Lord Chief is Peter Taylor, who came from my circuit: I know him well. He is no Establishment dinosaur. He went to a grammar school and is Jewish. He began well, by holding a press conference. Lord Lane never did that; he refused to speak to the media, regarding them as the enemy. Taylor even gave an interview to Fenton Bresler, which the *Daily Express* published on 6 August 1992. Taylor had already called for the maximum sentence for killing by reckless driving to be raised to ten years, and said that judges should be able to pass fixed-term sentences for murder instead of 'life' only. He apologised to two men wrongly convicted of murder. Lane never did that. Taylor wants judges to retire at 70 instead of 75. I agree. He has rightly criticised the new Criminal Justice Act for restricting judges' right to consider defendants' previous convictions, stating that the public might find this strange and get the impression that judges were 'going soft'.

On 17 October 1992 I went to a dinner at Middle Temple Hall in London for barristers and judges on the north-eastern circuit to celebrate Taylor's promotion and that of three other judges. Lord Taylor went out of his way to speak to me, despite the criticisms of him in this book. Gilbert Gray was absent, so the confrontation between us was post-poned: there is a price to pay for his self-indulgence.

In November 1992 Lord Taylor gave the televised Dimbleby lecture. I was disappointed. He showed the complacency I noted in him previously, and which all top judges seem to have. He asserted that judges have modernised their attitude, but I have not noticed that. He defended the system whereby the Lord Chancellor alone makes all judicial appointments. One of the few changes he did advocate was the abandonment of wigs – which seems unlikely to happen.

The most notable critic of the judicial system has been

Lord Williams of Mostyn QC, Chairman of the Bar Council. At the Law Society (solicitors) conference in October 1992 he attacked the system for selecting judges as 'bizarre and farcical'. He said 'Secret files are kept on individuals, and the individual has no redress. Are any of us happy with that? The cruellest error may be in it. You cannot put it right. It is carefully kept under lock and key by a graduate of the Franz Kafka school of management'. The Lord Chancellor's department refused to let the Bar Chairman review the files. Lord Williams said two lists were kept: an A list of those likely to become High Court judges and a B list of those thought unsuitable. The last time he looked at the B list, one barrister on it had been dead four years!

Lord Williams went on to say that judges' training is lamentable. High Court judges get none after appointment, and circuit judges get a week's seminar every five years. He considers the listing of cases 'a scandal – wasteful of cash, legal aid and people's time. We have to move from the totemic belief that no judge must ever be kept waiting'. He wants the Judicial Studies Board to monitor performance and advise judges who fall short.

Lord Williams' frankness is as admirable as it is rare. I assume he has no ambition to be a judge himself: frankness is not one of the qualities the Lord Chancellor looks for.

The law cries out for reform in so many areas. Delays disfigure our criminal and civil courts. Going to court is much too expensive and can be ruinous. The division between barristers and solicitors is inefficient. Judges are selected secretively, trained insufficiently and sit on geriatrically. The criminal law needs an overhaul, so that Britain may cease to be a land fit for criminals to live in.

The key to reform is replacement of the antiquated office of Lord Chancellor by a Minister of Justice sitting in the House of Commons. He would give all his time to manning and running the courts and prisons, laying down penal policy and introducing law reforms. A judicial commission would advise openly on judicial appointments and performance. Despite recent welcome signs, I cannot envisage these changes coming about in my lifetime. The legal and judicial systems are held too strongly in the grip of the three Cs – conservatism, complacency and conformity. But I hope this book may help to loosen that grip.

APPENDIX 1

My article 'Kilmuir Rules – OK?' published in the *Guardian*, 14 February 1986

I have things to say that must be said. On 23 January Hugo Young wrote in this newspaper: 'The Voices You Can't Hear Under The Woolsack.' It was about Lord Chancellor Hailsham's influence in inducing judges not to speak in public outside court. In a letter published on 27 January, Lord Hailsham replied, relying on the 'Kilmuir Rules' which a majority of judges has on several occasions approved. The Lord Chancellor stressed that he wishes to guarantee independence for judges.

What are the 'Kilmuir Rules'? In 1955 the BBC asked Lord Chancellor Kilmuir if serving judges could give a series of radio lectures on the Third Programme about great judges of the past. In rejecting the suggestion, Lord Kilmuir wrote that the overriding consideration was to keep the judiciary insulated against controversies of the day. (It is not clear how the lectures would have offended against that.)

> So long as a judge keeps silent, his reputation for impartiality remains unassailable; but every utterance he makes in public, except in the course of the actual performance of his judicial duties, must necessarily bring him within the focus of criticism. It would moreover be inappropriate for the judiciary to be associated with any series of talks or

anything which could fairly be interpreted as entertainment.

The 'Kilmuir Rules' seem much too wide now. Surely a judge could today give a lecture on radio or TV about a former judge, without offending anybody? And the rules are no longer strictly adhered to, in practice. Senior judges have in recent years been in radio and television programmes on topics such as sentencing. Lord Denning, while Master of the Rolls, was on *Desert Island Discs*. Presumably Lord Hailsham agreed to those broadcasts. Did they do any harm?

Lord Kilmuir did not define 'entertainment'. Any radio or television programme must try to entertain, in the sense of holding the attention pleasurably of those at whom it is aimed.

Lord Hailsham says that the 'Kilmuir Rules' are justified because most judges accept them. But we are not running a private company. The public and what they think matter most. What do they think about the rules and how Lord Hailsham applies them? I would like to know.

The judiciary should have the confidence of the public as a whole. Individual judges should have the confidence of the parties in cases they try. They should, ideally, be seen to have impartiality, wisdom, learning, common sense and patience. It would be wrong for a judge to rush into the media at every opportunity, airing his views on a variety of topics and appearing to be unbalanced. Lord Hailsham is right to be against that. But there are areas in which a judge can make a real, even unique, contribution to public discussion. Where is the line to be drawn?

While a judge should be wise and detached he should not be or seem arrogant, remote, and out of touch and sympathy with ordinary folk and their problems. We have that image with many people. We must adjust it. In doing so we should be guided, but not fettered, by precedent, or no progress will be made.

Lord Hailsham's rigid application of the 'Kilmuir Rules' is not supported by all judges. An increasing number of us is becoming restive. Unless a judge renounces, as I have, all claims to any sort of promotion, honour or favour – all of which flow from Lord Hailsham's overflowing hands – it is dangerous to step out of line. Recently two lord justices of appeal lamented, in court, the proposed statutory abolition of a right to appeal. Lord Hailsham induced both to write him letters of apology. One of those judges was recently made a law lord by the Lord Chancellor. Would he have been had he refused to apologise?

On 25 June 1979, Lord Scarman spoke at the annual general meeting of Justice on 'The Judge In Public Life'. He said there are areas of public life outside his court room in which a judge has a valuable role to play. He should be free to take part in the press, radio and television on major social and legal issues. Before his recent retirement, that great judge set out his views on such subjects as the need for a bill of rights and the pros and cons of introducing into our law the European convention for the protection of human rights and fundamental freedoms.

Lord Scarman considers that judges should contribute to such subjects as contempt of court, the right to privacy, the development of administrative law, the ways and means of sustaining the rule of law, and sentencing policy. But a fine line has to be drawn. For example, in the relations between the state and trade unions, we should be able to comment on what the law can do, but not on what the law ought to do. I am a Scarmanite.

Following Lord Scarman's address, Lord Hailsham wrote to all judges on 25 January 1980, after consulting the heads of various sections of the higher judiciary. While he *had no power to give direction to fellow judges* [my italics] he hoped that any judge who was invited to broadcast would approach him or his office, so that the judge could be advised on the basis of precedents 'and so enable the judiciary as a whole to maintain consistency of practice in this sensitive field'.

It should be noted that in October 1983, paragraph 77 of the Lord Chancellor's Handbook for Circuit Judges was amended by permitting judges to write articles for or letters to the press on legal subjects, provided they do so with discretion.

How does Lord Hailsham operate the Kilmuir system in practice? In December 1981, the producer and presenter of a BBC *Panorama* team came to see me. They were preparing a programme on prison overcrowding and sentencing policy and they wanted me in it. I said they would have to ask the Lord Chancellor. I doubted whether he would agree, as my ideas did not conform with Government policy. According to the producer, Lord Hailsham did not object to my taking part. A lord justice of appeal was interviewed at length in the programme.

No harm was done by my exclusion; I would not have added anything new. Might it appear however that the 'Kilmuir Rules' may tempt a Lord Chancellor to prefer 'safe' pro-Government judges to those with new or dissenting notions? Might the barrier between the executive and judiciary – which Lord Hailsham says he wants to maintain – be further blurred? I am not accusing the Lord Chancellor of doing anything he knows to be wrong, but pointing to problems.

BBC Radio Leeds telephoned me on 5 April 1984, asking me to record an interview later that day about a radio play of mine. I had already rejected an approach by BBC TV. I telephoned the Lord Chancellor's office, and Lord Hailsham and his permanent secretary, Sir Derek Oulton KCB, were consulted. Both said I should not give the interview. This is how control is achieved. Lord Hailsham may say he is only giving advice; but having asked for it and received an answer, it is hard for a judge to reject it. Usually an approach is dealt with by a civil servant, who is almost certain to say 'no'. The Lord Chancellor is too busy with non-judicial matters to deal with most such requests.

On 22 March 1985 the *Daily Telegraph* published an article by me, 'A Place For Punishment'. It concerned Government pressure on the judiciary to shorten sentences, parole and the inadequacies of the prison system. It arose from years of frustration at the failure of the higher judiciary to stand up to the Home Office. The public was not being protected. On the same day Sir Derek Oulton wrote to me. Lord Hailsham considered my article prima-facie 'judicial misbehaviour', a ground which he has for dismissing a judge under section 17 of the Courts Act 1971, the other ground being 'incapacity'.

So a prima-facie finding of guilt came with the summons. What would the Lord Chancellor say if I tried Crown Court cases like that?

My detailed reply was delayed by my going on holiday. Sir Derek Oulton then wrote that if my comments were not in his hands by 26 April, the Lord Chancellor would 'in any event proceed to consider your future on the circuit Bench'. What now about the Lord Chancellor having no power to give directions to fellow judges?

I had referred in a letter to Sir Derek that I had to give a public memorial lecture. He wrote that on my return from holiday I should immediately get in touch with him about that. 'I will wish to know what kind of occasion it will be and what you plan to say, so that Lord Hailsham can consider whether you should go ahead with it.' I ignored that. In fact the lecture was on radio drama. This illustrates the extent to which attempts are made to control judges, while supposedly guaranteeing their independence.

Mere circuit judge though I am and proud to be, I decided to stand up to the great and powerful Lord Chancellor and his powerful cohort. I wrote that I was appalled that Lord Hailsham should threaten to dismiss me. I would protect my position and reputation by any means available to me; if necessary I would make representations to both Houses of Parliament and the media.

The extent to which a minister should threaten and harry a judge for what he has chosen to say in the public interest was of high constitutional importance. It deserved parliamentary and public scrutiny. In deciding whether to sack me, Lord Hailsham was complainant, prosecutor, judge and jury. That could not be right and the public would not like it. It went against elementary principles of natural justice. I ended: 'My overriding duty must be to the public at large. When all the facts are put before it, I feel confident that the public will vindicate me.'

Lord Hailsham replied with a (subjectively) blistering letter. 'It has long been considered undesirable for a judge to contribute articles to the press, particularly on matters of current controversy.' The Lord Chancellor referred to previous complaints about me. If there were space I would go into these now. In nearly ten years on the Bench I have upset some people. In trying to do right, I have on some occasions gone wrong. The Lord Chancellor went on that it was no part of my duty to express a motivation to serve and protect the public, save in connection with cases which came before me.

'Recent events and in particular your article in the *Daily Telegraph* show that you have not heeded the warnings which those senior to you have given. This must be the result of foolishness or a complete lack of sensitivity.'

I had to treat this letter as a serious warning. He would not hesitate to set in motion the necessary procedure for dismissing me if I offended again. (Was he still trying to guarantee my independence, or threatening to get rid of a dissident?)

I replied that

. . . the basic difficulty is that I am a radical and you are a

248

conservative. I believe in changes based on public need;
you seem reluctant to make any changes. I am more than
ever sure that it is my duty to try to improve things in
certain areas that I know about (from experience and
study). If necessary, I should bring the defects and my
proposals for reform before the public. These areas include
judges and the media; the causes and remedies for crime;
the jury system; plea bargaining; delays in court cases; the
organisation of the legal profession; the appointment, control and dismissal of judges and magistrates; pressure by
the executive on the judiciary for political reasons; and
whether the office of Lord Chancellor should be abolished
and replaced.

The Daily Telegraph of 7 August carried an article by me,
'Justice Delayed Is Justice Denied'. It began by referring to
the previous article and went on: 'The Lord Chancellor then
wrote threatening letters to me. But I do not work for the
Government. I work for the public and if I feel there are
facts it should know I will not be stifled.'

The Lord Chancellor then set the Lord Chief Justice on to
me. Respectfully, Lord Lane is a good man and a good
judge, for whom I have genuine respect. When I saw him at
his request on 18 September, he was courteous and restrained. No reference was made to dismissing me. I
volunteered an undertaking not to write further newspaper
articles. For reasons I cannot go into here, I have since
withdrawn that undertaking.

Lord Hailsham and his top advisers have inherited their
attitudes from others. They have tremendous power and
influence over lawyers and judges. I do not attribute bad
motives to them. I do feel that underneath there is more to
the 'Kilmuir Rules' than guaranteeing judicial independence
(which is necessary).

The same attitudes which have made our society so secretive have influence here. 'Don't let the side down. Keep in

line. Don't let the public know more than is necessary. Don't do anything that hasn't a precedent for it.' These notions are holding Britain back in many areas, including the law.

As Lord Acton said: 'All power tends to corrupt and absolute power corrupts absolutely.' It is an inevitable process, not caused by any man's wicked nature but by the human nature in us all. The office of Lord Chancellor and the roles of his senior civil servants need looking at. Their power and influence, especially over those who hold, or would hold, judicial office should be brought under close scrutiny and distributed more widely, with checks and balances as in the US constitution.

APPENDIX 2

My 'Diary' article, 'A Few More Choruses of Stormy Weather', published in the *Guardian*, 4 March 1989

February was not created for boating, but it was mild as we left Penton Hook Marina on the Thames in my 28ft motor-cruiser, *Retreat* (not named by me). It was its final journey, or rather mine. I was giving up this appallingly profligate pastime – I have said that before – so for sale we headed for a boat yard near Hampton Court Palace.

We hoped we hadn't turned towards Windsor in error: I am that sort of navigator. At sixty-three you start throwing things overboard and I was throwing the boat (like disappearing up your own exhaust pipe?). Thirty-five years of happy times, glorious times, dangerous times. I managed okay in windy Windermere in the sixties in *Sally*, our 10ft wooden dinghy with one red sail and a mast that slotted through a hole in the thwart. I am bad on nautical terms; I don't understand tide-tables, the rate and set of the tide or obscure symbols on many-lined charts, and 'thwart' may be wrong, but it is a flat piece of wood near the front. I did okay in rocky, castellated Brittany; we towed *Sally* there. Our three kids learned to row and sail and outboard in her, and she never capsized though we pushed her hard. A faithful family boat.

I got ambitious – lawyers do – and successive cruisers grew as big as my head felt when West Stockwith Yacht Club near

Gainsborough made me president, and then I realised they wanted my name and title on the notepaper: it looked good to outsiders. It certainly wasn't for my seamanship that they chose me, with one dissentient whose identity I never discovered.

They knew it had taken me three days to get to Grimsby, stranding twice and being towed in by a yacht. They did not know that early one cold dark April morning in bird-sanctuaried Ravenglass, Bill – my careful Methodist navigator – had fallen overboard at the front where it was high, while I dozed below, and I could only see distant lights and there was nothing to hear except birds (possibly) and desperate Bill.

I never thought so fast, even in front of the smartest high court judge. 'Hurry up, Jim,' called Bill, 'I'm going,' meaning passing out. 'Don't go yet, Bill,' as I pulled him with a rope to the back and muscled him on board, and I didn't have to tell his wife that careful Bill had not worn a life-jacket when last seen.

Retreat hummed and undulated slowly – the journey to my boating graveyard had to be slow – past boats, boats, boats, winterised and still. Past flocking swans, Londoners' paint-peeling shacks, Arabs' silent mansions and marinas that are full and know that Monopoly is more than a game played for toy money. If some car salesmen are descended from horse-thieves, some marina men have raping and pillaging Vikings as forebears – but not those we touched or passed that day.

In two years and a bit I shall tie up at the judicial breakers' yard called Retirement, to the relief of many, led by me. I know every mean man's mendacity, every dodgy lawyer's jape, every Government minister's head-in-the-clouds-and-the-sand-at-the-same-time vote-hungry posture. And yet, I pondered as we slid through lonely locks aided by amicable keepers, those final couple of years will take me through foaming, fuming waters, and I prefer storms to doldrums.

As I looked over the stern at the brackish, tumbling wake

of the last four years, I thought of the dramatic turn-around. On 22 March 1985, the *Daily Telegraph* transmitted my message to the public, 'A Place for Punishment', on prisons, parole etc.

Lord High Admiral Hailsham then called my small boat from his battleship – a ponderous, noisy, obsolete craft. He flashed that if I did not heave-to he would sink me. I went full-speed ahead, chart-less, and the world knows the rest. Or the minuscule part of it that knows and cares does. Keep it in proportion. My problems did not compare with Mr Rushdie's. Lord H never threatened to have me knocked off, though if I had fallen overboard like Bill and perished, I doubt if H would have ordered the largest wreath permitted by civil service regulations.

Lord Admiral H was forcibly retired (hurt). His successor, Lord High Havers, was soon directed back to port (at the Garrick Club?) by She Who Rules Every Wave, the Woolsack being replaced by a cushioning £40,000 a year pension. Not bad for four months dolled like a dame in panto.

Then She called down one Mackay from Scotland; the son of a railwayman, few of us had heard of him then.

Now he wants to reorganise the fleet, modernise it, but there is mutiny led by old H, in his mothballed, moth-eaten ship; his guns fire blanks now – noisy but harmless. Vice Admirals Lane in HMS *Complacency* and Donaldson in *Conservatism* are rallying rebels, helped by Rear Admiral Ackner in *Conformity*. I not in *Retreat* – but advancing – am on the side of the new Lord High Admiral. What a turn-round!

Seriously, in my forty years in the law I have dealt with many lawyers and judges, met them at meetings. Few are wicked or malicious; all are intelligent; most are pleasant and polite; some are erudite. Yet I cannot recall any lawyers or judges proposing any reform unless it benefited themselves. Your average High Court judge fusses more over his coffee being five minutes late than over the five years the case he is trying has been delayed.

The law takes most of its recruits from the conservative middle class. All professions are controlled by those who have been immersed in practices and traditions for so long that they assume established ways are correct. Young lawyers soon learn that those who straggle and stray get left behind by the herd. Bar and Bench are still dominated by men from public school and Oxbridge – towering temples of tradition.

Lord H held up progress in too many areas to list fully here, but they include scandalous court delays, extortionate legal costs, an indefensible system for judicial appointments, barristers' and solicitors' restrictive practices, and law centres. Lord Chief Justice Lane, a nice man and a good judge, is as complacent in out-of-court matters as Donaldson, Ackner, Denning *et al*. Lawyers and judges will have to be dragged into this century. They will not go willingly.

In coming conflicts, Lord Mackay will have my support. We and others are not hampered by pampered patrician backgrounds. We can outgun and outrun those capital ships. I long for the sea again already, and I am priming my guns.

APPENDIX 3

My Judgement in the Michelle Renshaw case, 10 March 1989

On 12 November 1988, Michelle Lorraine Renshaw, who is a single woman aged twenty-four and is now before me for contempt of court, went to the police in Bradford and made a statement. In it she accused her former boyfriend Michael George Williams, also twenty-four, of assaulting her repeatedly. In particular she said that on that same day he had come to her flat, forced her to the floor and kicked her repeatedly on the head and body. He then hit her on the forehead with a mop handle, she said.

There are photographs and medical evidence as to her injuries, which consisted of bruising in various parts of her body.

Her statement included the words, 'After I continued pleading with Michael he just stood there and said that if I contacted the police he would kill me and it wouldn't bother him going to prison. I believe in my mind that Michael is capable of carrying this out and I am frightened for my own safety.' Any such fear of Williams had not inhibited her from going to the police; indeed, she had gone to them for protection, she implied.

When the case against Williams for assaulting Miss Renshaw causing her actual bodily harm came before me yesterday, prosecuting counsel told me that the Prosecution had decided not to proceed with the charge, as Miss Renshaw wished to drop it. I said that the decision was not hers to make, and after considering the matter the Prosecution decided to proceed, albeit reluctantly.

When Miss Renshaw was called into the witness-box and sworn, she said she did not want to give any evidence against Williams. Tearful, she said she wanted to put it behind her and get on with her life, adding that she had been told that she could not be compelled to testify. In the absence of the jury I explained, as clearly as I could to Miss Renshaw, that she was obliged to give evidence and that her refusal would be contempt of court, one of the penalties for which is imprisonment. I then adjourned for fifteen minutes for her to speak to her father. Upon her return, not showing the distress which had been apparent earlier, she said she was still not prepared to give evidence. I do not know what advice, if any, her father or anyone else had given her, or whether she was acting on any such advice, but if anyone had said to her that I did not mean what I had told her and that her contempt would go unpunished, that advice was bad advice.

The Prosecution had to abandon the case against Williams for lack of evidence and he was acquitted. What the jury's verdict would have been if the case had gone on we shall never know. It would be wrong to assume that Williams would necessarily have been convicted, nor is it alleged by anyone that he personally had a hand in the sinister-sounding events about which I was told after he had left court.

I granted legal aid to Miss Renshaw and then consulted Mr Justice Michael Davies, who is sitting in this building, and he decided that I should deal with Miss Renshaw's contempt.

Her counsel called before me as witnesses Miss Renshaw herself, her friend Miss Suzanne Brown, and her mother Mrs Renshaw. I was told for the first time that Miss Renshaw's decision not to give evidence was not solely for the reason she had given in the witness-box earlier. She said the main reason was fear of further violence upon her. I was told that between the end of December and early January she began receiving threatening phone calls at her flat. She said she did not recognise any of the callers' voices but they were telling her that if the case went against Williams she would suffer. She did not at first tell anyone except Miss Brown about the phone calls. She never asked for her ex-directory number to be changed or for phone calls to be intercepted, although she is a secretary and Miss Brown is an administrator with a responsible job.

Miss Renshaw told me that on two occasions she was followed around Morrison's Supermarket on Westgate, Bradford, by different men, neither of whom spoke to her. She thought one of them was a friend of Williams; she did not know either man's identity.

After discussions with her mother, Miss Renshaw went to the police and made a further statement on 23 January saying she wished to withdraw her complaint against Williams and giving as the reason that continuing it would not benefit her or her son from a previous relationship. She added: 'I would also like to say there have been no more incidents involving Michael and he has kept away from me and my family. I would just like to apologise for any inconvenience that I have caused the police.'

There is no reference in that statement to threats, although on the day she made her statement she did tell a policewoman that she had been threatened. There is a note made by another police officer on the following day that Miss Renshaw was adamant about withdrawing her complaint and that she said she was being harassed.

If threats did cause Miss Renshaw to refuse to give evidence it is a very serious state of affairs. The temple of justice has been undermined. These are gangster tactics alien to this country. I am sure that the police will take all due steps to deal with such a situation but, of course, they can do nothing without people who come forward and are courageous enough to give evidence. But was Miss Renshaw motivated by a fear of violence? Certainly any threats made to her by telephone fell short of duress in law. I am not satisfied that the men in the supermarket, if they existed, had anything to do with the Williams case.

In the end I am not primarily concerned with Miss Renshaw's motives for refusing to testify but with the refusal itself. Her motives may well have been mixed. She is a confused young woman for whom I have some sympathy. She has probably been ill-used by more than one predatory male. She has been left to bring up her child unsupported by a stable relationship. She is vulnerable in a society containing some wicked, brutal, insensitive men, but her very vulnerability underlines the seriousness of what she has done.

In crown and county courts I often have to deal with cases in which women complain of physical ill-treatment by men; sometimes their husbands, sometimes their lovers, sometimes their co-habitees, sometimes their ex-boyfriends. Some of the women come before me with broken limbs, black eyes or other signs of some man's brutishness. These women deserve the law's protection, and where it is appropriate they receive it from judges and magistrates. Sometimes we send the men to prison. But we can do nothing unless the women come forward and give evidence, otherwise the men concerned go unpunished and their wickedness is reinforced.

The law has to compel any witness who has relevant evidence to give it. Refusal to do so perverts justice and cannot be accepted. Miss Renshaw's stubbornness, despite my very clear warning, is not the worst type of contempt of court. But she and others who daily are in her unhappy plight have to understand that justice must prevail and their perversion of it by refusing to give evidence will not do. Witnesses who are threatened will receive protection from the police. Those who threaten them will receive long prison terms if the evidence is sufficient.

Usually the sentence in a case like this will be heavier than the one I feel obliged to pass. In Miss Renshaw's case it is imprisonment for seven days. She may go down.

APPENDIX 4

My article 'A Place in the Sun' published in the *Guardian*, 18 March 1989

It has been an odd sort of a week but it has taught me a lot about the media. On Friday, 10 March I went to Durham University to speak at a law students' dinner. What a gem of a city. If there is reincarnation I'll study at Durham.

I was very tired but managed to stay on my feet during my speech and only fell asleep after I had sat down. Surprisingly no one else appeared to nod off, during or afterwards. I did not say so, but I had been up from 2 a.m. to 4 a.m. the previous night, writing my judgement in the Renshaw case at Leeds Crown Court. There was nothing unusual about that. On the few occasions when I don't give judgements or sum up off the cuff, I sometimes do a nightshift (I am writing this at 3 a.m.).

I first knew the Renshaw case was causing a fuss after I had looked round Durham and its soaring cathedral on Saturday morning. I happened to meet a don who had been at the dinner, and he had heard on the radio that Bob Cryer MP was denouncing my decision in some case.

Only two of the national papers seemed to have got the story on Saturday: the *Star* and *Today* had it on the front page. Had it not reached the others, or had they not seen its news value?

By lunchtime that day television were on to it and ITN and Yorkshire came to my house. One group rang from their van on the motorway. They are presumably less likely to get rebuffed that way than by phoning before they set off. I gave brief interviews, which is all TV news need – not very satisfactory in a complex case.

Then TV-AM asked me to appear on Sunday morning. At first I declined. Only one judge had ever discussed one of his cases in detail on TV, and that was me.

After centuries of enforced reticence, judges were liberated within days of enlightened Lord Chancellor Mackay entering office in November 1987. Judges now decide for themselves whether to respond to media approaches. When LWT's *Eyewitness* programme asked me in January to do a live interview about the case where I put a man on probation for two years I said at first I would not discuss it. Then it occurred to me there could be no objection to my telling viewers what they could have heard for themselves if they had been in court.

I followed my own precedent when I went on TV-AM. I was being attacked, and even a judge should be able to defend himself. MPs and media did not know all that had happened in court but I did, so I submitted to Anne Diamond's charm, though sadly she was in London and I in Manchester.

I had intended to say no more to the media, but the story developed rapidly, and BBC TV asked me to go on Monday's 1 p.m. news. Eventually I agreed: I had to be fair to both groups. As I walked to the Leeds studio it struck me as remarkable that in a few minutes I would talk to millions, live, yet I felt relaxed. Whether this was maturity or senility, others must decide. I had found a means of addressing the public (who pay me and to who I am answerable) in their living rooms. I must do it in a dignified responsible way, and it can only happen rarely. I look forward to peace from the media till I retire in July 1991.

At BBC Leeds, I was for the first time besieged by the press 'rat pack', and I had to dodge into a taxi. Press men ran after the car poking cameras at the window and calling

'Sir', but I looked straight ahead. When I got back to the crown court there was 'rat pack 2', but I managed to avoid all but one photographer who ran ahead clicking.

What was that all about? Why were so many press men anxious to snap me in the street? Were they hoping to show me hiding my face or running away? I did neither. Why did only one photograph make the nationals? And why was I keen to avoid them? I don't know any of the answers.

Some left-wing MPs – including my own, Alice Mahon – have gone for me, not for the first time. Clare Short leads that pack, and she has called me 'barmy', doubting my sanity. That must be defamatory of a judge and I thought of telling her to get the advice of her barrister husband, Alex Lyon – I have known him for thirty-five years – about being disqualified from Parliament if she couldn't pay damages and went bankrupt. But dear Clare – I quite like her really – has no sense of humour, so I desisted.

I heard that the *Sun* in an editorial – if it can be thus dignified – had called me a 'plonker' so I had to buy it (I usually glance at copies left in trains). I have never parted with 20 pence so grudgingly. I saw immediately something was wrong. The Page Three lady had disappeared so Page Three itself looked bare. She had fled to Page Seven.

This unnerving switch was not explained. Was it some sort of moral uplift? I think we should be told. It is confusing for barmy judges when Page Three suddenly becomes Page Seven and I trust it will not happen again.

I looked up 'plonker' and the dictionary said 'see plunker'. This is 'a large marble'. I don't get it. Does this link up in some way with Clare Short, who thinks I am losing all my marbles?

I'll buy the *Sun* a dictionary when I eventually do them for Jeffrey Archer damages, causing Rupert to reach for his pregnant wallet and being able to satisfy the *Sun*'s calls for my resignation. I'll resign for half a million any day.

John Stalker – a soul mate, though I have not yet met him

– came out for me in the London *Evening Standard*, as did Lynda Lee-Potter in the *Daily Mail*. An *Independent* leader called my decision 'unexpected but not perverse'. I'll settle for that. The heavies were coming on to my side but the nastier tabloids were – well, nastier.

The *Guardian*'s leader writer stated, 'Judge Pickles is being censored.' Nobody censors me, though censure is OK: why should any public person be exempt? Maybe I'll buy the *Guardian* a dictionary, though I am unlikely to sue a newspaper I have read all my life, and my father before me.

APPENDIX 5

My sentencing remarks in the
Tracey Scott case, 2 January 1990

Tracey Scott, in your favour are these factors: you have
pleaded guilty; you assisted the police in identifying the
other thieves, most of whom would probably not have been
before the court but for your help in identifying them on
video film; you are nineteen and will be twenty next month;
you have no previous convictions. Your early life was frag-
mented through no fault of yours; you did not have the
normal unbroken love and affection from two parents which
is desirable for young people. Your life now appears to be a
lonely one, living on your own with a baby, deserted, for
most purposes, by the father of your baby. I have a great
deal of sympathy for you. You appear to have benefited very
little from all these thefts, very little financially at any rate.
The next factor is that there has been delay in this case.
There is delay in many cases. The fact is that it is over a year
now since you were seen by the police as to these offences. It
is the third time you have been before a court for sentence.
On two previous occasions I adjourned the case so that,
should you lose your liberty, the Home Office could arrange
for your young baby to accompany you. They have now
made such arrangements, and I am grateful to them.

I am concerned about your young baby. I worry for that
child. I do not want her to be standing where you are in
nineteen or twenty years' time. The baby was born on 26
October 1989, and was presumably, therefore, conceived

after your course of theft came to light and you had been seen by the police. I do not, however, find that you deliberately became pregnant with a view to avoiding a custodial sentence. The possibility, however, that other women may do that is one of many factors I have to bear in mind in this difficult case.

Against you are these factors: you were an experienced shop assistant. After working in other stores you worked as a check-out operator for Pound Stretcher for over a year; they thought well of you and trusted you. It was an essential part of your duty to prevent people from stealing goods at that store. In actively participating in thefts on many occasions over three months – that period is one which you yourself state was the relevant one – thieves stole goods on a substantial scale, estimated by you at about £4000. Some of the thieves were strangers to you. When questioned by the police you did not then say that you took part in offences because of threats, although two people in the case apparently, you said, assaulted you at some time previously.

I have read all papers in the case relating to you. I have read about, though I have not seen, video films which show apparently you allowing people time after time to take substantial quantities of goods without paying anything, or only paying token amounts. We all know that stores lose millions of pounds every year through thefts by staff and customers. Here we have a member of staff actively helping customers to steal. Stores are entitled to be protected against staff who have broken the trust put in them. I have to think of other trusted employees of other stores, who may be subject to the temptation to steal and do what you did. Of course, usually they steal for their own benefit. In this case, as I say, that does not seem to apply, but that is no consolation to the store, to know that you personally did not benefit. The fact is that there was a loss on a big scale.

I have also to think of the short sentences of custody served by five of the thieves who appeared with you on this indictment.

Of the possible objects behind any sentence the relevant ones here are punishment for you and deterrence for other people. I adopt a non-custodial approach wherever I can. I value and support the day centre at Kirklees and similar places, some of which I have visited. Constructive work is done there by dedicated probation officers; problems are sorted out in conditions of liberty; prison overcrowding is reduced, and it is much cheaper than prison. But that type of approach, although relevant and applicable in many cases, cannot be called punishment as I understand the word; it cannot be called deterrence.

I have grappled with crime and criminals for forty years. I have prosecuted, defended and judged in criminal cases thousands of times, I suppose. The one question most accused people want answered is, 'Will I lose my liberty today?' Any other sentence is usually shrugged off as tolerable. Only a custodial sentence is feared by almost all offenders and some potential offenders and so acts as a deterrent to many people in my view, although it is difficult to prove it satisfactorily.

When all is said, and it has been very helpfully said by your counsel, this remains in my view, a bad case. It is much too serious for a non-custodial approach. The least sentence I can pass on you is one of six months' detention in a young offenders' institution. You may go down.

APPENDIX 6

Note of a meeting between the Lord Chancellor and Judge Pickles, 2 November 1990

1. Judge Pickles and the Lord Chancellor met informally, with no officials present. The Lord Chancellor said that the matters concerning him about Judge Pickles' conduct were; first, that following the decision of the Court of Appeal, Criminal Division, in the Tracey Scott case, Judge Pickles had, on his return from leave, called a press conference in the Inns of Court Public House in Wakefield in order, as he put it, 'to put the record straight'. At that press conference he had stated that criticisms of him, which had been made in the judgement of the Court of Appeal, had not been correct in certain respects, and he went on to refer, in the press conference, to the Lord Chief Justice as 'like a dinosaur of a previous age'. The Lord Chancellor reminded Judge Pickles that, following correspondence about the Renshaw case earlier, Judge Pickles had given an undertaking not to discuss in public any case in which he had participated judicially in such a way as to identify the case, and what had happened on the occasion of the press conference was in breach of that undertaking. The Lord Chancellor also said that he felt that the reference to the Lord Chief Justice as 'like a dinosaur' was a demeaning remark for one holding the responsibility of judicial office to make and one very likely to attract a headline.

2. Secondly, the Lord Chancellor said that he was concerned that it was reported that at the Fylde Medico-Legal Society Judge Pickles had, in the course of an after-dinner speech, repeated the reference to the Lord Chief Justice in the presence of at least one person with press connections. As a result of which action the remark was again reported.

3. Thirdly, the Lord Chancellor referred to the report that Judge Pickles had appointed an agent to arrange engagements for him on commercial terms, said to require a fee of £800 a night.

4. In reference to the first of these matters, Judge Pickles explained that he had been abroad when the decision of the Court of Appeal, Criminal Division, in the case of Tracey Scott had been reported. When he came home, he found his home besieged by representatives of the media. He felt that some of the criticism directed at him by the Court of Appeal, Criminal Division, had been unfair and in particular that the Lord Chief Justice had said: 'the Judge seems to us to have been concerned more with the public impact of what he was doing and saying, rather than with the justice of it.' In the pressure of events when he came home Judge Pickles felt that it was right for him to seek to correct these matters.

5. In addition, Judge Pickles felt that he had been misreported as having said that he had imposed a custodial sentence in order to deter women, who were the subject of police complaint, from becoming pregnant with a view to avoiding custodial sentence.

6. With hindsight Judge Pickles now agreed that he should not have called the press conference, or made any public comment on the case, and he also accepted that he should not have made the remark he did about the Lord Chief Justice. He had already publicly apologised for that remark in the television programme called *Talking to Myself*, which apology was also contained in the account of that programme which was published in the *Listener*.

7. As to the second matter, the dinner in question was

essentially a private one and the remark was certainly not made with a view to publication. The apology already referred to covered it and the remark had never been repeated since then.

8. With regard to the third matter, Judge Pickles had made an arrangement with an agent, through whom engagements could be made on his behalf, but the fee quoted of £800 was a gross exaggeration. The fees which Judge Pickles in fact received were a good deal less than that. The highest he could recall being £500, in respect of a programme where a great deal of effort was called for on Judge Pickles' behalf, and which involved his house being open and available to the camera crew for a full half-day. Judge Pickles pointed out that he had given many interviews and undertaken many engagements for which no fee had been taken, or where any fee offered had been given to charity. He felt that judges had written books, in respect of which royalty arrangements might be assumed to have been made, without apparent objection by anyone to that practice.

9. The Lord Chancellor said that what he felt was objectionable was that a person serving in the capacity of a full-time judge should have a commercial arrangement with an agent, under which his services were being made available in a way that, in the very least, depended on the fact that the person offering his services was a serving judge. The Lord Chancellor said that he felt that that was inconsistent with holding office as a judge and he invited Judge Pickles to undertake that, for so long as he served as a judge, he would not accept fees for appearances and engagements of this kind. Judge Pickles agreed to consider this and to let the Lord Chancellor have his conclusion in writing. Judge Pickles had already undertaken some commitments in this connection, which he would find it difficult to break. The Lord Chancellor invited Judge Pickles to deal with that matter in his written undertaking.

10. Judge Pickles emphasised to the Lord Chancellor his

view that it was important that the judiciary should be able to participate in matters of public interest in a responsible way; that he had tried hard to do that. The Judge said that he did not go to the media, they came to him, and that he sought to do his best to carry out his judiciary duties properly and to give effect loyally to the judgements of the Court of Appeal, Criminal Division. He had been sitting as a judge part-time since 1963 and full-time since 1976, and it was only in a rather fortuitous way that in 1986 he came to the attention of the media, which he had certainly not courted.

11. The Lord Chancellor concluded the meeting by stating that, after he had received a letter from Judge Pickles dealing with the undertaking referred to,* he would consider carefully what action was required and he would require to make a public statement about it.

Addendum

12. Following the preparation of this record, Judge Pickles raised the question of newspaper articles. The Lord Chancellor responded that, in his view, it was not appropriate generally for a serving full-time judge to receive payment for newspaper articles about matters to which the writer's capacity as a judge was relevant.

* I sent it. It cost me several thousand pounds – I had to present a BBC *Byline* programme on drugs without fee.

INDEX

Aarvold, Carl, 37
absolute discharge, 201
Ackner, Lord, 239, 253, 254
Acland, Sir Richard, 49
Act of Settlement (1700), 175
Acton, Lord, 250
addicts, drug, 147, 215, 229–31
affidavits, 86
alarms, burglar, 137
alcohol, 115, 147, 225, 231
All Souls' College, Oxford, 39
Armley Prison, 197
assizes, 55, 58
Association of Chief Police Officers, 132
Association of Chief Probation Officers, 223
Attorney-General, 94
attorneys, 94
Australia, 98, 103

bail, 203, 222
Baker, Geoffrey, 22, 29, 42, 52
Bakewell, Joan, 154, 178
Bar Council, 11–12, 95, 105, 126, 130, 241
barristers, 45–6, 63, 88, 94; fusion with solicitors, 87, 94, 102–9; Inns of Court, 9–10, 95, 126; JP's views, 108–9; partnerships with other professions, 101, 108; pre-trial reviews, 87–9; pupillage, 10–11, 12; specialisation, 104; working class barristers, 126
Barristers' Clerks' Association, 27
BBC, 23, 134, 142, 152, 153, 154, 161–2, 170, 178, 243, 246, 261–2, 270
Benson Commission on Legal Services, 102
Beverley, Frank, 24, 39
Beyfus, Sir Gilbert, 17–18
Birkett, Norman, 126

Birmingham Law Society, 43
Birmingham Prison, 197, 204
Birmingham Six, 122, 123–5, 126–7, 180
Blundeston Prison, 206–7
Bough, Frank, 142
Bourne, Sir Wilfred, 61, 62–3, 166
Boyle, Sheron, 171
Bradford County Court, ix, 57, 83, 155
Bradford Law Centre, 76
Bradford Law Society, 60, 83–4
Brady, Ian, 221
Bresler, Fenton, 240
Bridge, Mr Justice Nigel, 123–5
Brighouse, 49, 50
Bristol, 93, 113
Brittan, Leon, 199
brothels, 146
Brown, Suzanne, 256, 257
Budgen, Nicholas, 186
burglar alarms, 138
burglary, 218
Butler-Sloss, Lord Justice, 65
Byline (BBC programme), 170, 270

Callaghan (Birmingham Six), 124–5
Cambridge University, 12, 59, 64, 68, 126, 180, 214, 254
Canada, 103, 227
cannabis, 134, 135, 147–8, 215
car thefts, 137
Carlisle Report, 199
Carman, George, 105, 106
Carson, Edward, 40
Challoner, Detective Sergeant, 118
Charles II, King, 111
children: and divorce, 77, 140–1; protection of, 216
Christ Church, Oxford, 7
Christian, E. B. V., 102
Christianity, 139
Churches, 139–40, 141, 142, 147

271

INDEX

INDEX